D0782753

AMIGAS Y AMANTES

Families in Focus

Series Editors
Anita Ilta Garey, University of Connecticut
Naomi R. Gerstel, University of Massachusetts, Amherst
Karen V. Hansen, Brandeis University
Rosanna Hertz, Wellesley College
Margaret K. Nelson, Middlebury College

AMIGAS Y AMANTES

Sexually Nonconforming

Latinas Negotiate Family

KATIE L. ACOSTA

RUTGERS UNIVERSITY PRESS

NEW BRUNSWICK, NEW JERSEY, AND LONDON

Library of Congress Cataloging-in-Publication Data

Acosta, Katie L., 1980–

   Amigas y amantes : sexually nonconforming Latinas negotiate family / Katie L. Acosta.
      pages cm. — (Families in focus)
   Includes bibliographical references and index.
   ISBN 978–0–8135–6196–7 (hardcover : alk. paper) — ISBN 978–0–8135–6195–0 (pbk. : alk. paper) — ISBN 978–0–8135–6197–4 (e-book)
   1. Lesbian mothers. 2. Hispanic American lesbians. I. Title.

   HQ75.53.A28 2013
   306.874'308664—dc23   2013000430

A British Cataloging-in-Publication record for this book is available from the British Library.

Excerpts from my article "The Language of (In)Visibility: Using In-Between Spaces as a Vehicle for Empowerment in the Family," *Journal of Homosexuality* 58, nos. 6–7 (2011): 883–900, reprinted by permission of the publisher, Taylor & Francis Ltd., http://www .tandf.co.uk/journals.

Copyright © 2013 by Katie L. Acosta

All rights reserved

No part of this book may be reproduced or utilized in any form or by any means, electronic or mechanical, or by any information storage and retrieval system, without written permission from the publisher. Please contact Rutgers University Press, 106 Somerset Street, New Brunswick, NJ 08901. The only exception to this prohibition is "fair use" as defined by U.S. copyright law.

Visit our website: http://rutgerspress.rutgers.edu

Manufactured in the United States of America

For Josiah and Camila,
with hopes of a more accepting world for you both

CONTENTS

ACKNOWLEDGMENTS

I came to the study of Latina/o sexualities at the most opportune time. I was a graduate student at the University of Connecticut and one of my mentors, Marysol Asencio, had just received a Ford Foundation grant to map the nascent field of Latina/o sexualities. She hired me as her research assistant on this project, which involved the bringing together of all of the top scholars in the area to discuss the advancements which had been made and to identify the multitude of work left to be done. That project culminated in a much awaited anthology, *Latina/o Sexualities: Probing Powers, Passions, Practices, and Policies.* Over the course of working on this project, I received an unprecedented amount of support from everyone involved. Unlike many sexualities scholars in the academy, I never felt marginalized. On the contrary, from the beginning I felt as if I were becoming part of a vibrant and growing community of researchers whom I respected and who were rooting for my success. I am very grateful to Marysol Asencio for giving me the invaluable opportunity to be part of such a collective and to all of the members of the Latina/o sexualities board for their enthusiasm for my work. This experience gave me the confidence I needed to write *Amigas y Amantes.*

I also need to thank Nancy Naples, Bandana Purkayastha, and Carlos Decena for extending their relentless loyalty and support to me while I was a student and in the following years as I wrote this book. I'm indebted to Nancy for helping me see the hidden potential in my data and for continuing to advise me during the writing of this book until the very end. I am thankful as well for Bandana, who has always kept me grounded with sound professional advice about my career goals, and for Carlos for all of his feedback on chapters and for the many conversations we've had over the years, all of which have helped me grow exponentially as a scholar. Thank you all for caring about me as a person in addition to caring about me as a student and later a colleague, always recognizing how my personal needs shaped my research.

During the data collection process, many key figures and organizations at the University of Connecticut supported my efforts. I extend a special thanks to the Puerto Rican/Latino Studies program for funding me during my years as a graduate student. In particular, I thank Anne Theriault for her instrumental role in soliciting funds for me to attend conferences to present my preliminary research findings. The Rainbow Center at the University of Connecticut supported me by creating a welcoming space in which I could discuss my ideas. I also benefited from the University of Connecticut's Multicultural Fellowship, which I received for the duration of my time in graduate school.

When I set out to write *Amigas y Amantes,* I had a strong sense that this work had a mind of its own. I imagined *Amigas y Amantes* as a living being with its own agenda and myself as the surrogate entrusted to carry out the mission. This feeling came from the myriad people who, both silently and audibly, were pushing and longing for its creation and existence. In addition to my colleagues, who shared my excitement for this project, were the study participants who themselves wanted to have their stories told. This book would not have come to fruition without the overwhelming support I received from my respondents, who opened their lives to me in such intimate and uninhibited ways: all of the times they included me in their events and the innumerable times they shared their fears, joys, frustrations, and triumphs. It is by no means an easy task to share so much of oneself in the ways in which the participants in this study opened themselves and their lives and stories to me, and I remain overwhelmed and indebted to them for doing so with such bravery and candor. I also thank the participants for the ways in which they have helped shape me as a person over the years. In the academy, we rightfully spend much time exploring how the researcher can change the participants, alter their environments, or potentially cause them harm. However, while I hope I have benefited my participants by yielding a voice to their too often silenced stories, my experience has been that I, too, have grown, changed, and evolved over the years on account of my involvement in the LBQ (lesbian, bisexual, and queer) communities where I conducted this research. Thank you all for holding me accountable, assisting me in my journey by sharing yours, and helping me grow by including me in your lives. I hope to have done justice to the complexities, the beauty, the pain, the joy, and the individuality and communality of your experiences in these pages.

I would not have survived the writing of *Amigas y Amantes* were it not for my phenomenal colleagues at Tulane University. A special thanks to Yuki Kato, David Ortiz, Stephanie Arnett, and Michele Adams for reading draft chapters and offering new directions and insight for me to consider. I am also indebted to Martha Huggins for her belief in me as a scholar and support of my work. I also owe many thanks to my student worker, Callie Wise, who has aided me in writing this book from the very beginning. Thank you for your loyalty and commitment to this project. My writing group, Sistah Circle, is also deserving of my gratitude not only for providing me feedback on all the chapters in this book, but also for creating a space for me within which to write without feeling isolated. Beretta Smith Shomade, Nghana Lewis, and Rebecca Chaisson, thank you, my writing "sistahs," not merely for your collegial support, but also for sharing your personal struggles of balancing writing and parenting and reminding me that I am not alone in this endeavor. I am, in addition, indebted to the Newcomb Center for Research on Women, which provided the grant that made possible the solidarity and support I received from Sistah Circle. In addition to this grant, I received a great deal of additional support from Tulane University to help bring this book to publication. I must express my sincere gratitude to the Newcomb College Institute for providing me with a fellows grant to help support this research as well as to the COR Fellowship program, which provided me with two internal grants (one in 2010 and the other in 2012) to help see this project through to completion. I would also like to acknowledge Tulane's School of Liberal Arts for the subvention grant I received to help cover the costs associated with preparing this manuscript. I am deeply grateful to Anita Ilta Garey, one of the editors for this series, for her generous support, guidance, and mentorship, as well as Peter Mickulas, my editor at Rutgers University Press, for his support and guidance through the publication process.

Last, but certainly not least, I could not have written this book without the unfailing support of my families of both choice and origin. My cousin Jennifer and my aunts Nury and Iro provided me with much needed practical support, and provided housing when I traveled to conduct interviews, rides from the train station when I arrived late at night, and directions to navigate the various cities in which I found myself for data collection. They also helped by passing out fliers for me at pride parades, looking over my recruitment materials, and accompanying me to events. Joan and Stephen Ostertag were also both extremely instrumental during the data collection phase of research by providing a variety of much needed academic and emotional support as I engaged in interviewing and participant observation. I especially need to thank my partner, Hilary, and my son, Josiah, for their patience and understanding, particularly as I obsessed over the book's chapters for hours and hours. Thank you, Josiah, for all of your unconditional encouragement and your unfailing enthusiasm, which I dare say could be matched by few others your age. This support means more to me than you will ever know. Thank you, Hilary, for calming me down every time I wanted to cry, for reading every chapter I asked of you, and for making me laugh when I most needed a smile. I am very fortunate to have such a strong familial support network, and I thank you all for the sacrifices you have made to help me along this journey. Your efforts have neither gone unnoticed nor underappreciated. Les quiero de gratis.

AMIGAS Y AMANTES

INTRODUCTION

I was raised that your family is the most important thing. And it wouldn't feel
right for me to not have my family around, even though they are the only ones
that cause me pain.   —Luisa, a bisexual Ecuadorian woman

I started my field research on lesbian, bisexual, and queer Latinas at a difficult
point in my life. My beloved grandmother had recently died, and on her deathbed she told her best friend that she lamented the fact that she would not get a
chance to meet the new grandchild whose arrival the family was so anxiously
awaiting. The grandchild she referred to is my aunt's daughter, whom her partner had conceived via alternative insemination six months earlier. The statement
that my grandmother made on her deathbed was the closest she had ever come
to publicly acknowledging my aunt and her partner of more than ten years as
a family. It was the first time my grandmother had ever acknowledged that the
child they were bringing into the world, while not tied to her biologically, would
indeed be her grandchild. Months after the funeral, I continued to return to
this incident in my head. I thought about the tacit relationship my family had
with my aunt: the way they never acknowledged her lesbian existence while all
the while accepting her partner as part of the family. I had been well trained in
these tacit arrangements, never mentioning my own relationships with women
to anyone in the family. For them, alternative sexualities was a tacit subject; even
when it was understood, it was never discussed, and through the lack of verbal-
ization we maintained familial ties (Decena 2011).[1] These experiences solidified
my desire to conduct research on lesbian, bisexual, and queer Latinas.[2] At this
point, through my own experiences and those I had witnessed in my family, it
had occurred to me that no one was writing about the curious ways that Latinas
negotiate sexuality and the family.

Throughout my research, in interview after interview, study participants
shared remarks like those provided by Luisa above. As I sat down with the mas-
sive amounts of data I had collected through both participant observation and
in-depth interviews, it became clear that the study participants shared a collective

familial experience. While they did not always envision themselves as a unified group or even as part of the same community, they shared an experience in the ways in which they negotiated the family. This negotiation has become the centerpiece of this book.

Amigas y Amantes approaches an understanding of how lesbian, bisexual, and queer Latinas live and operate in their daily lives while managing the conflicting needs of families of choice and those of origin. Employing an intersectional lens, I explore the ways that race, class, gender, nationality, and sexuality are interrelated in shaping lesbian, bisexual, and queer (LBQ) Latinas' experiences with their families. *Amigas y Amantes* traces sexually nonconforming Latinas' relationships with partners, families of origin, children, and friends. It provides a gendered analysis of how these women develop and maintain sexual identities, reconcile their sexualities with family members, negotiate cultural expectations, and combat compulsory heterosexuality.

In accordance with feminist standpoint theory, this work uses the lived experience as a site for the production of knowledge (Harding 2004; Smith 1987). For Dorothy Smith, this experience becomes a point of entry for the scholar to begin to understand the relations of ruling that land in women's lives. Following this premise, I am committed to validating women's experiences as a legitimate source for knowledge production and challenging the relations of ruling that have silenced the voices of sexually nonconforming Latinas. One does not need to look beyond the academy to see the ways in which sexually nonconforming Latinas have been silenced. In this day and age, despite the many advancements made by gender and sexualities scholars alike, there continues to be a marked absence of nonwhite sexually nonconforming women in scholarship. The research on nonheterosexual women has overwhelmingly focused on white and middle-class groups (notable exceptions include Arguelles and Rich 1984; Espín 1997; Moore 2011; Zavella 2003a, 2003b). In addition to this fact, research on Latina/o sexualities and same-sex relationships has focused overwhelmingly on men (Almaguer 1993; Cantú 2009; Díaz 1998). While empirical work on Latina lesbians is nearly absent, there is a wealth of creative work being done in this area. Scholars like Cherríe Moraga and Gloria Anzaldúa (1983), Carla Trujillo (1991), and Catrióna Esquibel (2006), among others, have made significant contributions by way of creative writing on lesbian desire, the creation of safe spaces, and the establishment of community. These contributions have made the absence in social science scholarship even more apparent. I, along with many other scholars, have for years now questioned the academy's dismissal of research on sexually nonconforming Latinas. Why is no one doing this work? My own experiences in the academy have led me to believe that the academy as a patriarchal institution has not been ready for research that explores the lives of racial minority women who have chosen to build families for themselves without men. While the academy is often considered to be a progressive space, I have found that it is ultimately burdened by the same ideas of heteronormativity that are pervasive in the rest of society. For instance, as part of a report for the American Socio-logical Association, the Committee on the Status of Gay, Lesbian, Bisexual, and Transgender Persons in Sociology included a report on the number of articles published in major sociology journals on LGBT issues from 2001 through 2008. The findings show only three articles published during this time period focused on lesbians and none focused specifically on bisexual men or women (Weedon 2009). The result of this absence has been a less than welcoming environment for research that explores the lives of women who love other women, especially if those women are not white. *Amigas y Amantes* is an exploration into the lived experiences of a predominately overlooked group of women whose narratives, when explored, provide us with a richer understanding of gender and sexual relations in Latina/o families. With it, I hope to join other scholars in beginning to close this empirical gap.

The absence of this research in social science scholarship is more than just an empirical gap: it also may feed the misconception that there is nothing to be learned from a work that centers on sexually nonconforming women of color. This misconception, in turn, further feeds the misconception that the experi-ences of LBQ Latinas can be subsumed by the existing work on white lesbians. However, in conducting this research, it became evident that a project centered solely on sexually nonconforming Latinas introduces a variety of issues rarely addressed in the existing scholarship on same-sex relationships. Among such issues are the struggles affecting interracial/interethnic same-sex couples and those affecting poor and undocumented LBQ mothers. I address these and other issues in *Amigas y Amantes* with the hope of advancing our understanding of the intersections of race, gender, sexuality, and the family.

The Politics of Naming

Understanding the importance of and my desire to conduct research on women who love other women, I quickly recognized the significance of terminology. Who gets left out when we use words like "lesbian" to describe the complexities of women's same-sex intimacies? Luz Calvo and Catriona Esquibel (2010) point out the difficulties associated with accessing sexually nonconforming Latinas because these women do not always identify with labels such as lesbian. The authors suggest that researchers use a broader term so as not to exclude Latina women who, while holding intimate feelings for other women, do not necessar-ily adhere to the lesbian label. Furthermore, Lisa Diamond (2008) finds that for women, sexual fluidity can result in their changing identity categories in order to adopt broader labels that better portray their sexual variance. She notes that non-exclusive attractions are the norm for many women, and when these attractions trigger fluidity, women can develop authentic desires that are inconsistent with their initial sexual identity categorizations. Diamond notes, and the responses in this study support, that differing degrees in sexual fluidity are not an indication of a more or less authentic lesbian identity. On the contrary, women's varying degrees in fluidity may only help us understand if and when they experience nonexclusive attractions throughout their lifetime. Hence, given the complexities and malleability of sexual identity categories, in recruiting subjects for this study, I advertised for women who self-identify as lesbian, bisexual, or queer. In doing so, I was able to broaden the range of participants' experiences to include women who fall outside of the heterosexual norm but who may not necessarily choose a lesbian identity for themselves. This broadened sample allowed me to learn a great deal about how the study participants felt about sexual identity categories and the ways in which they manipulated these categories at different times in their lives. Consider this statement from Laura:

> I think if you imposed a definition on me, you might say lesbian, but for me and my gender studies stuff, I learned the history of lesbians and where that comes from, and I absolutely don't feel connected to that history or that movement or that generation. I'm definitely not a lesbian and like I haven't hooked up with a guy in a long time, but if I ever got the urge there's not anything stopping me. Even now, I still hook up with guys every now and then because they're so easy. The women of color I know who identify as lesbian have really essential-ist politics about womanhood and are transphobic and into the butch/femme binaries and into monogamy and that kind of stuff. It's all stereotypical, but that's not what I want to be associated with. I like to be associated with queer because I've also dated or hooked up with trans women. I think that's why I call myself queer. I'm really into transgender politics and fluidity of gender.

For Laura the term "lesbian" implies an exclusivity and monogamy that she is not comfortable with. While she admits that her relationship patterns (she has been in an open relationship with a woman for five years) mean that others would label her a lesbian, she finds the term stifling. Laura's sexual fluidity means that while her primary emotional connections and attractions are to women, she does occasionally have sex with men because they are available, and she has dated transgender women as well. Given her experiences and her nonexclusive attractions, the term "queer" best fits her overall experience.

Another study participant also discussed the limitations of sexual identity labels during our interview. Like Laura, Luz identifies as queer but admits that this identity is situational. She explains, "I identify as queer but I say bisexual to be clear with people because a lot of people just don't know what queer means. If I'm around queer people I say queer because they'll know what I'm talking about. But when I'm talking to people that don't know much about LGBTQ [les-bian, gay, bisexual, transgender, and queer] stuff, I'll just say bisexual. I always shy away from that term (bisexual) because my first relationship was with someone who wasn't really identifying as a man or a woman. I don't like to say bisexual because it implies that those are the only two options." At the time of the interview, Luz was in a relationship with a man. She still identifies as queer, and because all of her previous partners as an adult have either been women or transgender men, Luz was very careful about sharing information about her new relationship with her family of origin. They had become comfortable with her queer existence, and she did not want to give them the impression that this new relationship meant a change in her sexual identity. As she explains, "I didn't tell them for a long time because I didn't want them to be really happy. I really waited until I felt like things were really serious. It was almost like coming out to my parents again. I think this is a really solid relationship. My family really likes him. I wouldn't bring a guy around unless I felt like this was a really long-term relationship because I didn't want them to be like, 'Oh, thank God, she's seen the light,' and then it turns out that I'm not going to be with that person."

Participants like Luz struggled with other individuals' inability to recognize the degrees of their sexual fluidity. They found themselves trying to conform to other people's preconceptions about the static and essentialist nature of sexuality, despite the fact that their realities were far more complex. My decision to conduct a study on lesbian, bisexual, and queer Latinas was driven in part by a desire to understand how these women negotiated this messiness with their families of origin, partners, and children. These women's interviews yielded an incredible amount of sexual variance: from monogamous women with exclusive attractions to other women to women in open relationships who expressed nonexclusive attractions. While at first glance it may appear that women with such varied sexualities would have little in common, in actuality, these women's experiences are very similar in that, irrespective of their sexual fluidity, they are marginalized subjects in a heteronormative society. The respondents shared the experience of having significant attractions for other women, which they were forced to negotiate both with themselves and those they loved. For most of the women, these same-sex attractions resulted in long-term relationships with other women. But for others these attractions led to short-term same-sex relationships or open relationships with both men and women. Given the disparities in the participants' experiences with desire, attraction, and sexual encounters, I settled on the term "sexually nonconforming Latinas" to describe these women in an effort to be inclusive of more Latina women whose sexualities are marginalized for a variety of given reasons. This term is attractive in part because it eliminates hierarchies between women based on their level of same-sex attractions or experiences. It also eliminates sexual identity labels, which have the potential to divide women into categories of more or less authentic sexual minorities.

Without question, terminology is unavoidable, and any given term has its limitations, as does sexually nonconforming. As a concept, the term "sexually nonconforming" can reduce women's experiences to solely their sexual acts. This was not at all the purpose behind my use of the term. "Sexually nonconforming," for me, is a term that ties together those individuals whose love interests set them apart from the dominant society and leave them vulnerable to stigmatization. While this group is indeed diverse and does not always acknowledge its affinities with one another, their experiences are often oversimplified by the dominant society in ways that obfuscate their differences. In writing about lesbian, bisexual, and queer women simultaneously, my intent is to point out their places of convergence as well as to highlight the intricacies in the experiences that make them different. While these women used different terminology to self-identify, I found that their experiences and sexual histories were not nearly as distinct as the labels would imply. How these Latinas self-identified had more to do with how they understood their sexual histories rather than their experiences specifically. Thus, in writing this book my focus has been on the experiences these women share in common: their love, commitment, and desires for other women and their difficulties negotiating family. Despite recognizing its limitations, I found the term "sexually nonconforming" to best meet the goals I sought to accomplish in recruiting participants for this study. In using it, I highlight the ways in which this diverse group of women can learn from one another's strategies in negotiating family.

I engaged in similar reflections regarding the use of the term "Latina" to describe and recruit study participants. For the purpose of this study, Latinas are defined as women who are of Mexican, Central American, South American, or Spanish Caribbean descent and who now reside in the United States. Clearly, the term "Latina/o" is limited in that it implies the homogeneity of very diverse groups of people. However, despite the limits of pan-ethnic labels, I use the term Latina for multiple reasons. Unlike white immigrants, immigrants of color often have ethnicities imposed on them and are often left without the choice of which, if any, ethnic identities to adopt for themselves (Waters 1990). Furthermore, recent work has shown that Latina/o immigrants are increasingly identifying pan-ethnically (Diaz-McConnell and Delgado-Romero 2004).

Despite the fact that, for the purpose of the census, Latina/os are not recognized as a racial group, we know that Latina/o is a general label that holds racialized meanings for actual people (Itzigsohn 2004). In the 2000 census, 47.9 percent of Latina/os categorized themselves as "white," but another 42 percent chose the category "other," writing in their nationality instead (C. Rodriguez 2009). This issue is complicated by generation in the United States. Latina/os have the highest disparity between parents and children in terms of racial identification on the census. Second-generation Latina/os are much more reticent than their parents to choose the category "white" for their racial identity and are instead choosing the category "other" and writing in the pan-ethnic label Latina/o to describe themselves (Rumbaut 2009). Jose Itzigsohn (2004) notes that Latina/os are a pan-ethno-racial group, and the differences we see in how they racially identify are a product of their variances in phenotype and their different experiences with racism in the United States.

In this work, I acknowledge the situational nature and fluidity of racial/ethnic categories and thus prefer to use the pan-ethnic label "Latina" in order to allow for a broader nonexclusive sample selection. However, I also honor the fact that there are significant differences among Latinas and do not seek to minimize these differences in this work. These women's experiences are diverse on account of class, generational status, immigrant status, racial identity, and sexual identity. Nonetheless, these women share a social position in the United States, a devotion and obligation to family, and a mestiza consciousness. For Gloria Anzaldúa (1999), a mestiza consciousness emerges as a way to reconcile the contradictions one experiences from living within opposing worlds. She defines mestizas as the outcasts who face rejection at every turn on account of their race, ethnicity, language, class, sexuality, and/or immigrant status: the mestiza is torn because of plural identities. Anzaldúa develops a mestiza consciousness to help her transform her marginalization and the many contradictions she faces into a form of resistance. Developing a mestiza consciousness allows her to convert the feeling of being split or torn on account of her conflicting identities into something positive.[3] This consciousness and the other commonalities that the study participants share cannot be ignored and have resulted in the collective struggle, which I outline in the subsequent chapters.

Methods

Deciding which methods to use in our research, how to implement these methods, and how to analyze the data is ultimately shaped by our epistemological stances (DeVault 1999; Naples 2003). My decisions regarding how to conduct this study are driven by my background in feminist scholarship and my commitment to an intersectional analysis and to the establishment of a Latina feminist standpoint. Such an epistemological stance lends itself to the feminist qualitative methods that I use in this study.

Amigas y Amantes draws from forty-two in-depth interviews with sexually nonconforming Latinas and fourteen months of participant observation. Participants were obtained through various networks in the LGBTQ community as well as through referrals from social service organizations and support groups. I worked with the Lesbian, Gay, Bisexual, and Transgender Community Center in New York and used referrals from its support staff to locate potential participants.[4] The center also served as an advertising space: I posted on the bulletin boards located throughout the center. I also posted a call for study participants on their website and on a variety of Queernet online community groups. Furthermore, in order to reach a larger population who may not frequent the center, I ran ads in the *Rainbow Times* and the *Village Voice*. The *Rainbow Times* has 250 distribution points and services in Massachusetts and northern Connecticut. The *Village Voice* is a much larger paper, with over 200,000 distribution points throughout New York City, including the outer boroughs of Brooklyn, Queens, the Bronx, and Staten Island. In addition to their distribution points, both papers had electronic subscribers who received the paper via email.

The formal in-depth interviews were conducted with Latinas who identify as lesbian, bisexual, or queer. Twenty-four of the interviewees were born and/or raised in the United States. Eighteen interviewees were women who immigrated to the United States as adults and were raised predominantly in a Latin American or a Spanish-speaking Caribbean country. The women were all at least eighteen years of age. The first-generation Latina migrants had all resided in the United States for at least one year prior to being eligible to participate in the study. The women used twelve different labels to identify their ethnic backgrounds, including Puerto Rican, Dominican, Peruvian, Mexican, Chicana, Colombian, Cuban, Nicaraguan, Ecuadorian, Honduran, Panamanian, and Guatemalan (see appendices A and B). The interviews were conducted in English and/or Spanish and lasted from one to two hours. Those interviews that occurred in Spanish were later translated; however, here I include the original Spanish text so as to preserve the original meaning of the participants' words (for a discussion on my decision to include the original Spanish text, see appendix C).

In addition to in-depth interviews, I also conducted fourteen months of participant observation with various social groups. I attended LGBTQ social events throughout 2007 and 2008 in order to remain connected to the community and to engage in recruitment through these network ties. The participant observation took place in several informal groups throughout New York City, Boston, and in Connecticut. I also attended the respondents' family events, including baptisms, picnics, birthday parties, and the like. In addition to participant observation being a useful way to recruit potential participants for the study, it also allowed me to interact with a wider range of women who did not formally participate in the interviewing process. Furthermore, the participant observation alongside the in-depth interviews gave me a distinct angle on some of the participants' lives because I was able to compare their taped interview responses to the behaviors I observed them engaging in with their families and friends. This added a layer of complexity to the participants' initial interviews and allowed me to reconsider the discrepancies I found in what they said versus what they actually did.

The Participants

The first-generation Latinas were mostly college-educated women who were afforded a relatively comfortable standard of living due to their families' lucrative professions or businesses in their countries of origin (see appendix D).[5] Of the first-generation participants, all but two were college educated and many came from college-educated parents. A few had even obtained graduate degrees in their countries of origin. Those who reported a lower-middle-class status in their countries of origin were predominantly raised in single-parent households. Thus, their relative lower economic status can be attributed to the financial burdens of a one-income household and not to their lack of professional employment.

As is often the case with first-generation immigrants, the majority of these study participants, irrespective of economic class status, were working in the service sector or in factories in the United States. In some cases, this can be attributed to a lack of citizenship status, in other cases, to an inability to transfer their professional degrees from their countries of origin to US labor markets. Others still struggled with inadequate English language proficiency. Puerto Rican migrants were the exception because of their status as US citizens. While some Puerto Ricans reported struggling with the English language after migrating to the Northeast, they fared relatively better in the United States in that they were often able to obtain work in their chosen professions. Because these women are citizens, they had an advantage in the labor market, which protected them from downward economic mobility post migration. All of the immigrant participants and those who migrated from Puerto Rico came to the Northeast of their own accord as adults. I made this a prerequisite for participating in the study in order to ensure that the sample only included Latinas who had the choice to stay in their countries of origin or in Puerto Rico and still elected to move.

The second-generation participants were mostly raised in poor, working-class communities of color in the United States. Nonetheless, many of these women had achieved social mobility through obtaining college and, in some instances, professional degrees. Among them are a high-level employee in the finance district, a public health worker, a social worker, and a lawyer. Those who had not yet achieved social mobility via education were mostly still attending four-year prestigious and Ivy League colleges.

The Couples

The majority of the study participants who were partnered were in relationships with someone of a different race or ethnicity. Only eight of the study participants were in a relationship with someone of their same nationality. Another eight of the participants were in relationships with other Latinas with different national origins; twelve of the Latinas were in relationships with white women; three were in relationships with black women, and eleven of the participants were single at the time of the interview (see appendix E). Participants' experiences negotiating these interracial and interethnic relationships, as well as the cultural clashes created with their families of origin on account of these relationships, became an important venue for exploring emotion work (see chapter 3).

Positionality

Scholars have long debated over the advantages and disadvantages to having an insider status as a researcher. However polarizing, insider/outsider status does not account for the complexities of these statuses. Becoming an insider or outsider is an interactive process, and these statuses are not fixed (Naples 2003). There are multiple layers of similarities and differences that shape a researcher's relationship to the community (Trinh Vo 2000). We are often insiders and outsiders simultaneously. My own position in sexually nonconforming Latina communities is indicative of the constant negotiation researchers encounter between insider and outsider statuses. I am a dark-skinned, queer, Dominican woman. My status as a US citizen and researcher, my English fluency, and my education level have all privileged me over many of the women in this study. These privileges contribute to my outsider status. My queer identity sometimes contributed to my outsider status and sometimes made me more of an insider. Queerness for me means experiencing love and intimacy in a way that is not limited by the gender binaries. When I first entered the field, I was dating a woman whom I brought with me to events occasionally. Under these circumstances, my presence at events was rarely questioned. But I later was in a relationship with a man. The few participants who knew this fact were particularly wary of my presence in LBQ communities. In this way, my choice in partners caused me to shift between insider and outsider status.

Being a woman of Dominican descent and a fluent Spanish speaker helped me achieve a certain level of "insiderness."[6] The high numbers of Dominicans in the communities where I conducted this research helped me gain legitimacy with the women I interviewed. The women often introduced me to their friends with statements like "This is Katie. She's Dominican from Puerto Plata." In other instances women would come to me and say, "Tú eres dominicana, ¿verdad? Porque tienes el plátano en la frente" (You're Dominican, right? Because you have a plantain on your forehead).[7] Furthermore, my phenotype and gender presentation helped me assimilate physically with the women I studied. Gender, nationality, and language played a big role in creating my acceptance within the community. In a few instances, my identity as a mother also helped facilitate my acceptance with some of the respondents who had children. The few sexually nonconforming Latinas raising children whom I met in the field were often excited to connect with another mother. This meant that my son and I would sometimes get invited to their children's birthday parties, religious events, or play dates. Furthermore, we sometimes attended child-friendly events put on by various LGBTQ organizations together.

Collaborative Research

I strove to involve the participants in every aspect of the research process, ultimately making this work a coproduction of knowledge. Before I began interviewing participants, I met with counselors and support staff from the Lesbian, Gay, Bisexual, and Transgender Community Center in New York in order to learn about what they considered to be the unique needs of sexually nonconforming Latinas. Their suggestions, as well as those from the research participants, helped to shape the interview guide I used in the field. While initially I had broadly framed the project goals as being about LBQ experiences, the participants kept bringing the focus back to their struggles with family. It was with the encouragement of the study participants themselves that I decided to focus on the family in *Amigas y Amantes*. While a researcher ultimately uses her own lens to interpret the data she collects, she evolves, learns, and grows through interacting with the participants (DeVault 1999). In the end, my obligation is to interpret the data collected, but only after engaging in much reflexivity regarding my own social position and how it has shaped my understanding of these women's experiences. Therefore, this work is a collaborative project because I started this study aware of my ignorance and open to the participants' interpretations and experiences. My interactions with these women ultimately shaped my interpretative lens. This transformation of myself permeates the work and has ultimately informed the standpoint I developed through community involvement (Collins 2004; Hartsock 2004).

Sexually Nonconforming Latinas in the Borderlands

As I was studying sexually nonconforming Latinas and the ways in which they negotiate family, Gloria Anzaldúa's writings resonated heavily with me. Anzaldúa left the academic world many gifts before her untimely death in 2004. *Borderlands/ La Frontera* and her subsequent writings provide us with a theoretical framework with which to analyze forms of oppression, a theory of transformation, and a map for the stages of developing and strengthening a mestiza consciousness (Anzaldúa 1999, 2002, 2009). In *Amigas y Amantes,* I use Anzaldúan theory to map the path of resistance, transformation, resilience, and growth experienced by sexually nonconforming Latinas. Anzaldúa's writings help crystallize the strategies these women used to simultaneously negotiate families of both choice and origin. The contributions she makes in *Borderlands/La Frontera* and her subsequent essays serve as a backdrop to this book because they best encompass the work involved in managing family and the contradictions of the plural self. Her collective writings are useful here in that they emphasize the work that women who hold multiple marginalities do to develop a consciousness that can withstand life's contradictions.

Following Anzaldúa, in *Amigas y Amantes* I explore the in-between, unspoken spaces inhabited by the mestiza. Anzaldúa (2002) came to call this ambiguous space "nepantla," a place where one lives in a constant state of displacement. Mestizas spend so much time in nepantla that it becomes "a sort of home," albeit a place where one is vulnerable (Anzaldúa 2002, 1). I use nepantla here to describe the space that sexually nonconforming Latinas negotiate with their families of origin and choice: the space where they negotiate the visibility and invisibility of their sexualities. In this way, the women whose experiences are shared in this book are nepantleras; they are always in between spaces, always in transition.

In *Borderlands/La Frontera*, Anzaldúa theorized about one's ability to develop *la facultad*, a deeper level of cognition that one can achieve through self-reflection and digging "below the surface" (1999, 60). In an interview with Christine Welland in 1983, Anzaldúa further outlines la facultad. It is a tool that provides marginalized people with the power to resist the detrimental messages others hold about them. It is an intuition that helps the mestiza survive her oppression. La facultad helps her stay grounded. Achieving la facultad requires one to undergo a process of transformation. I trace this process of transformation for the sexually nonconforming Latinas who participated in this study as they come to develop a deeper level of understanding of themselves, their families, and their religious beliefs. In *Amigas y Amantes*, I use Anzaldúa's theories to explore sexually nonconforming Latinas' journeys toward developing a mestiza consciousness and using this consciousness to make sense of their relationships with those they value most in their lives—their families of origin and choice. In *Amigas y Amantes* I expand upon some of Anzaldúa's key concepts: mestiza consciousness, borderlands, nepantla, la facultad, and Shadow-Beast.[8] I explore the mestiza's need for visibility and her struggle to determine if and when to make her Shadow-Beast visible. The struggle for visibility/invisibility is central to the experiences of the sexually nonconforming Latinas in this study. Their need for visibility clashed with their families of origins' preference for invisibility, creating a fundamental obstacle in their efforts to do family.

The women who participated in this study are mestizas who are always living on the fringe of multiple contradictory cultures. As Latinas in the United States, they struggle with finding belonging among the dominant society. They are othered on account of their accents, immigration status, phenotypes, and cultural traditions. As sexually nonconforming Latinas, they struggle to find acceptance and visibility among their families of origin. They work to gain familial approval of their romantic relationships and familial support of their sexual nonconformity. The study participants grapple with the contradictions that emerge from seeking visibility and acceptance from institutions like the family and religion that marginalize them.

Amigas y Amantes is an exploration of sexually nonconforming Latinas' acts of resistance. As women who have chosen to build their lives with other women, they are resisting societal and familial norms. *Amigas y Amantes* is about these mestizas' journeys to reconcile the contradictions in their lives as mothers, daughters, and lovers and to learn to live with their plural identities and to develop borderlands where they can become whole. Mostly, however, it is about how Latinas build families and the roles that their contradicting identities play in the process.

"Queering" Emotion Work

Emotion work is an invisible labor that people perform daily, consciously and subconsciously, for the sake of the family. Scholars have used the phrase "emotion work" to describe both the physical acts of cleaning, feeding, and caring for the family, as Arlie Hochschild does in *The Second Shift* (1989), and the cognitive acts of making others feel secure, happy, and safe, as she does in *The Managed Heart* (1983). For Hochschild, the process of emotion work is about people suppressing and shaping their feelings of disappointment, resentment, and anger in order to present themselves in a particular way, but it can also be about evoking positive feelings or suppressing those one believes to be inappropriate in a given situation. Hochschild's contributions, along with those of many others, have advanced our understanding of emotion work as labor that is taken for granted as a production of motherhood and femininity.[9]

Emotion work in the family has rarely been used outside of a heterosexual context. Most of emotion work scholarship has focused on the heterosexual nuclear family (DeVault 1991; Duncombe and Marsden 1995; Erickson 1993; Hochschild 1989). This work often seeks to understand the gendered division of labor in these households and how that affects the overall happiness and success of married couples. But emotion work is also produced in nonheterosexual and/or alternative families. However, with the exception of Christopher Carrington's (1999) work on how "lesbigay" families manage the division of labor and Carla Pfeffer's (2010) work on women caring for their trans male partners, we know very little about how emotion work is done among alternative families.[10] Carrington's and Pfeffer's works help to illustrate the ways in which emotion work can be an inherently gendered process that confines the men and women who do it to specific gender ideologies. While this research has begun the process of "queering" emotion work in the family, there is still much work to be done. I know of no studies that look at emotion work exclusively in sexually nonconforming women's households. This is curious given that so much research has focused on emotion work as women's burden in the home. This absence begs the question, how does emotion work play out in the households of sexually nonconforming women who do not adhere to stereotypical gender roles? In *Amigas y Amantes*, I contribute to the queering of emotion work by exploring the lengths that sexually nonconforming Latinas go to in caring for families of choice and origin.[11] I consider the ways sexually nonconforming women integrate not only their friends, partners, and children but also their parents, grandparents, and other extended families of origin into their own personal support network. This work adds to our understanding of same-sex families and the struggles they face in building and preserving familial ties.

Previous research has shown that socioeconomic status shapes how sexually nonconforming individuals create families of choice.[12] But we need to better understand how that process is complicated by race, ethnicity, and immigration status. In *Amigas y Amantes*, I focus on the emotional management aspect of emotion work, not the domestic tasks individuals engage in. I focus on how women feel and negotiate the feelings of others in their efforts to establish a collective familial network that bridges families of choice and origin. While families of choice are often studied in isolation from the families of origin that LGBTQ individuals are born into, the experiences of the sexually nonconforming Latinas described in this study illustrate that these women simultaneously engage in emotion work with both families. The invisible labor involved in managing the emotions of both families is an ongoing, interrelated, and overlapping negotiation that often results in LBQ Latinas compromising their own needs for the sake of family. These women learned how to manage the care needs of families of origin at times when they conflicted with the care needs of families of choice. I found that the sexually nonconforming Latinas in this study engaged in just as much emotion work as previous scholars found to be the case for women in heterosexual relationships; and, consistent with previous research, they engaged in this emotion work without complaint, hesitation, or even acknowledgment that this emotion work was a form of invisible labor. However, the emotion work the study participants engage in has some distinct qualities. The study participants begin from a place of seeking visibility, acceptance, and redemption from their families of origin. They seek visibility of their families of choice and redemption from the stigmas that they believe their sexual nonconformity brings upon the family. In this way, sexually nonconforming Latinas do emotion work from a very distinct place from heterosexual women who may take visibility for granted and who may not be burdened by these stigmas. These basic differences lead sexually nonconforming women to develop distinct ways of doing family. Thus, in *Amigas y Amantes,* I seek to address the following questions: What do families of choice and origin look like for those individuals who are both sexually nonconforming and Latina/o? Do sexually nonconforming Latinas/os ever merge families of choice and origin? What would a space that allows such a merging look like?

We know very little about the ongoing relationships that LGBTQ individuals maintain with their families of origin post disclosure or irrespective of disclosure and how those relationships are affected by their families of choice. We know even less about if and how LGBTQ individuals are able to merge families of origin with their chosen families. In *Amigas y Amantes,* I provide an analysis that moves us away from the stereotypical image of LGBTQ couples as separate and disconnected from biological families and begin exploring the ways in which families of choice negotiate relationships with biological families. I delve into the social constraints that sexually nonconforming Latinas face as they shoulder the burden of negotiating families of choice and origin. *Amigas y Amantes* is about how sexually nonconforming Latinas manage the costs associated with these negotiations. It is about the tensions that arise as Latinas learn to negotiate the parts of the self that contradict one another and to manage their emotions based on the constraints they experience from juggling families of choice and origin. All of the findings illustrated in the following chapters help us to better understand the distinct ways in which sexually nonconforming women do family and, in doing so, contribute to the queering of emotion work.

OVERVIEW OF THE BOOK

In each of the chapters in *Amigas y Amantes*, I set out to produce a work that would add to our understanding of how sexually nonconforming Latinas experience family. However, the findings in this book are not only applicable to Latinas or other sexually nonconforming women of color. The findings in this book have implications for many sexually nonconforming women, regardless of race or ethnicity. Chapter 1 explores the theme of femininity and how LBQ Latinas reconcile the messages they received growing up about the appropriate way to do gender with the gender expectations they confront in LBQ communities as adults. This chapter takes an in-depth look at the meanings of femininity for mothers and daughters and the ways in which femininity influences familial reactions to their kin's sexual "transgressions." Chapter 2 explores the role of religion in LBQ Latinas' lives. Specifically, this chapter emphasizes the ways in which family members can use religion as a platform from which to reject or judge their kin. Furthermore, this chapter explores the ways that LBQ Latinas reconcile the religious messages they received growing up about same-sex sexuality with their experiences as adults. Chapter 3 explores how LBQ Latinas and their families deal with interracial or interethnic same-sex relationships. In this chapter, I set out to map how issues of race, ethnicity, immigration status, gender, and sexuality play out in the family and how the burdens that result from these intersections influence the respondents' interpersonal relationships. Chapter 4 explores the barriers that LBQ Latinas face in their efforts to gain citizenship and rear children. The mothers and the undocumented women in this study faced the most adversity in creating families of choice, due to poverty and legal status. These women needed families of origin more than other participants, whose financial stability and citizenship afforded them options in circumnavigating the structural barriers that same-sex couples face in trying to gain protection and recognition for their families. Chapter 5 explores LBQ Latinas' experiences trying to negotiate integrating their families of choice and origin and tending to their care needs. Here I explore the ways in which respondents manage their feelings and those of their loved ones in an effort to balance the needs of both families. All of these chapters contribute to queering emotion work. They highlight the labor involved in doing family and the particular constraints placed on women who are marginalized on account of their race or ethnicity, sexualities, class, and immigration status. Apparent in each chapter is the resiliency of these LBQ participants and the ways in which they cope with the many constraints that land in their lives. Their resilience contributes to their mestiza consciousness and to their collective experience.

CHAPTER 1

"AS LONG AS YOU WEAR A DRESS"

GENDER CONFORMITY AND SEXUALITY

As a girl in the Dominican Republic, I remember the powerful women in my family teaching me to embody femininity. As young as five, I vividly remember slouching comfortably over a chair watching cartoons and my *madrina* (godmother) straightening me out. "No te conviene andar con la espalda jorobada. Tienes que sentarte derecha con las piernas cruzadas. Así es que se sientan las señoritas." (It's not in your best interest to go around with your back hunched over. You have to sit up straight with your legs crossed. That's how young ladies sit.) I consistently received messages such as this one from the women whom I respected the most and thus learned very early on how much femininity mattered. I took these experiences with me to the field when conducting interviews with sexually nonconforming Latinas. I soon found how similar the participants' childhood experiences were to my own. Their experiences revealed a recurring tension in the family regarding femininity and sexual conformity, a tension that played out most profoundly between mothers and daughters.

In this chapter, I explore why proper socialization of femininity was so important to the study participants and their families. By femininity I refer to the characteristics, physical appearances, and behaviors or mannerisms that these women and their families associated with appropriate womanhood. In looking at both the study participants' physical presentations of self and the behaviors they associate with a coveted femininity, I begin to disentangle the correlation that these women and their families made between sexual conformity, outward physical appearance, and femininity. For the study participants, doing femininity was central because they believed that gender conformity through their embodied physical appearance and their behaviors sent messages to others about their identities and their families' social status. Given this, how these women deployed femininity was a cause of constant tension in their families of origin. Familial concerns regarding femininity deployment are intertwined and cannot be extracted from the reservations those families of origin had regarding their children's alternative sexualities. Together, these tensions add a layer of complexity to our understanding of familial "acceptance" in these Latinas' homes.

In a theoretical piece on gender hegemony, Mimi Schippers (2007) argues that there are multiple and hierarchal femininities. Pariah femininities, she offers, are those that, when embodied by women, challenge the hierarchal and complementary relationship between masculinity and femininity. Those who are promiscuous, hold erotic feelings for other women, or are sexually aggressive embody pariah femininities. Those whose behaviors subscribe to stereotypical "womanly" characteristics and maintain a hierarchal and complementary relationship with hegemonic masculinities embody hegemonic femininities. Justin Charlebois (2011) adds oppositional and dominant femininities to this hierarchy. Oppositional femininities are those that resist hegemonic femininities but that are not necessarily deviant or stigmatized, as is the case with pariah femininities. Dominant femininities are those that are widely accepted and celebrated in a given context but that do not complement or support the ascendancy of hegemonic masculinities. Charlebois's work (2011) allows for an analysis that recognizes that individuals can embody more than one of these femininities simultaneously. They may embody an oppositional femininity through their behaviors or sexual practices while also embodying a dominant femininity through their physical appearance. By virtue of their relationships with and erotic desires for other women, the participants in this study embodied pariah femininities. Their awareness of the stigmas inherent in these embodied femininities fueled their desires to simultaneously adopt an outward appearance of dominant femininity. For the study participants, the desire to exude dominant femininities came from an understanding that "appropriate" gendered presentations of self could afford them opportunities in the social world. Their mothers were most committed to this display after their daughters entered relationships with other women. This, I argue, is because they wanted to minimize stigma for their daughters and for their presentation of self to signal their womanhood to others. Most of the LBQ Latinas in this study, then, embodied femininities that were simultaneously dominant and pariah. Most embodied an outward presentation of self that to varying degrees fit societal expectations for gender conformity while simultaneously engaging in behaviors that defied heterosexual norms.

Both the study participants and their mothers used physical appearance to cover the stigmas associated with their or their daughters' erotic desires. By maintaining an outward appearance of dominant femininity, the study participants can ensure that their stigmas remain discreditable rather than discredited.[1] Most of the participants in this study were committed to keeping their sexualities as discreditable stigmas around their families. Sometimes they aimed for this in order to pass for a nonstigmatized "normal." In these instances, some participants did not disclose their alternative sexualities with their families of origin, choosing instead to keep their erotic desires for other women separate from them. At other times, the participants covered their discreditable stigmas by displaying a dominant, feminine outward appearance so as to minimize the stigma of their sexual nonconformity. Regardless of whether the study participants aimed to pass for "normals" or to cover a discreditable stigma, they, along with their mothers, understood that a non-gender-appropriate physical appearance could serve as a stigma symbol. Given this understanding, to varying degrees and at various points in the study participants' lives, outward displays of dominant femininities and gender conformity played a more central role.

THE POWER OF FEMININITY

In *Beauty Secrets* (1986), Wendy Chapkis describes beauty as something women actively pursue in their efforts to gain validation and respect from the larger patriarchal society. Chapkis writes, "Appearance talks, making statements about gender, sexuality, ethnicity, and class. In a sexually, racially, and economically divided society, all those visual statements add up to an evaluation of power" (1986, 79). The value of beauty lies in its link to femininity, which is then linked to womanhood (Freedman 1986). Producing appropriate femininity can exonerate an individual of social stigmas associated with nonconformity. When one produces femininity appropriately, one conveys aspects of her identity to others. In evaluating if and how we do femininities, others can deduce information about our sexualities, our class, and our social status. The assumptions others make about our identities based on how we do femininity may be inaccurate, but, nonetheless, these assumptions shape our interactions with others. These assumptions have the power to shape the opportunities available to us.[2] The production of femininity, then, is more than just a personal decision: attached to it are social consequences that supersede the personal realm. The very power of femininity can be constraining; we are often compelled to achieve certain displays of femininity based on the social opportunities we hope will be opened for us by doing so.[3] Femininity can be a double-edged sword, and women stand to pay a big price for not conforming to ideal standards of beauty (Berry 2008). This price can affect both their financial security and their social status.

Understanding the economic value of feminine beauty contextualizes why physical appearance played such an important role in the lives of sexually nonconforming Latinas and their families of origin. These women were socialized to understand the power of feminine beauty and its relationship to their economic mobility. In particular, the eighteen study participants who were raised in Latin America reported being confined by the relationship between gainful employment and physical appearance. Their employment options were limited and based not only on their credentials and the availability of jobs, but also on their physical appearance and age. During our interview, Vanessa, a thirty-five-year-old Colombian woman, explained her frustration with employment in the labor market prior to immigrating to the United States:

> En Colombia, nunca conseguí un trabajo porque allá, no solamente por la situación económica, sino por todos los requisitos que quieren. Tú puedes tener un GPA casi de 3.5, foto, edad, pero si tú tienes más de veinticinco años . . . Forget it, too old . . . En Colombia los trabajos son como segmentados, ¿no? Entonces le cierra a uno todas las puertas. Yo trabajé con mi papá, pero él para ayudarme.

> (In Colombia, I never found a job there, not only due to the economic situation, but also because of all the requirements they want. You can have a GPA of almost 3.5, a photo, be of legitimate age, but if you are more than twenty-five years old. . . . Forget it, too old . . . In Colombia the jobs are kind of fragmented. So they close all the doors on you. I worked with my father, but he did it to help me.)

Vanessa is a college-educated woman from a solidly middle-class home. She is highly proficient in English but still struggled to find employment in Colombia. Despite performing gender and femininity appropriately, Vanessa found her age to be an obstacle to her professional advancement. While these kinds of employment discriminations also occur in the United States, they can be particularly detrimental in certain Latin American countries with very high unemployment rates and limited options for social mobility. These circumstances created social and economic implications for achieving or not achieving hegemonic or dominant femininities. Those implications impacted the LBQ Latinas in this study, as well as their entire families, and solidified their commitment to outward displays of dominant femininities through physical appearance.

FEMININITY AS A FEMALE-CENTERED ACHIEVEMENT

Doing dominant femininity is quite often about seeking the approval of other women, therefore making it a commonly practiced accomplishment in female-centered spaces. As Dorothy Smith (1988) notes, women are not merely passively reacting to existing discourses of femininity. They can manipulate these discourses into their own versions of femininity. They engage in this process together, taking in the criticisms they receive from one another and adjusting their appearances accordingly (Smith 1988). Thus, dominant femininity is a female-centered production and one that women engage in irrespective of their desires to attract men or to advance economically in the world of work.

When women collectively engage in the production of femininity, the end result can be a culturally scripted beauty ideal. Our imaginings of what is beautiful and feminine are often racialized into a specific, ideal type. This is particularly the case when doing femininity and beauty occurs in collaboration with other coethnics or family members.[4] The family is one of the spaces where women collectively create dominant femininities for themselves and others. Looking back at my own history, achieving dominant femininity was a way for female kin to bond. I spent hours in the kitchen with my mother, aunts, and female cousins, everyone getting their hair straightened to smooth out the natural curls. "El que quiere moño bonito tiene que esperar" (Someone who wants good hair must wait) they would say when I got impatient and wanted to play. When I complained that it hurt to have every strand of hair on my head tugged into straight submission, my mother would remind me that "el pelo bueno no viene fácil" (good hair doesn't come easily). For family gatherings, the ritual of taming my hair was coupled with the need to wear the perfect dress, shoes, and other accessories. In these instances, femininity was about displaying a carefully mani-cured version of the self to the extended family members in order to gain their approval. We used discourses of middle-class femininity as a way to measure our own productions and help one another succeed at doing gender.

The study participants reported that, as children and adolescents, producing dominant femininities was about obtaining approval from their mothers. A suc-cessful production of femininity served as a point of pride for middle-class fami-lies, and daughters often aspired to provide their families with this honor. Many of the study participants described doing femininity as an accomplishment in living up to their mothers' expectations, matching my own experiences. Alexis, a twenty-year-old woman of Colombian descent, describes the feminine messages she received growing up in the following way: "We're Colombian, and with Colombian culture women dress themselves up a lot. You take care of your hair; you take care of your nails. You look presentable at all times. My mother did emphasize looking good with what you had. She gave me an etiquette book and had me read it. But I never saw it centered around catering to a man or how to behave around a man. It was mostly about behaving as a woman and being very proper." The idea of behav-ing like a "proper" young woman permeated women's recollections of the mes-sages they received from their mothers regarding femininity. These women were taught to physically adorn their bodies in feminine ways and to behave according to specific rules of etiquette attributed to dominant femininities. In this way, doing femininity with and for other women became the norm. Rarely did the partici-pants describe these lessons as being about desirability to men. In exploring the respondents' experiences with doing gender in the home, my goal was to better flesh out the links that the study participants and their mothers create between gender conformity and sexual orientation and the influences that these correla-tions have on familial acceptance. My goal was to better understand why maintain-ing celebrated, nonstigmatized femininities was important in these families, even when the approval of men was not sought or needed.

Overwhelmingly, the study participants attributed doing femininity to pro-ducing womanhood, as Alexis describes. The sooner they learned to take care of their hair, apply makeup, and tweeze their eyebrows, the more adult they would become. It signaled to family and community members that they had matured and had accepted appropriate gender norms. As these women entered adolescence and beyond, the expectation was that being a woman would involve doing dominant femininities.

The study participants often looked toward their mothers when trying to gauge if their attempts to produce femininity were successful. In these instances, mothers became the standard by which LBQ Latinas measured their performance of femininity. Consider, for example, this description provided by one study participant named Sara. Sara was born in Puerto Rico and raised in the United States. She is twenty years old and attends an elite university in New York City. She describes her experiences learning about dominant femininities at an early age in the following ways:

> My mother would always want to brush my hair. . . . And she would get lit-
> tle bows to put in my hair. Everything was always centered around my hair. I
> always felt pressure when it came to my extended family. When we had fam-
> ily gatherings, I would always compare myself to my cousins. There are four
> of us, four girls, and all of us have the same middle name: Cecilia. So it is
> Maria Cecilia, Melanie Cecilia, Raquel Cecilia, and me, Sara Cecilia. There's
> always been an unspoken contest to see who out of the cousins was the pretti-
> est. I always remember wanting to dress more feminine to match them or even
> exceed them. But it never worked. They always had more style than I did. And
> also there was the whole money issue. We couldn't afford nice clothes.

Sara recalls the value her mother placed on producing femininity. The contest she describes between herself and her three cousins was also a contest between their mothers. Each mother wanted her daughter to be the best dressed at family events because their daughters' successful performances of femininity were a reflection of their motherhood. Sara's insecurities regarding her physical presentation of self were driven in part by her knowledge that her single mother did not possess the financial resources to keep up with the other girls in the family.

Accomplishing a certain class categorization does not occur independently of how one accomplishes gender and femininity. Ultimately, these are simultaneous accomplishments (West and Zimmerman 2002). The pursuit of privileged femininities is often described as a middle- and upper-class concern because it is those women who have the resources and the capital to keep up a feminine ideal.[5] However, regardless of actual class status, women strive to achieve specific femininities because they are cognizant of the ways in which physical appearance marks social class. In recent studies, women were able to categorize each other into class groups based on their presentation of self: markers such as clothing, hair styles, and manicured nails aid individuals in making these distinctions (de Casanova 2004; Lee 2009).

Thus, producing hegemonic and/or dominant femininities makes a statement not only about a mother's success at motherhood or a daughter's evolution into womanhood, but also about the financial means of the family. Producing appropriate femininities sends a message to the community about the family's social and economic position overall. The fact that she was raised by a single mother made Sara particularly concerned with succeeding at the performance of dominant femininity because it signaled to the family whether or not her mother was succeeding at motherhood on her own.

The study participants used their mothers' productions of femininities to evaluate themselves. Those whose mothers embodied dominant or hegemonic femininities recalled making a conscious effort to try to measure up to their mothers. This was the case even for girls who were comfortable not measuring up to their peers. Luisa is an Ecuadorian woman in this study who recalled not being overly concerned with femininity as she was growing up, but as she matured she recognized the importance of this production for her mother. As she notes, "My mom is very feminine. She's very pearls and high heels. Always looks put together. And I remember around twelve years old thinking, 'Okay, I'm not going to be that femmy, girly-girl, going-to-the-mall-and-looking-for-clothes kind of person.' Right around that time, I got a book to help me learn how to do it right. My mom gave me this binder Mary Kay gave out that had sections on makeup and how to do your eyebrows and how to dress right. And I remember studying it and being like, 'Okay, this is what I need to do.' By the time I got to high school, I knew what I was doing." Luisa looks at the displays of femininities from her peers and from her mother in an effort to develop her own individual form of femininity. Understanding her role as the reproducer of feminine ideals, Luisa's mother provides her with the necessary tools to help her transition into womanhood. By giving her the book from Mary Kay and by modeling a privileged, nonstigmatized form of femininity, Luisa's mother sets the process of replicating appropriate femininity in motion for her daughter.

Alexis, Luisa, and Sara internalized the subtle message that doing gender and privileged femininities were important for the family's social position and therefore made a conscious effort to accomplish this goal. Dominant femininities became something desirable to the participants in adolescence not only because it brought them closer to womanhood but also because it earned them approval from the respected female figures in their homes. Throughout their childhood and adolescence, the study participants strove to achieve dominant femininities that had little if anything to do with attracting men or maintaining heterosexuality and everything to do with gaining the acceptance of their mothers. Producing femininity became one of the ways respondents did emotion work in exchange for familial approval. Long before these women understood the economic value of femininity, they understood its value in the family, and thus they started the process of doing emotion work by doing dominant femininities long before they became adults.

Doing Gender and Familial Acceptance of Alternative Sexualities

As adults and particularly within their relationships with other women, the study participants reported having more tensions with their families regarding outward displays of femininities. Parents assumed that because their daughters were entering relationships with other women, they were somehow going to adopt an unfeminine or masculine physical appearance. Controlling dominant femininities became a tool that mothers used to mitigate what they believed to be a diminishment of their daughters' womanhood on account of their stigmatized status as LBQ women. Mothers, it seemed, were more comfortable accepting their daughters as lesbian, bisexual, and queer women if these daughters maintained the outward displays of dominant femininity instilled in them as young girls. Dominant femininities became a way for mothers to validate for themselves and for the larger community that their daughters were still women even when they were in relationships with other women. I argue that mothers become more committed to dominant femininities as their daughters matured into sexually nonconforming women because they wanted to ensure an outward presentation that could not clearly mark the stigmas of their sexualities.

While the research has shown that parents are less concerned about teaching young daughters how to be gender conforming at early ages than they are about sons (Kane 2006), the findings from the participants in this study suggest that gender conformity becomes most important for daughters as they become adolescents and adults.[6] However, while the participants in this study overwhelmingly remarked on their mothers' commitment to privileged, outward displays of femininity, they did not so much attribute this commitment to a direct promotion of heterosexuality. Rather, the participants' descriptions point to their mothers' promoting dominant displays of femininity in order to afford them the privileges of heterosexuality, irrespective of their sexualities. In other words, the participants believed their mothers encouraged them to achieve dominant femininities not as a way of promoting heterosexuality but as a way to protect them from further rejection and potential harm.

Mothers who knew that their daughters were in relationships with other women struggled equally with the sexual transgression they believed was taking place and their fears that gender transgression, the failure to embody a societally celebrated form of gender presentation, would also take place. The respondents explained that some of their mothers were even more concerned that their daughters might engage in gender transgressions than they were about the same-sex relationship itself. As an example, Luisa and her partner, Courtney, are getting married. For Luisa, getting her mother to accept their relationship and to agree to attend the wedding was a very difficult process; however, at the time of the interview all of Luisa's family had agreed to be at the wedding, and Luisa was busy making plans. She described a recent conversation she had with her mother about what she will be wearing on her wedding day. She stated, "My mother asked me, 'So you'll both be wearing a dress, right?' And I [Luisa] said, 'I think so.' And she said, 'You have to. If she's [Courtney] wearing a dress, you have to wear a dress.' And I asked, 'Why?' I told her 'I'm comfortable in a suit. I look good in a suit.' And she said, 'Yeah, but you have to wear a dress because I don't want anybody coming to the wedding to think that you're the guy in the relationship because you're not.'" Luisa's mother's acceptance of her relationship with Courtney is separate and apart from how she feels about Luisa's presentation of self. She needs her daughter to display gender conformity on her wedding day so as to send a clear message to others that despite identifying as bisexual and despite marrying a woman, she was still a woman. Luisa's mother attempts to minimize the stigma of her daughter's alternative sexuality by ensuring she wears a dress to overemphasize her womanhood. In this way, LBQ Latinas reported that their mothers were sometimes intent on policing their daughters' gender performance, in part, I would argue, because they could not control their daughters' sexualities. Luisa's description of this interaction with her mother implies that if she were to achieve an outward display of dominant femininity, it would somehow make her mother more comfortable about the ways in which she and Courtney are disrupting heteronormativity and hegemonic masculinity. In this way, the commitment that mothers like Luisa's had to their daughters' presenting dominant femininities through physical appearance added an additional layer of complexity to their level of acceptance of their daughters' sexualities.

The prospect of a gender transgression evoked anxiety and created an added barrier in parents' ability to "accept" and connect with their daughters after they had openly entered relationships with other women. Gender nonconformity served as a second barrier to acceptance between study participants and their families. This is illustrated in Jasmin's description of her father's reaction when she first told him she was a lesbian. She recounted their conversation as follows: "I was like, 'I want you to know I'm a lesbian.' He didn't say anything for a second. Then he said, 'Well, I guess I should have guessed that since I haven't seen you bring a boy home in six years.' And I was like, 'Yeah, I guess that's a pretty good indicator.' Then he asked if it was because he played sports with me a lot when I was little. My dad is kind of old fashioned the way that he thinks that girls should dress like girls and boys dress like boys. And then he asked, 'Are you going to start dressing like a boy?' I was like, 'No, Dad. I'm still the same person I was before.'" Immediately after learning of Jasmin's lesbian existence, her father asks if she attributes her lesbianism to him playing sports with her as a child. He questions if, by playing sports with her as a child, he somehow contributed to the disruption of her potential hegemonic femininity. His question illustrates his ideas regarding what is a successful embodiment of hegemonic femininity. It demonstrates fear that when girls play sports they are going outside a prescribed gender script of hegemonic femininity, something he begins to associate with deviant sexualities. When he probes whether or not she will begin "dressing like a boy," he illustrates his fear that if Jasmin is attracted to other women, it must be because she is somehow less of a woman herself. When he asks Jasmin if being a lesbian means that she will begin "dressing like a boy," he is trying to mitigate his concern that Jasmin's sexual preference will diminish her outward displays of dominant femininity. For as long as Jasmin continues to be gender conforming, her dad has reassurance that Jasmin will not face adversity due to the stigmas of simultaneously embodying a pariah femininity. Jasmin's outward displays of dominant femininity, I argue, make it easier for her dad, as it does Luisa's mother, to accept her lesbian existence.

Jasmin's experience also points to another important issue regarding how these families negotiated femininities in their homes. Just because mothers were the socializing agents of dominant femininities does not mean that fathers were not equally invested in this performance. The work of producing the feminine self mattered to fathers just as much as it did to mothers. Previous scholars have already started to disrupt the stereotypical notion that teaching appropriate gender socialization is solely the work of mothers in Latina/o families (González-López 2004; Gutmann 1996). This study supports their findings as evidenced by LBQ Latinas' beliefs that their fathers played an important role in their appropriate gender socialization. The participants didn't experience their fathers' investment in their femininities as motivated by a desire to compliment hegemonic masculinities. Rather, they experienced their fathers' investments in these femininities as similar to their mothers' teachings. Fathers wanted their daughters to be taken up by the larger society as well-socialized, appropriate, gender-conforming women. Some fathers made their expectations regarding femininity abundantly clear to their daughters. For example, Mariela's father always insisted that her nails be painted even though she never expressed an interest in manicures. Other fathers, however, were less direct about their expectations, using the mother as a vehicle through which to convey their opinions. Lucy, a Mexican immigrant who currently lives in New York City, describes this dynamic well. When she was a girl in Mexico, her mother always stressed to her the appropriate attitudes and behaviors that were expected of her as a young woman. Her mother encouraged her to use her older sisters as role models of proper "lady-like" behavior. Lucy, however, much preferred to run around with her brothers, never quite bonding with the other women in the family, as her mother would have hoped. In this quote, she describes how she perceived her father's role in all of this:

> Mi mamá le preocupaba que yo tomara las actitudes o las conductas de mis hermanos. Pero en realidad es que yo tenía mi propia cuerda. Mi padre nunca se metió mucho en eso, aunque si le decía a ella. Básicamente, ella era el canal de imponer ciertas conductas, porque mi papá rara vez se metía en eso, aunque con su forma de ser siempre nos puso autoridad.

(My mother worried that I would adopt the attitudes and behaviors of my brothers. But in reality, it's that I did my own thing. My father never got too involved in that, even though he would tell her to. Basically, she was a channel to impose certain behaviors, because my father rarely got involved in that, even though his nature was to always assert his authority over us.)

Here Lucy describes the way her parents distributed the task of enforcing a feminine comportment. While it was her mother who stressed to her the importance of feminine behavior, Lucy was always aware that this issue mattered equally to her father despite his silence. The study participants' recollections of these familial dynamics emphasize gender socialization as a familial process. Even though these dynamics most often played out between mothers and daughters, it is clear that fathers were equally complicit in maintaining appropriate gender boundaries in their homes.

The study participants carried the messages they received early on in life about femininity and its significance for social class status and womanhood with them into romantic relationships. In doing so, study participants learned that their productions of femininity had implications beyond the family. As the participants began to seek out queer spaces from which to meet potential partners, they learned new forms of producing gender and femininity in order to achieve new goals. To varying degrees, all of the participants learned to manipulate their gender displays in order to attract potential partners and to "fit in" at female-centered spaces. These new forms of femininity, like the participants' new romantic interests, added yet another layer of complexity to their relationships with families of origin.

Situational Femininities

There is no one kind of femininity: it evolves according to time and space. The multiple configurations of femininities are situational and can vary according to culture and region (Charlebois 2011). In their interviews, the study participants described the multiple cultural expectations that influenced how they produced femininity. They emphasized family and the larger society in both the United States and Latin America, as well as the expectations from their lesbian, bisexual, and queer communities, as social constructors of their femininities. As they became adults, the study participants sometimes shed the outward displays of dominant femininities imposed on them in adolescence and created their own distinct gender presentations to fit their individual lifestyles. These changes were most drastic among the eighteen participants who immigrated to the United States as adults after having been socialized into Latin American forms of dominant and hegemonic femininities and among those raised in Puerto Rico. Those women were likely to adopt Western ideals for dominant femininities into their lives as adults. They sometimes embodied alternative femininities, adopting gender displays that marked them as women but that placed them outside of the confines for celebrated and privileged femininities, thus subjecting them to stigmatization (Holland 2004). Displays of alternative femininities can include excessive tattoos, body piercings, and unconventional haircuts and hair dyes. A few participants adopted a more transgressive outward presentation of self. "Transgressive" is a term that Mignon Moore (2006, 2011) uses to describe black lesbians whose outward appearances can be described as masculine through their use of men's clothing and adoption of masculine mannerisms. On account of these various shifts, these women at times experienced a disjuncture in familial approval. This tension sometimes led participants to adopt "situational standards of femininity": achieving one ideal type of a dominantly feminine physical appearance when among families of origin and a distinct outward display of femininity when around friends in the United States. Maritza, a study participant from Peru, described her situational femininities in this way:

> Yo era muy femenina desde chiquita. Siempre usaba vestidito. Lo hacía siempre. Ahora, cuando estoy con mi familia uso falda. Me visto bien femme pero sólo cuando estoy con ellos. Cuando estoy acá sola me visto así (T-shirt and jeans). Todavía me pongo vestido, falda y todo pero tampoco es que me gusta mucho usar faldas. Pero yo lo hago.

> (Since I was little, I've been very feminine. I always wore dresses. I always did it. Now, when I'm with my family, I wear skirts. I dress very femme but only when I'm with them. When I'm here alone, I dress this way (T-shirt and jeans). I still wear dresses, skirts, and everything, but it's not that I like to wear skirts. But I do it.)

After moving to the United States, Maritza became more comfortable wearing short hair, for example, something she perceived others would read as unfeminine in Peru. Her dress style in the United States often involves wearing jeans and T-shirts with a feminine cut. Her overall look embraces Western standards for dominant femininity but does not overemphasize femininity. This style appeals to her in part because of its low maintenance. Her hair doesn't require hours of blow-dryer mistreatments, her jeans don't need ironing, and her tennis shoes are comfortable for walking around the city subways. Doing dominant femininity in Peru involved wearing her hair longer and more dresses and skirts, all of which resulted in more maintenance and care. Both styles are feminine; however, Maritza describes her look in Peru as being more carefully and meticulously produced, something that was required of her for the purpose of work and familial gatherings. She has found a bit more freedom to expand her feminine options in New York. Maritza describes the process of doing femininity in Peru as harder to achieve. She describes it more as a process that requires work, rather than a display of one's natural beauty. This is not to say that the same pressures do not also exist in the United States, but rather that Maritza felt she had more options of femininities available to her in New York City. These options, I would argue, stem from the freedom she has gained living in the United States, away from her family of origin and the constraints of being accountable to them. The geographical distance between herself and her family relieved Maritza of the responsibility of protecting the family's social status through conforming to rigid standards of dominant or hegemonic femininities. This autonomy has allowed Maritza to embody a feminine self that is more comfortable for her: one that does not require much maintenance but clearly identifies her as a woman.

In choosing to revert to a feminine style that requires more maintenance and care when around family, Maritza is making a conscious effort to manage her family's anxieties regarding her presentation of self. She is altering her image in order to create a look that is consistent with the expectations of her family of origin. For Maritza, the emotion work of managing her presentation of self manifests itself in situational femininities. For her, the work isn't just in producing a socially acceptable standard of femininity but in producing distinct, socially acceptable standards for femininity based on location and audience.

Producing beauty is a process throughout which one negotiates contradictory cultural discourses (Hammidi and Kaiser 1999). The Latinas in this study used situational femininities when negotiating the cultural discourses of femininity that prevailed in their homes, dominant cultural discourses of femininity that they received from the larger Western society, and the cultural discourses they learned in their LBQ communities. They used this situational strategy among families of origin, but also within other social environments as they negotiated distinct cultural discourses. In becoming part of LBQ communities in the United States, these women learned to subtly alter their outward displays of femininity in order to fit the type of women they hoped to attract. This is something they negotiated with family members who adhered to specific ways of displaying femininity and struggled to accept alternative forms of femininities. In this process, the study participants moved across various femininities in order to negotiate relationships (Denner and Dunbar 2004).

Gendered presentations of self are fluid, and thus at various points in their lives these women produced themselves differently based on the partner they were with, the communities they were a part of, and where they were in their lifecycles. By the time I interviewed Sara, she had long stopped aspiring to surpass her cousins as the "most feminine" at family gatherings. She wore a very short haircut, a loose-fitting T-shirt, and ripped, loose-fitting jeans. She had also pierced her tongue, lip, and eyebrow. Here Sara highlights how her gender presentation has evolved through the years: "I think I can attribute my gender presentation to the partners that I've been with. With Lydia [Sara's former partner], there were very strict roles. She was the more butch one, and I was the femme one. I had my nails done, my hair long, lip liner, all of that. And then, you know, with Alexis, that's when I started feeling more comfortable, being a little more androgynous." I asked Sara what her mother thought of her current gender presentation, and she explained that her mother was very upset when she shaved all her hair off and that her mother was always giving her subtle hints about how much she liked her hair when she wore it longer. Sara admits that the biggest issues that she has with her mother right now are not about her queer identity but about her physical appearance. Part of what makes this process difficult for Sara's mother is the evolution of Sara's gender presentation over time. As a newly out queer woman, Sara found herself confined by rigid roles for gender and sexuality in her first relationship. Her partner Lydia embodied a transgressive outward display and Sara embodied dominant femininity. In her current relationship, Sara has had more flexibility to explore alternative femininities. Sara uses the term "androgynous" to describe her outward physical appearance. However, her physical appearance marks more of a shift from a dominant display of femininity to an alternative display of femininity. Sara experiences this gender presentation as androgynous because it does not fit conventional norms of celebrated femininities. Sara feels her more androgynous presentation of self fits her current relationship and lifestyle, but this may also be confusing and anxiety producing for Sara's mother.

When Sara and the other study participants found new ways to do gender, they faced the task of renegotiating family. The vast majority of the study participants described themselves as embodying a dominant femininity, an alternative femininity, or a gendered appearance that mixed feminine and masculine styles. Moore (2006, 2011) has termed these women "gender blenders." The shifts in their outward presentations of self did not coincide with what their mothers had envisioned for them. This meant that they spent a lot of time justifying their choices in less dominant or alternative femininities to their mothers. In some instances, participants even had to make these justifications with their partners' mothers. The dual processes of doing family and doing femininity strained the participants' romantic partnerships. It was yet another way in which the study participants labored with the emotion work of the family. Mariela received messages about femininity that were very similar to those described by other participants. As an adult, however, she no longer felt comfortable embodying dominant femininity, opting instead for a more transgressive appearance. Mariela's resistance to a celebrated or privileged form of femininity has created tensions not only with her own family but also with her partner Jasmin's family. She describes here the problems that her gendered presentation of self has created with her girlfriend's mother:

> I feel more comfortable in "guy shorts," the baggy pants. I'm not one to dress very feminine, which is something [Jasmin's mom] thinks is a requirement to being female. So when I'd go over, my girlfriend would ask me, "Can you dress more feminine? Can you wear tight jeans and a tight shirt?" And at first, I did it, but then I realized that there was no need for me to do that.

> One day in particular, I was wearing a wife beater and cargo shorts and [Jasmin's mom] said, "Oh, why are you dressed like that? Were you outside working on something?" And I said, "No, I'm coming from the house." And she said, "Oh, well, why aren't you wearing something else?" I'm like, "Because I wanted to wear this." And that's all she said. It was never too over the top, but she made it a point to point out that she didn't like how I dressed.

Jasmin's mom is very committed to conventional standards of beauty and femininity. Her preference for dominant and hegemonic femininities is challenged when her daughter Jasmin comes out as a lesbian. This ideal is further challenged when Jasmin enters a relationship with Mariela, whose outward presentation of self is more transgressive. Mariela embodies a more intense form of pariah femininity than Jasmin does in that she prefers masculine attire. Both her outward presentation of self and her lesbian existence challenge hegemonic masculinities. While at first Mariela does situational femininities by presenting a softer, more feminine look when around Jasmin's mother, she ultimately becomes resentful of having to do this work. Mariela faces the task of reconciling conflicting discourses of femininity.

Doing situational femininities is one of the ways that sexually nonconforming Latinas do emotion work in their quotidian lives. On the one hand, these women are mindful of the way gender conformity can facilitate familial approval of their sexualities. They are equally mindful of the ways that gender conformity can lead to opportunities in the larger society, particularly with partners, with employers, and in larger LGBTQ communities. However, these women are also aware that idealized depictions of dominant femininities vary across time and space. Using situational femininities is a strategy that women like Sara, Maritza, and Mariela employ to alter their presentation of self to cater to the audience receiving them. This process is more complicated than simply choosing a more professional appearance in the workplace versus a relaxed look for the weekends. Situational femininities are meticulously planned and involve an array of physical appearances. Doing situational femininities requires the actor to consider her audience and the expectations for gender performance within this specific space and to produce that specific version of femininity in order to gain access. Yet despite the careful planning involved in cultivating these socially acceptable presentations, the participants did not usually conceptualize these behaviors as work. At most, participants interpreted these processes as anxiety producing. Take Luz, for example, who described to me during our interview feeling really confined by butch and femme roles in lesbian communities. She stated, "I think the anxiety is really more about the butch/femme thing. When I'm going to a lesbian club, there is still going to be something when I'm deciding what to wear. It's going to be present in my mind." That presence in Luz's mind causes her to adopt situational femininities. She considers carefully what she will wear to the lesbian bar because in many ways it is different from what she will wear when around family of origin or work colleagues. She is acutely aware that her presentation of self will send messages to others in the bar about who she is and whom she is interested in. This understanding preoccupies her mind as she decides how to produce an outward display of femininity.

I'm Still Feminine; I'm Not a Man

As adults, the study participants' situational femininities sometimes included more relaxed and less pronounced expressions of gender. This created anxiety for them that, by resisting the dominant femininities imposed on them through familial discourses and other societal forces, they would somehow be perceived as inferior women. Samantha Holland (2004) found similar anxieties in her work on women who embody alternative femininities. She notes that women went to great lengths to adopt nontraditional femininities while simultaneously fearing that their alternative appearances made them unfeminine. In Holland's work as well as in mine, the anxiety stems from not wanting to be aligned with men or masculinity. The study participants sometimes wanted to embody an alternative to the dominant or hegemonic femininities imposed on them in the home, but they did not want to cease being feminine in the process. Even while LBQ Latinas made a conscious effort to resist the discourses of femininity imposed on them by mothers, they feared how their resistance would be read by others. Despite their desires to resist, they did not wish to compromise the social status that inherently comes with gender conformity. Thus, in addition to managing their families' feelings about their less dominant, alternative, or transgressive displays of femininity, these women also managed their own feelings about this resistance. The study participants did the work of manipulating and resisting dominant discourses of femininity in order to adopt a presentation of self that best fit their lifestyles or a given situation; however, in doing so, they learned to assuage their own insecurities regarding their new, gendered appearances. They labored to convince themselves that they were still feminine women, in part, I argue, because their outward appearances did not display dominant, privileged femininities. Take Cynthia, for instance, who, during our interview, expressed insecurities about not fitting dominant or hegemonic discourses for femininity in Peru:

> First of all, my relationships always ended because I was a tomboy. My boyfriends would say, "Don't do this; it's not for girls." The guys always changed me for other more girly girls. And it was too much for me. I thought, "Why can't I have long hair or use makeup?" But I tried it for a few days and I was like, "Forget it. Where's my baseball cap? I love it." I was never mad with the guys. I was mad with myself. I would think all the time, "It's my fault because I'm not feminine, because I'm not like my friends. I don't have long hair or put on makeup, no long nails or nice clothes." I would think, "Why am I always

wearing long shirts and shorts or pants and boots?" I would think, "Come on, my look is more like a guy." And actually my father would tell me that all the time. I remember one time I cut my hair, and my father looked at me and said, "You look like a boy."

Cynthia attributes her lack of success with dating men in part to her failure to embody hegemonic femininity. Her insecurity stems from being cognizant that her presentation of self doesn't fit with what other young women her age embodied. Her response to this perceived shortcoming is disappointment in herself for failing to measure up to hegemonic femininities in Peru. Her words highlight the strong correlation that she, her father, and previous boyfriends make between her outward appearance and her womanhood. These strong correlations breed insecurities in Cynthia that she must then manage and curtail.

One of the ways that study participants grappled with the insecurity of not meeting dominant standards of femininity was to establish boundaries of gender transgression. Study participants drew clear lines delineating what they considered to be too transgressive and the kinds of femininities that were acceptable even if not dominant. In this way, LBQ Latinas participated in maintaining hierarchies of femininities (see figure 1.1).

Those participants who didn't embody dominant femininities compensated by redefining the boundaries of appropriate, acceptable femininities to include their own physical appearances. The more the study participants perceived that their gender presentation could potentially be read as masculine, the more intensely they evoked boundaries of gender transgression around displays of femininity. Kayla, for example, is a Puerto Rican lesbian from New York. She struggled to define her gender presentation during our interview, settling ultimately for describing herself as "in the middle . . . not feminine and not masculine." Consistent with Moore's definition for women whose physical appearances were similar to hers, Kayla embodied a gender-blender appearance. She describes herself as "I'm not that, I'm not the typical . . . I'm not like a hard-core kind of butch woman. And I'm not the ultra-femme either. I'm really, really middle of the road. . . . I'm very much attracted to natural beauty in a feminine sort of way." Kayla knows what she is not, and she knows what she is attracted to. Her description of her physical appearance stems from understanding these aspects of herself. In stating what she is not, Kayla is better able to explain her embodied femininity. She also begins to outline the hierarchy of femininities as she perceives them. Her tone during the interview makes it clear that she perceives the "hard-core butch woman" to be an inferior form of femininity. Furthermore, she illustrates the ways in which femininities do not just complement or reject masculinities but also how they complement and reject each other. She is not striving for either a transgressive appearance or a display of dominant femininity, and by placing those parameters around her presentation of self, she carves out her own space in the middle.

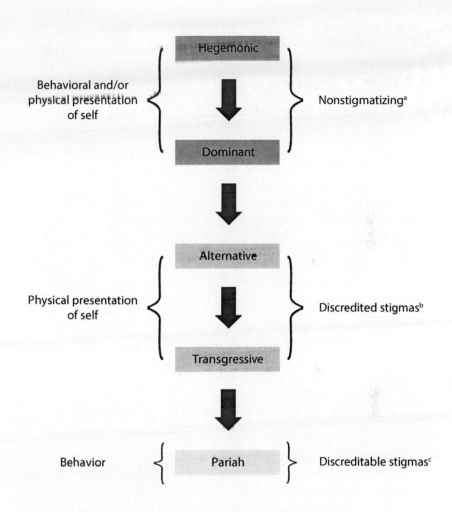

Figure 1.1. Hierarchy of Femininities

The content within the figure:

Behavioral and/or physical presentation of self

Hegemonic

Dominant

Nonstigmatizing[a]

Physical presentation of self

Alternative

Transgressive

Discredited stigmas[b]

Behavior

Pariah

Discreditable stigmas[c]

[a]The terms hegemonic and dominant femininities have been used previously by scholars to describe both behavior and physical presentations of self. These femininities are societally accepted and nonstigmatizing.

[b]The terms alternative and transgressive femininities have been employed by scholars to discuss physical presentations of self and the ways in which they may create stigma associated with gender nonconformities.

[c]Pariah femininity is a term that, in general, describes behavior, specifically, sexual deviance, as a way to corrupt femininity. Goffman (1959, 1963) would describe a pariah identity as discreditable in that it does not have to be immediately apparent to others but is societally stigmatized.

The participants' desires for clearly established gender boundaries were driven in large part by their awareness of the power of femininity. They understood the benefits that come with embodying a gender-conforming presentation of self. This knowledge not only made some study participants reluctant to adopt an outward appearance that embodies an alternative femininity or a transgressive look, but also led participants to feel uncomfortable around others whose outward presentation of self did not fall in line with the ideals of dominant femininities.[7] Yanira is a participant who felt strongly against a transgressive outward appearance. Interestingly, she is one of the participants who previously had a rather long "tomboy" phase, which lasted into her twenties. By her own account, Yanira *parecía un nene* (looked like a boy) when she was growing up. Yanira resisted embodying dominant femininity until after leaving Puerto Rico as an adult. I asked her about this transformation and what it meant to her.

> Las muchachas que se ven así bien nene, como que las discriminan más. Hasta yo la discrimino a veces. Es como ellas actúan en todo: su forma de ser y sus manerismos. Y se agarran allá [entre las piernas] yo no sé qué. . . . Para conseguir trabajo y pareja también es mejor ser femenina. Yo encuentro que desde que fui más femenina como que atraigo a más [mujeres].

> (The girls that look very boyish, it's like they're discriminated against more. Even I discriminate against them sometimes. It's the way they act in everything: their way of being and their mannerisms. And they grab themselves there [between their legs] at what I'm not sure. . . . To find work and also to find partners, it's better to be feminine. I find that when I become more feminine, it's like I attract more [women].)

For Yanira, adopting a dominant femininity was strategic and motivated by her desire to gain the societal privileges associated with gender conformity. However, since this shift, Yanira has come to look down on other women who do not embody similar presentations of self. She doesn't point to their physical appearance as the source of the offense. Instead she admits that she is disgusted by these women because of the way they carry themselves. She supports her feelings by arguing that transgressive, sexually nonconforming women mimic masculine ways of walking, standing, and using their hands. In this way, Yanira makes a distinction between women who may embody a transgressive outward appearance, as she once did through masculine dress, and those whom she believes are attempting to mimic hegemonic masculinity through their behaviors and mannerisms. She draws a distinction between those women who may "look masculine" because of their attire and those whom she believes want to be men not only by embodying a transgressive outward appearance, but also by abandoning ideals of feminine, lady-like behavior.

As I conducted interviews and observed women's interactions in the field, the hierarchies of femininities that sexually nonconforming Latinas helped maintain became abundantly clear. While the study participants expressed diverse forms of femininity, most were careful not to cross the line to embodying a transgressive appearance. They did not want to be confused for men and therefore made conscious decisions to alter their presentations in carefully calculated ways so as to not lose their identities as women. Not all study participants were as vocal as Yanira about the boundaries they preserved between the feminine and unfeminine. Most participants articulated in subtle ways their disapproval of an overly masculine gender presentation. Others simply overstated that femininity was central to their identity. In doing so, they didn't explain how they view their presentation of self as much as they explained what they strive for. As Eileen, a Peruvian immigrant, explains, "Para mí la feminidad va antes que todo. Y eso es lo que yo también aprendí de ellos [mis padres]" (For me femininity comes before everything. And that is what I also learned from them [my parents]). In this way Eileen doesn't make any negative judgments against others or how others do gender, but she makes clear what matters to her and what she strives to achieve in her gender presentation.

Issues of race and class can exacerbate hierarchies of femininities for sexually nonconforming women. Moore (2006) found that black lesbians have a heightened awareness that gender nonconformity or transgression can potentially create another layer of "other" in their lives. In an attempt to minimize the discrimination they already experience on account of their race, black middle-class lesbians can be unsupportive of transgressive displays within their communities. The Latinas in this study expressed concerns similar to those Moore writes about. Yanira specifically notes a concern about being discriminated against on account of gender transgression. She adopts an outward appearance of dominant femininity in part to avoid this kind of discrimination and increase her social acceptance. Yanira's desire to remain a middle-class woman also motivates her to display a more feminine self. She notes that it was easier for her to find employment when she started to conform to societal ideals of dominant and hegemonic femininities. Her motivation to find stable employment is coupled with, as she states, a desire to attract more potential partners. She observes through participation in Latina lesbian social scenes in the Northeast that other women are not supportive of community members whose physical presentation is transgressive. In her desire to fit in, therefore, Yanira learns to transform her gender presentation. While the power of femininities is something that constrains all women, it has particularly damaging effects for women of color who are already struggling with racism and/or anti-immigrant sentiment. It is these women who stand to lose the most from nonconformity and for whom embodying alternative or transgressive outward displays of femininity can be most destructive.

There were only a few Latinas (three) in the study who could be described by themselves and others as transgressive. These women transgressed gender boundaries by adopting stereotypically masculine behaviors and forms of aggression. Not only were these women not the norm, they were isolated from the larger LBQ communities. Because so few women in this study fit this category, it is difficult to make any definitive statements about how they negotiated familial relationships. But it seemed from their interviews that those women had come to accept that by adopting a transgressive presentation of self they had also crossed the boundaries of womanhood. Moore (2011) highlights similar findings, noting that black transgressive lesbians described themselves as boyish and masculine. Further work is needed to better understand how mothers of transgressive daughters come to reconcile these particular pariah femininities.

CONCLUSION

In this chapter, I have highlighted the central role that embodied femininities played in the study participants' abilities to gain familial acceptance of sexual nonconformity and womanhood. These motivations are interlinked and together had large implications for the participants' relationships with their families of origin. When mothers came to terms with their daughters' same-sex relationships, a residual layer of anxiety remained around preserving their womanhood and protecting them from stigmatization. These LBQ Latinas' experiences suggest that heteronormativity was only part of the concern for mothers; the other equally important concern was preserving their womanhood. Their desires to minimize stigma for their daughters led mothers to try to preserve their daughters' womanhood through enforcing dominant femininities. LBQ Latinas' own insecurities regarding their gender presentation also stem from a desire to validate themselves as women. Mothers and daughters both negotiated these intricacies and negotiated their relationships with one another accordingly.

Mothers' anxieties around gender nonconformity stem from its potential to mark alternative sexualities. By not doing gender appropriately, daughters could potentially make their sexual nonconformity more visible to others. The stigmatization that stems from gender nonconformity made doing dominant femininity essential to so many of the study participants' mothers. The mothers' commitment to preserving some facet of dominant femininity in their sexually nonconforming daughters is understandable at multiple levels given that these stigmas could potentially lead to violence or physical abuse. While the participants often described their mothers as overly concerned with the potential judgment and rejection from others, it is also plausible that mothers feared for the safety of their daughters. LBQ Latinas employed situational femininities as a way to help ease their mothers' discomforts regarding their presentation of self and their alternative sexualities more generally. Producing situational femininities was one of the ways study participants secured acceptance. The respondents did it strategically in order to reassure their mothers and themselves that they were still women.

I have noted the power that femininity holds for the study participants' social and economic well-being. I have unraveled its many complexities and the ways in which it shaped the participants' familial relationships. The Latinas in this study were not just deciding between gender conformity or nonconformity; they were also negotiating how to embody femininity. The vast majority of the participants desired to be read as women, and they therefore played with femininity, manipulating and negotiating it in order to adopt a version of femininity that was most comfortable for them. At every level, hierarchies of femininities shaped their decisions, forcing them to continue the process of emotion work in order to manage their presentation of self. Their experiences, nonetheless, are not unique to Latinas or to sexual nonconformity, rather they are indicative of a much larger process of doing gender in a society that values specific standards for femininity. The ways in which the study participants managed theirs and their families' insecurities regarding their physical presentation of self are indicative of the extent to which gender matters and the breadth of its potential influence in everyday life.

The tensions that LBQ Latinas negotiated with their families of origin regarding displays of dominant femininities highlight the complexities of the visibility versus invisibility issue in these families. Respondents reported that their mothers' commitment to their dominant femininities was driven by their desire to ensure that their daughters' sexual nonconformity was less visible and therefore less stigmatizing. While the participants ultimately adopted situational femininities based on their audience, they too revealed being preoccupied with presenting an acceptable outward appearance to the larger society. In both cases, there is a preference to make visible a less-stigmatizing gender presentation of self in order to elevate one's position in a hierarchy of femininity. In this chapter, LBQ Latinas and their families of origin share a goal: to make less visible that which can be socially stigmatizing. However, as the subsequent chapters will highlight, when the study participants desired more visibility of their sexual identities and chosen families from their families of origin, much bigger tensions began to emerge.

CHAPTER 2

"AND THEN THE
FATHER SET ME FREE"

RELIGION AND SEXUALITY

When Carmen and Cassandra's daughter was born, they decided they wanted to baptize the baby in a Catholic church. They picked Carmen's sister and brother-in-law to be the baby's godparents, and since they did not have a church of their own, they baptized the baby in the new godparents' church. We all stood in front of the altar: the baby, her two mommies, the godparents, myself, and a variety of other family members, waiting for the priest. Everyone seemed uneasy, unaware of how he would react to this alternative family. Upon entering, the priest asked for the baby's parents, and both mothers raised their hands. The priest looked befuddled and asked, "Where is the baby's father?" to which someone nervously replied, "There is no father." "So then who are you?" the priest asked, pointing at Carmen. "I am the baby's other mother," she said. The priest rolled his eyes, sighed, and went on performing the ritual without another word. Later, as I pondered over this scenario, I wondered why Carmen and Cassandra, who are not practicing Catholics, would want to have this ceremony performed on their child. Why would they choose to participate in a religion that does not recognize their family? I soon learned that there are no simple answers for what motivates LBQ Latinas to practice non-gay-affirming religions. Their experiences with religion and family are as diverse as their levels of commitment to organized faith.

As I delved through months of field notes and interview transcriptions, I found participants at all different points on a journey to reconcile religious teachings with their sexualities. Almost all of the study participants reported being raised Christian. Over 50 percent of these women were raised Catholic. Even those participants who were not currently active in organized religion reported religion playing an important role in their upbringing. Given their religious backgrounds, the participants often described the turmoil they experienced with religion after acknowledging their desires for other women. The coming-out process for the study participants and their families of origin evoked a plethora of questions regarding God, Christianity, and their religious commitments. The respondents reported experiencing their coming-out journeys and their spiritual journeys as interwoven processes (Shallenberger 1996). Their recollections point to one of the many contradictions with which they struggled daily: accepting themselves as women who love other women even though their religious instructions taught them that same-sex desires are wrong. Their stories illustrate the ways in which these women learned to live with the contradictions (O'Brien 2004) of loving God and loving other women. These contradictions influenced how the study participants validated themselves. Their descriptions demonstrate the subtle ways in which these women made sense of their religion's stance on homosexuality and their family members' interpretations of this religious stance. What evolved is a complex web of emotions that influenced how the study participants felt about religion, their same-sex relationships, and the reactions of their families of origin to the tensions between the two.

LIVING WITH THE CONTRADICTIONS

Aracely was very active in her Catholic church in Peru. She sang in the choir and did community service with her church's food-for-the-poor program. All of this came to an end when Aracely met Ana Julia. When Aracely started a relationship with Ana Julia, she found it difficult to return to church. When I asked why, she replied, "Porque sé que estoy participando en algo que Dios no acepta" (Because I know that I am participating in something that God does not accept). I thought, "How does one have so much respect for God and the Catholic Church while wrestling with the belief that this institution condemns the love you feel for another woman?" One path to reconciling this dilemma is to embrace the idea that it is God's will for one to be gay, making religious rejection of homosexuality more about man than about a higher being (Thumma 1991). Scott Thumma finds, while researching gay evangelicals, that redefining certain Bible scriptures and challenging traditional evangelical beliefs about homosexuality can help one develop a more affirming gay identity. Sometimes individuals are able to reconcile the tension between religion and their sexuality by embracing the contradiction and interpreting it as a burden placed on them by God so that they may assist in reforming nonaccepting religious institutions (O'Brien 2004). In challenging the rejection from religious entities, one may adopt an ideology that it doesn't matter whether one's partner is of the same or opposite sex, but rather that one lives a life consistent with Christian ideals of morality in their relationships (Yip 1997b). However, most of the participants in this study did not choose these paths in reconciling the tensions between their religions and their sexualities. Like Aracely, some had chosen to abandon their religious journeys and move away from the alienating institution. Nonetheless, regardless of their current level of commitment to religion and Christianity, the study participants had to grapple with the knowledge that most Christian denominations are not accepting of homosexuality, and they had to learn to make sense of their existence in spite of it. To do so, the respondents did a great deal of work to shift their ideologies regarding their sexualities, their religions, and their families' perceptions of the tensions surrounding the two.

The study participants utilized several strategies to cope with the contradictions between their religious and sexual identities. Almost half (twenty) intentionally chose to leave the church altogether or create significant distance between themselves and the religions of their upbringing on account of their sexualities. Some of these women abandoned religion altogether, and others were in the process of searching for an alternative, more accepting denomination. About a quarter of the participants (ten) became inactive in the church as adults but do not attribute their leaving to tensions between religion and their sexualities. Another four participants chose to maintain their religious upbringings and tried to gain some acceptance from the church community, either through visibility of the LBQ identity or through invisibility. And one study participant chose to leave the church where she was raised for another that she found to be more accepting of her alternative sexuality. Irrespective of the strategies used, the participants were burdened by the emotional challenges associated with their decisions. My interest in exploring this theme is in understanding the emotional challenge LBQ Latinas face in coming to terms with the strategies they use to deal with tensions between religion and sexuality.

In a study on the experiences and attitudes of lesbians, bisexuals, and gay men within organized religion, Gary Comstock (1996) found that the most common reason study participants gave for why they chose to remain members of antigay churches was because of their familiar, home feeling. This answer was closely followed by those who felt their antigay churches represented their familial background and upbringing. These responses beg the question: How do LGBTQ individuals stay in churches that believe homosexuality is a sin? Comstock notes that these individuals often stay by developing more tangential relationships with the church. Others, he notes, stay because of their commitment to changing these denominations. Jodi O'Brien (2004) notes similar findings, adding that gay and lesbian Christians sometimes reconcile their participation in antigay churches with the belief that their sexuality is created by God and their existence as gay or lesbian Christians is part of God's plan so that they may be instrumental in the expansion of Christian belief systems. However, most of the LBQ Latinas in this study who remained connected to the church were not actively trying to change their religious institutions. Rather, these women were mostly struggling with the feelings of rejection from their churches. Those who chose to remain members of the religious institutions under which they were socialized were tasked with reconciling their commitment to their faith and the stigmatization they felt as sexually nonconforming women within their faith. Most study participants eased this contradiction by limiting their religious involvement. As Comstock found, by establishing more tangential relationships with their religious upbringings, the study participants were able to avoid the constant tensions between their conflicting identities. However, in spite of these tangential relationships, the study participants were pained by the lack of acceptance and visibility they received from their churches. When pressed to consider the foundation of their continued belief in the institution, the participants consistently referred to their family values as the reason for why they stayed members of antigay churches. Consider the following example: Eileen was raised in a very Catholic family. She completed all of her sacraments and was an active church member before immigrating to the United States. I asked her to tell me about her current relationship with Catholicism and her feelings about the church's stance on homosexuality:

> EILEEN: Yo creo en el catolicismo. . . . Yo creo mucho en los valores religiosos de la gente. No voy a la iglesia frecuentemente. Rezo, pero no todos los días. La tensión entre la religión y la homosexualidad es un tema espinoso. Yo comparto su posición como iglesia pero no comparto por el lado nuestro. Yo le veo los pros y las contras para ciertas cosas. Pasan muchas cosas en la iglesia católica que tamblén no son bien.
>
> KATIE: O sea, ¿tú aceptas la religión con sus defectos?
>
> EILEEN: Sí.
>
> KATIE: Y ¿la religión te acepta a ti?
>
> EILEEN: Yo creo que no. Mientras no acepte el matrimonio entre dos personas del mismo sexo no me está aceptando a mí. Pero por el otro lado, soy de una familia que es creyente, y por el amor de la familia es que respeto esos valores.
>
> KATIE: ¿Entonces es más una cosa familiar para ti?
>
> EILEEN: Sí, pero creo que existe un Dios.
>
> EILEEN: I believe in Catholicism. . . . I believe firmly in people's religious values. I don't go to church often. I pray, but not every day. The tension between religion and homosexuality is a thorny subject. I share its position as the church but I don't share it on our side. I see the pros and the cons for certain things. Many things go on in the Catholic Church that are also not right.
>
> KATIE: In other words, you accept religion with its defects?
>
> EILEEN: Yes.
>
> KATIE: Do you think your religion accepts you?
>
> EILEEN: I don't think so. As long as it doesn't accept marriage between two people of the same sex, it's not accepting me. But on the other hand, I'm from a practicing family, and I respect those values for the love of family.

KATIE: So it's more a family thing for you?

EILEEN: Yes, but I believe that God exists.

Eileen's description of her relationship with Catholicism highlights the balancing act she must play. She rationalizes the church's stance on homosexuality and then laments the marginality created by this stance for LGBTQ families. In her work on evangelical lesbians, Kimberly Mahaffy (1996) found participants were more likely to remain connected with the Christian community despite the tensions and dissonance they experienced and learned to alter their own beliefs or interpretations of the Bible in order to come to terms with the tensions they experienced. But Mahaffy's work cannot illustrate what remaining in the church and altering one's cognition does to an individual and how one might make sense of the emotion work involved in changing one's views about religion and homosexuality in order to reconcile the tensions. Eileen points to the church's limitations, acknowledging its lack of acceptance while simultaneously reaffirming her continued belief in God and the values of the church. Her connection to her family of origin has been essential to her continued connection with Catholicism, but the family is not the only factor at play. Irrespective of family, Eileen believes that God exists, and this belief does not allow her to abandon Catholicism all together, despite the marginality she experiences within this institution. As long as Eileen believes that God exists, she is unwilling to abandon the only vehicle she knows with which to connect to this God. This is her inner struggle: to participate in a church that stigmatizes her sexuality in order to fulfill another important part of her existence, connecting with a higher being to whom she feels accountable.

As is often the case with LGBTQ individuals who experience a disjuncture between their spiritual life and their sexuality, some of the study participants pulled away from religion altogether. Their recollections of leaving their religious upbringings behind led me to question how the study participants felt about pulling away from the church. I wondered if these types of exodus from the church would in themselves result in an alleviation of the contradiction one feels between religion and sexuality. In her work on black lesbian families, Mignon Moore (2011) finds that the goals of black churches are at odds with those of gay black congregants. The black church, she notes, uses religion as a way to control gay people, while gay individuals use the church to gain support for their sexual identities and remain connected to black communities. Leaving the church would thus result in a loss of social networks and support systems. While these motivations are consistent with those I found in this study, a large number of the study participants still chose to leave their churches of origin by the time they were interviewed. This resulted in deep feelings of loss for those participants who held a strong connection to their religious institutions. These women's internal turmoil and the ways in which they managed their emotions in order to come to terms with their exodus from the church are central to our understanding of the invisible work these women do in their everyday lives.

Yvette was raised a Jehovah's Witness. As a young girl, she dreamed of becoming a missionary in Latin America. She studied the Bible daily and played an active role in her church's youth group. However, as she started to develop feelings for other girls, she no longer felt connected to the church in which she was raised:

> YVETTE: But when I finally kind of realized that I was really liking girls a lot more than I should, it became a lot harder to go to the religious meetings, because Jehovah's Witnesses are only beginning to admit that, yes, there are people that are gay. . . . They are only beginning to see that, yes, there may be Jehovah's Witnesses that are gay. But they believe you have three choices. You completely ignore the feeling and get married, and you continue living your nice little perfect Jehovah's Witness little life. You remain celibate, but you remain a Jehovah's Witness. Or you decide to live your life how you choose to and not follow God and you lose your religion. The thing is, the first two, getting married or being celibate, have another restriction on it. They believe being gay isn't a sin; acting on it is. Thinking about it is an action.
>
> KATIE: So you have to fight the thought?
>
> YVETTE: You can't think about it; you can't do it; you're basically destroying that part of you. And I don't know how that works for people. . . . And, you know, just hearing at meetings the brothers or sisters that I had grown up with and had known my whole life say certain things about homosexuality would always make me think, "Wow, that's what you think about me." . . . So, I stopped going to meetings that often. Occasionally, I do just to get my mom off my back. But, yeah, not so much. This year I found an organization called A Common Bond. They are either former Jehovah's Witnesses or current Jehovah's Witnesses who identify as queer. . . . It was really cool to come across their website and to see them going to Pride and things like that. I'm like, "Wow, I'm okay. I'm not alone."

Yvette's experience is not atypical for LGBTQ individuals in their early twenties. She attributes her decision to no longer attend religious meetings to not wanting to destroy or lose her lesbian existence. She notes that the reactions of fellow congregation members regarding homosexuality made the church no longer feel like a welcoming place for her. Still, in choosing to leave the church, Yvette is losing a part of herself. She loses the part that was committed to Bible study and had dreams of becoming a missionary. She loses the part of her that grew up committed to this religion and its teachings. Yvette's task, then, is to learn how to reconcile this loss and to love herself despite the knowledge that those within her congregation who have watched her grow up no longer approve of her life. Identity integration is often promoted as a healthy way for LGBTQ individuals to reconcile their sexual and religious identities (Rodriguez and Ouellette 2000; Wilcox 2003). Eric Rodriguez (2010) describes identity integration as a process through which individuals learn to develop a positive gay identity as well as a positive religious identity and rid themselves of the conflict between the two. Doing the work to integrate one's conflicting identities can help LGBTQ individuals cope with the feelings of rejection. A variety of different organizations have emerged both within organized religious institutions and outside of them to provide LGBTQ individuals a safe space to begin the process of identity integration (Wilcox 2003). Such religious communities can be instrumental in allowing Christian LGBTQ individuals to share with others in their spiritual journey (Shallenberger 1996). A Common Bond may eventually become such a place for Yvette. Such a group could eventually provide her with the community that is so important for this integration.

Most of the study participants appeared to be paralyzed by the rejections they felt from their respective Christian churches but unable to envision an alternative religious denomination as an equally valid form of worship. This was the case even for respondents like Yvette, who felt a strong need to leave the Jehovah's Witnesses and expressed an interest in finding a community for former LGBTQ Jehovah's Witnesses. When asked if she would consider participating in a more gay-friendly religious community, Yvette responded, "To this day, I don't think I could ever join another religion." A Common Bond appealed to her because it is a support group for LGBTQ former Jehovah's Witnesses but not a religious entity. Yvette is not actively seeking membership in an alternative religious institution. Study participants like Yvette tended to remain trapped in the rigidity of the Christian churches in which they were raised and from which they now felt excluded.

The academic research often endorses gay-friendly churches, like the Metropolitan Community Church (MCC), as providing a sacred space for individuals because of the way in which they promote the integration of one's spiritual and sexual identities (Rodriguez and Ouellette 2000). However, the participants in this study did not report connecting with MCC in this way. None were active members of the MCC at the time of the interview. In general, the respondents' attempts to switch to churches that welcome LGBTQ parishioners and their families were difficult and not easily accomplished (only one participant reported having succeeded at this). Consider Vanessa's thoughts on this issue. An immigrant from Colombia, Vanessa was raised a devout Catholic. At various points in her life, she became active in Christian churches from different denominations. However, since coming to the United States and coming out as a lesbian, Vanessa has not found a church to assist her in the process of identity integration:

VANESSA: Yo fui católica, apostólica, romana mayormente. Cuando tenía como dieciocho años me curioseaba una iglesia mormona que había al lado de la iglesia católica. Una muchacha que yo conozco me invitó. Ella también venía antes a mi iglesia católica y entonces yo terminé con los mormones. A mí me encantaba leer todo sobre espiritualidad. Leía libros y libros diferentes. Hasta que un día conocí a una niña cristiana que me gustaba. Bueno, fue mi mejor amiga, pero yo siempre vivía enamorada de ella. Entonces me volví cristiana con ellos. Pero luego cuando llegué acá [los Estados Unidos], nunca encontré una iglesia como esa en la alabanza. Y yo fui a varios sitios. Entonces me alejé mucho por lo menos de la religión como religión. O de un sitio físico.

KATIE: Y ¿te hace falta?

VANESSA: Pues, no sé hasta qué punto me haga falta. El problema es que la cristianidad es un poco rígida. Como mis amigos eran cristianos, tampoco me sentía bien con ellos porque sabía que no estaban de acuerdo con la homosexualidad. Entonces para mí era difícil. Era como sentirse uno medio hipócrita. Y acá las iglesias homosexuales no me gustan. Yo fui a una iglesia realmente gay. No, no, no. En esa iglesia se pusieron a hablar de política. ¿Usar la Biblia para hablar de política? No. Yo nunca más volví.

VANESSA: I was mostly apostolic Roman Catholic. When I was eighteen I was intrigued by a Mormon church that was next to the Catholic church. A girl I know invited me. She had also attended my Catholic church and so I ended up with the Mormons. I loved to read everything about spirituality. I would read books and more books. Until one day I met this Christian girl that I liked. Well, she was my best friend, but I was in love with her.[1] And so I became a Christian with them. But later when I came here [the United States], I never found a church like that one in terms of worship. And I went to various places. And so I distanced myself a lot, at least from religion as religion, or as a physical space.

KATIE: Do you miss it?

VANESSA: Well, I don't know to what extent I miss it. The problem is that Christianity is a little rigid. Since my friends were Christian, I didn't feel comfortable with them either because I knew that they didn't agree with homosexuality. And so for me it was difficult. It was like feeling part hypocrite. And I don't like the homosexual churches here. I went to one truly gay church. No, no, no. There they started to talk about politics. Using the Bible to talk about politics? No. I never went back.

While Vanessa found a very fulfilling religious community in Colombia, coming to the United States and coming out as a lesbian has made it more difficult for her to replicate this community in her new country. In Colombia, Vanessa tried different Christian denominations and was successful in finding one that would fit her spiritual needs. However, she was not out as a lesbian, had not yet had a relationship with a woman, and considered her Christian identity most salient in her life. In her church in Colombia, Vanessa was not burdened by the stigmatizations associated with same-sex desires and was thus able to maximize her religious experience. After she immigrated to the United States, Vanessa's sexual and religious identities began to hold equal prevalence in her life. As her identities came in conflict with one another, Vanessa was faced with the same dilemma many of the other study participants experienced. The Christian church she attended did not accept homosexuality and the gay-friendly church did not meet her expectations for religious worship. At present, Vanessa is most comfortable practicing religion privately, where she is not burdened with meeting the needs of one of her identities at the expense of the other.

Creating a religious community that honors both one's sexual and religious identities is an important step for identity integration. But the study participants' experiences of attempting to switch from the religions they were raised with to more gay-friendly denominations proved to be much easier said than done. Churches that honor diversity in all its forms can sometimes aim to be all things to all people. While these churches often succeed at creating a welcoming and nonjudgmental environment, they stand to lose parishioners who do not find their religious faiths appropriately represented in the church. Thumma (1991) noted a similar phenomenon among gay evangelicals whose religious faith was of primary importance to their identity and who saw their faith as informing other aspects of their identity. A participant in Thumma's study notes, "I left the Metropolitan Community Church because I felt that they were putting gay before God. . . . They just weren't evangelical enough for me" (1991, 338). For individuals like Vanessa or those in Thumma's study, whose Christian identity precedes a gay identity, participating in gay-friendly churches may have its limitations. While identity integration through membership in gay-friendly churches is an ideal solution for some, those who participate must find a balance in a space that can fulfill their needs as sexually nonconforming individuals as well as Christians.

The one participant in this study who was successful at switching religious denominations found relief in the contradictions between religion and sexuality, but she was also faced with a different conflict. Luisa was conflicted between her loyalty to the religion that she was raised with and the one that she adopted as an adult. Her partner Courtney introduced her to an Episcopal church, which is more accepting of them as a couple. This experience forced Luisa to grow in her faith in God as well as in her acceptance of herself. Despite the positive experiences Luisa has had with the Episcopalian Church, the switch did not come without its own set of conflicts. As she explains, "The church she goes to isn't Catholic; it's an Episcopal church. And for me it was like Catholic light; it's a wanna-be church [she laughed at herself as she said this]. In my head that's how I saw it. Catholics are so narrow-minded. They are like, 'We are the only ones who know the truth.' So when you grow up like that, anything else is wrong. I felt like I was cheating. I felt like I was sitting in a church cheating. It took me a long time." Luisa's experiences speak to the various levels of contradiction that the study participants lived with in their daily lives. They wrestled with their sexuality and its relationship to the religions they were raised with. But also those who didn't abandon religion altogether had to learn to either reconcile the tensions between their religions and their sexuality or affiliate with other religious entities that are more accepting of same-sex relationships. For Luisa, the Episcopal Church served this function. When Luisa mentions initially feeling like she is cheating, she notes the divided loyalties with which she must contend after choosing to join the Episcopalian faith. Thus, even after a relatively successful switch from one religious denomination to another, Luisa still faces divided loyalties. In Luisa's case, the conflicted loyalties are not about God but about the two religious denominations.

JUDGING THE REJECTER

When I pressed Aracely (whose experiences I described previously) to say more about her decision to not return to church, she explained, "Yo soy lesbiana y todo, pero yo sé lo que es bueno y lo que es malo. Y yo no fumo ni uso droga ni nada de eso." (I'm a lesbian and everything, but I know right from wrong. And I don't smoke or do drugs or anything like that.) Something in the way she said "I'm a lesbian and everything, but" gave me pause. As she continued to talk about herself as someone who did not use drugs or smoke, I realized she was convincing herself that she was a righteous person in spite of her lesbianism. She was changing a dominant discourse in her brain in order to fight the negative image of lesbianism as sinful. Aracely was engaging in what Erving Goffman (1963) calls covering as a strategy through which an individual attempts to minimize the importance of his or her stigmatized identity. Aracely tries to discredit the stigmas she believes are associated with lesbianism (immorality and drug use) by emphasizing her redeeming characteristics. Goffman describes this stigma management strategy as one that individuals use in order to gain acceptance from the "normals," or nonstigmatized others. However, Aracely's use of this strategy has a much more intimate purpose. Aracely knew me as a queer woman, had met my then partner, and thus, arguably, did not need to prove her morality to me. Aracely's words indicate that she is engaging in a process of self-affirmation that requires her to negate the self-deprecating ideas regarding sexual nonconformity that have been ingrained in her and reassure herself that her lesbianism does not make her a bad person. She uses covering not only to prove to others that she does not fit their stereotypes of lesbians, but also to reassure herself of this fact.[2]

In talking about religion, the LBQ Latinas in this study consistently took on the task of convincing themselves and those around them that their sexual nonconformity did not make them bad people. Aracely's words, "I'm a lesbian and everything, but," capture the work involved in reassuring oneself that the erotic desire one feels for other women does not make one immoral. In addition to mitigating the stereotypes of their stigmatized identities, one of the strategies the respondents used was to reassure themselves of their morality by finding wrong in the behaviors of others.

Conversations about religion became the only occasions when the study participants alluded to an underlying struggle with the morality of their sexual lives. In every other aspect of their lives, the study participants were affirming of their sexualities and their relationships with other women. But when talking about religion, they often hinted at an internal struggle. It was the one place where I noted that study participants defended their relationships and life choices by questioning the morality of others' behaviors. Mostly, this occurred when the participants felt rejected by those they loved. In these instances, rather than defending themselves and their commitment to an alternative sexuality, the study participants tended to point to the behaviors of their rejecters and use the language of morality and sin to question the lives of others. Andrew Yip (1997a) found that one of the strategies gay Christians used to manage the stigma of being rejected by the church was to discredit its teachings and question its validity. He found gay Christians chose to attack the institution from which they had been rejected. In her exploration of how Catholic Mexican women make sense of the contradictions between their religion and their sexualities, Gloria González-López (2007) found that these women pointed to the immoral and hypocritical behaviors that respected church leaders engaged in as a way of discrediting the church's attempts to regulate their sexual autonomy. By questioning the church's legitimacy as a teacher of sexual morality, these women were able to make decisions regarding their lives that best meet their needs, irrespective of the religious values disseminated through Catholicism. In analyzing sexually nonconforming Latinas' reactions to rejection, I noted a similar, albeit more complicated, stigma management strategy. Rarely did I note the study participants directly defaming the church or its stance on homosexuality as Yip and González-López found. Instead, I found study participants critiqued the individuals in their lives who were using religion as a basis for their rejection. In this way, the respondents mostly avoided questioning Christian teachings but instead focused on the selective ways in which these teachings were enforced by the people in their lives.

Take Kayla, for example. Her first relationship took place during her freshman year in college. Up until that point in her life, Kayla had never contemplated having a relationship with another woman. Perhaps too naive to recognize the potential for rejection by others, Kayla was taken aback when one of her friends in college for rejected her by stating that her religious beliefs were incompatible with Kayla's lifestyle:

> So when I was a freshman in college, in one of my first classes, the only other minority student was a black single mom, and we became study partners. I used to babysit for her, and we used to be lab partners. Eventually she realized that I was in a relationship with a woman, and I never thought that would be an issue. I really liked her. I depended on her for things. She was a really good

friend. One day, she says, "You know, Kayla, I was at Bible study this weekend, and I realized that I can't be friends with you anymore." I said, "What? Why?" She said, "Because you don't live the life that I think you should live." I was devastated. I said, "Because of Bible study, you got that out of a Bible?" She said, "Yeah." I made a decision at that point, I said fuck these people; they're hypocrites because here is this single mother fucking around with men left and right, and she's passing judgment on me. She's not even married with the father of her kid. I said, "Fuck you, girl."

The bitterness in Kayla's words was still apparent when I interviewed her ten years after this incident took place. As another nonwhite woman in a predominantly white college, far away from home, Kayla bonded with this friend. The friend provided Kayla with a certain solidarity that she could not get from many of her other college peers. However, she defends herself by questioning the sexual piety of her friend. Rather than simply defending her relationship and/or morality, Kayla undercuts the morals of another marginalized woman. I interpret Kayla's reaction to indicate that on some level, she, too, struggles with the morality of her alternative sexuality. On some level, she needs to convince herself that her friend is wrong to reject her by exposing this friend as a sinner.

In *Stigma: Notes on the Management of Spoiled Identity,* Goffman (1963) spends a great deal of time addressing the stigma management strategies individuals use to conceal, mitigate, or downplay their stigmatized identities in interactions with others. However, most of his analysis assumes that the audiences receiving these efforts are members of the public, unknown to the stigmatized individual or individuals not intimately acquainted with the stigmatized individual.[3] His analysis of the stigma management strategies used with intimates is under-theorized, leaving one to wonder how stigmatized others manage rejection from those they love and the effect that these deeply personal rejections have on the individual. As Kayla's description illustrates, when rejection and stigma stemmed from those the study participants were close to, their reactions tended to be more intense. In these instances, the classic strategies of covering, passing, normalization, deflection, and education often found by other scholars of stigma do not apply (Anderson and Snow 2001; Goffman 1963; Kraus 2010; Taub et al. 2004). When the rejection and stigma are coming from those who are deeply and intimately connected with the stigmatized other, the reaction can be much harsher.

Kayla's reaction was not an isolated incident. The study participants fought rejection by using the religious teachings of what is immoral versus moral. They defended themselves against rejection by scrutinizing the sin, morality, and virtue of others. Like Kayla, the participants were particularly quick to point to the promiscuity of other women in retaliation for feeling rejected. They used Christian teachings on sexual morals as a platform from which to defend themselves. These interactions were particularly harsh when they occurred between mothers and daughters. When daughters felt rejected by their mothers, they sometimes retaliated by bringing their mothers' sexual morals into question. Take, for example, Marta, who recapped for me a conversation she recently had with her mother:

> La semana pasada le dije, "Me enteré de que no se lo había dicho a sus hermanas todavía que yo era una lesbiana. Me enteré de que se avergonzaba." Yo le dije, "No te preocupes que te quite el peso de encima. Yo acabo de llamar a cada una de tus hermanas y se lo acabo de decir. Porque eso en mi libro está equivocado. Tú tuviste el descaro de poderle hacer infiel a mi papá y de salirte del matrimonio y yo nunca me avergüence de ti. Sin embargo tú te avergüenzas de mí. 'El que no tenga pecado que tire la primera piedra.'"

> (Last week I told her, "I found out that you haven't told your sisters yet that I'm a lesbian. I found out that you were embarrassed." I told her, "Don't worry; I took the burden off you. I just called every one of your sisters and I told them. Because that, in my book, is wrong. You had the audacity to be unfaithful to my father and to leave the marriage, and I'm never ashamed of you. But you're ashamed of me. 'Let he who has no sin cast the first stone.'")

To help her cope with her mother's judgments, Marta resorts to pointing out her mother's imperfections. She does not defend herself or her relationship with Rachel by affirming their lasting commitment to one another but instead points to her mother's wrongdoing. In so doing, Marta points to what she believes is "more" immoral in order to defend her actions, insinuating that at some level she struggles with the morality of her relationship. Her last statement here illustrates how this strategy is intricately tied to the teachings of religion. The religious passage she quotes reminds us that none of us is free of sin, which would lead one to question if on some level Marta sees her relationship with Rachel as sinful. When asked whether or not she believed her actions were sinful, Marta adamantly explained that she did not; however, her words left me wondering if Marta was convincing herself of this fact rather than truly believing it.

The respondents' words consistently pointed to the internal struggles they had with rejection, particularly when it came from their families of origin and most acutely when the rejection was presented as one motivated by religion. The participants' interview transcripts and the field notes I collected in their homes provide a glimpse into the work they do to manage their emotions and make sense of the contradictory ways in which they employ religion in their daily lives. González-López (2007) found that the emotional costs of guilt, shame, and anxiety that Catholic Mexican women felt on account of their need to control their reproductive rights were eased by the hypocrisy they witnessed in the Catholic Church. In her work on how the voluntarily childless manage stigma, Kristin Park (2002) found that individuals who had chosen to remain childless sometimes condemned others who had unplanned pregnancies or positioned those who chose to have children as selfish for doing so. In condemning the decisions of parents, the voluntarily childless position themselves as morally superior, based on the fact that they actively made the decision to not have children. In some ways, the LBQ Latinas in this study found similar strategies to ease the emotional costs of their sexual "transgressions." These LBQ Latinas pointed to others' questionable sexual behaviors as a way to justify their feelings about their own relationships. I interpret the participants' questioning the behaviors of others as a strategy not only to manage how they felt about the rejection they experienced but also, more importantly, to manage how they felt about themselves.

Families of Origin Using Religion as a Platform for Rejection

Despite the fact that some participants pointed to family values as one of the things that kept them connected to organized religion, it was not uncommon for families of origin to use religion as a platform from which to reject their sexually nonconforming kin. This was particularly hurtful for the study participants. Not only were they being rejected by their families of origin, but their families were using the next most powerful socializing agent of their childhoods as the basis for the rejection. This created a double loss for the study participants. They felt as though they were losing their loved ones and religion simultaneously. Families based their discomfort with nonconforming sexualities on religion. They also used religion as a basis to pass judgment on the study participants. Take, for instance, Luisa's godfather's reaction to her attempt to gain visibility and acceptance of her relationship with Courtney:

> We put together our first Christmas card ever two years ago. It's a black-and-white picture of the two of us and on the bottom in red ribbon it says "Happy Holidays." It's completely secular. My godfather mailed it back with a thank-you note saying, "Thank you for sending this. I'm sending it back because it doesn't reflect my belief in the Lord Jesus Christ. Love always, your godfather." At the time, I was on the floor completely torn. There was no need to do that. That was a slap in the face. And since then I've had conversations with him, and I'm like, "You are not allowed to hurt me. You don't have to agree; just don't hurt me."

Luisa has had to learn through her own spiritual journey to deal with the rejections from her family and to not allow their interpretations of the Bible to influence her own perception of her relationship with her partner or her connection to God. Still, when her godfather rejected her so bluntly and cited Jesus Christ as his motivation for doing so, Luisa was overcome with grief. Her grief was immediately apparent as she recounted this experience to me during our interview. How does she make peace with this, I wondered? How does Luisa continue to love herself, God, and her godfather after such a deeply hurtful experience? Living with these kinds of contradictions has aided Luisa and many of the other participants in developing what Gloria Anzaldúa (2002) described as *la facultad*: a cognition which allows one to achieve a deeper understanding of what lies below the surface of ours and others' actions. La facultad is awakened in the mestiza when one undergoes an emotionally disturbing or deeply traumatic experience. It is achieved through a process of transformation where one engages in self-reflection and growth, and with it one becomes more resilient to the oppression she experiences in life. Luisa's experiences with familial rejection and her journey through reconciling her religious faith with her sexuality have helped her develop la facultad, and in this achievement Luisa becomes stronger and better equipped to love herself, God, and her godfather in spite of the many contradictions she experiences. Through developing la facultad, Luisa is able to do the work of managing her feelings about this rejection. The emotion work she does allows her to steer her feelings away from grief and into forgiveness for her godfather. This work enables her to rise above being angry with God and to acknowledge the shortcomings of a beloved family member instead. She expresses this in the following statement: "I look at what my godfather said, and I say, 'Wow, I feel bad for you because you're so afraid and so homophobic and so backward in your thinking that you're using the Bible to hit people with it. Instead of using it to understand what it means to be open and love, you are using it as a weapon.'" Luisa's stance shows a growth that many of the other participants had not been able to reach at the time of the interview. She does not allow her godfather's rejection to lead her to question her own morality. She manages her feelings regarding this rejection in a way that places the blame completely on him or, rather, on his fear and homophobia, and not on her. By shifting her feelings regarding this incident, Luisa is empowered to straddle the contradictions of her sexuality and her religion and to make amends with the members in her family who have not succeeded in doing so.

Not all of the participants or their families were as committed to religion as Luisa's. Still, even among those participants who were not practicing Christians, families continued to cite religion as the reason for denouncing their kin. Kayla, for example, was raised Catholic but neither she nor her family had been practicing for many years. Nonetheless, Kayla's mother's reaction upon learning that her daughter was in a relationship with another woman was to urge her to see a priest. As with Luisa's example, the triangular contradictions between the religion, families of origin, and the study participants become manifest. Consider the following passage, where Kayla describes seeking advice from a priest:

Before you know it, I have to say, "Ma, I'm in a relationship with Destiny, with a woman." . . . And she said, "Your father and I are going to talk to you tomorrow night and before then you need to go speak to a priest." Well, she knew I was at a Catholic university, so being raised Catholic, that was one of the hardest nights of my life. I mean, all I could think about is what is going to happen; they want me to go speak to a priest?

The next day, I went and found where the priests lived on campus. I knocked on the door. I'll never forget him, Father O'Malley. He answered the door, and I started crying right there in the doorway. He goes, "My child, my child, what's the matter? Come in, come in." I was bawling my eyes out, and he sits me down in this little area that they have right by the door and he goes, "What's going on? What's the matter?" And I said, "My mother told me I had to see a priest. I just told my mom that I'm in a relationship with a woman, that I'm gay." He was so compassionate, and he says to me, "You know what? Let me tell you something. There are men in this priesthood who have killed themselves over this, because of their sexuality." And then he said something that set me free. He said, "There's nothing wrong with giving your love to another human being. There's nothing wrong with that, and that's all that you are doing." So he sent me into the church. We sat in the church for a little bit, and I asked him specifically, "Am I going to be kicked out of the church?" He's like, "No, no." I said, "Can I tell my mom that?" He said, "Yeah, yeah."

Kayla's words, "and then he said something that set me free," provide a glimpse into the constraints she felt as a lesbian woman: fearing the rejection of both family and religion. The intensity with which Kayla spoke of this experience and the influence it had on her life is indicative of the power which these two institutions (family and religion) have over how sexually nonconforming Latinas feel about themselves and their relationships. Kayla's parents ultimately disagreed with the priest and told Kayla that her actions were not in line with Catholicism, but it no longer mattered to Kayla. She had already been set free of the constraint of shame and embarrassment. From that point forward, Kayla was better equipped to handle her parents' reservations and to accept herself as a woman who loves other women. The judgment and rejection that often come from others no longer had the same effect on her because she had been released from the constraints so frequently imposed on these women by the church.

Visibility within the Church

Previous scholars have written about membership in a fully "accepting" church as necessary for successful identity integration (E. Rodriguez 2010; Wilcox 2005). However, I find the term "accepting" to be limiting when used in this context because it fails to capture the complexities of what the study participants are seeking to gain from their churches. The study participants sought more than acceptance. They wanted to be seen. This distinction is important because it is common for individuals to continue practicing religion as adults in churches that accept them only because they do not have to see and thus not acknowledge their alternative sexualities. Acceptance and visibility are related but distinct phenomena. Visibility implies a step above acceptance that could otherwise be done simply by ignoring the perceived transgression.

Visibility was an important step to help the respondents integrate their sexual and religious identities. However, many of the participants had not achieved visibility in their churches at the time of their interview. This was a nonissue for those who had abandoned organized religion altogether or for whom religion did not play a strong part in their lives. But others felt a sense of loss from their inability to obtain visibility in the church. This remained a weakness in these women's otherwise self-affirming identities. These women wanted their participation in organized religion to involve an acknowledgement of their same-sex partnerships. Take, for example, Mariela, who was raised Catholic but later renounced Catholicism entirely because of perceived hypocrisies and contradictions within her church. Her relationship with Jasmin, a Seventh-Day Adventist, has brought her back to church, but she struggles with feeling that she must hide their relationship in order to attend services:

> MARIELA: For a while, I didn't want to hear anything about it or read anything about it. But my girlfriend is Seventh-Day Adventist. And I've gone to church with her a few times. Recently, I've been trying. I wouldn't label myself as anything right now. But I believe that there has to be something else greater than me. I'm in the processes of having a stronger belief system.
>
> KATIE: So you do sometimes go to church with your partner?
>
> MARIELA: Yeah. But Seventh-Day Adventists don't agree with homosexuality. So when we go to church we can't act as a couple. It's one of the reasons that we don't go as often. We are both very out with everybody pretty much. So when we are in public, we want to act as a couple. We feel as though we have that right. So that's one of the things that holds us back from going to church. I listen to what the pastor has to say. I take it in. But I don't believe everything they believe, so I wouldn't categorize myself as an Adventist. I try to find the positives.

While Mariela is currently seeking a stronger belief system, she wants to be in a church where her lesbianism is seen as well as accepted. Her desire to attend a church where she and her partner can "act as a couple" is about wanting her religious community to see their relationship. She wants a congregation that fosters a comfortable environment for her and her partner as a couple as opposed to one that accepts her as an individual without ever seeing or acknowledging their relationship. For Mariela, who remarks on being out in every other facet of her life, losing that visibility in church creates a sense of loss.

Participants in this study found it much easier to gain acceptance from their religious communities if their alternative sexualities remained unseen and thus ignored. But this kind of acceptance without visibility is exactly what Mariela is trying to avoid. The visibility she seeks can be particularly difficult to find among Seventh-Day Adventists and has created a number of challenges for them as a couple. René Drumm (2005) notes that gay and lesbian Adventists with the most success at integrating their conflicting identities and becoming self-affirming were those who developed new role models. These role models, Drumm notes, most often came from the Seventh-Day Adventist Kinship International. Kinship is an organization that provides support to gay, lesbian, bisexual, and transgender Adventists. Through Kinship, LGBTQ Adventists are able to build community among others who share their religious beliefs and see their relationships as legitimate forms of loving. A group such as this one provides visibility for its members in a way that the traditional Seventh-Day Adventist Church does not.

Support groups like Kinship, A Common Bond, and Dignity can serve as borderland spaces for their religious LGBTQ members. Anzaldúa (2009) offers that when mestizas are disoriented by the contradictions they experience in life, they enter a state of "nepantla." This state becomes a way of being for mestizas. Through borderland spaces, the women in this study are sometimes able to integrate their religious and sexual identities and establish visibility by working through the tensions between religion and sexuality in their lives in their nepantla state. As Anzaldúa notes in her work, the borderland is home to the marginalized. It can be a physical location or an imaginary space that allows its inhabitants to house the whole self. Regardless of the form these spaces take on for the participants, borderlands provide the necessary space that mestizas need when they are in a state of nepantla. In her work on an African American LGBTQ church, Aryana Bates (2005) describes Liberation in Truth, a church that she terms a subaltern community. Much as I use borderlands and nepantla here, Bates (2005) finds this subaltern community to be a safe place for lesbian, gay, bisexual, and transgender individuals to explore the religious and spiritual dimensions of their identities. She notes that the power in this church comes from its ability to affirm the whole person and recognize that sexual identity is inherent in that whole person. Melissa Wilcox notes the existence of similar spaces within Catholic churches in her work on lesbians' religious affiliations (2005) as well as in her work on safe spaces among other religious denominations (2003). Despite some of their limitations, gay-friendly churches like MCC are also potential borderland spaces. Irrespective of what borderland spaces look like for the participants, they can be empowering because they have the potential to allow sexually nonconforming individuals to gain visibility in a space where they would otherwise be unseen.

Visibility comes in a variety of forms, and the participants in this study sometimes achieved visibility without joining religious support groups for LGBTQ individuals. In Kayla's case, it was the priest at her college who helped her develop a self-affirming identity. Because the priest is a religious leader, Kayla is originally anxious over how he will receive her confession. But this priest does more than just accept her as a lesbian: he assures her that being a lesbian does not mean she is not welcome in the church. Should Kayla chose to return to this church, she would be doing so with the understanding that its priest sees her and accepts her as a woman who loves another woman. It is this visibility that ultimately sets her free and is instrumental in her identity integration process. Another participant, Milagros, received a similar kind of visibility from her priest. Milagros's priest accepts her and supports her without ignoring her lesbian existence. He makes visible her lesbianism and uses his leadership position within the church to advocate on her behalf. As Milagros describes:

> Incluso yo llevé a mi mamá a una iglesia donde ya había hablado con el padre. Porque yo siempre quería como ese apoyo religioso. Ese padre era mi confidente. Yo le decía mis curiosidades, mis dudas, mis traumas. Yo siempre confiaba en él. Y él me ayudó bastante porque él me dio ese apoyo religioso. Él fue a donde mi mamá y le dijo que yo no estaba haciendo nada malo, que Dios me quería como yo era.

> (I even brought my mother to a church where I had been talking to the priest. Because I always wanted that religious support. That priest was my confidant. I would tell him my questions, my doubts, my traumas. I always confided in him. And he helped me a lot because he gave me that religious support. He went to my mother and told her that I wasn't doing anything wrong, that God loved me the way I was.)

By taking the time to advocate for Milagros, this priest takes visibility to another level. He sees, acknowledges, and accepts her lesbianism, and then he aids her in getting her mother to do the same. This kind of visibility was most instrumental in helping the study participants in the identity integration process.

When study participants were not so lucky as to receive this kind of visibility and acceptance of their sexualities from a religious leader in their churches, these women learned to navigate visibility in more subtle ways. This was the case for Eileen, who agreed to be the godmother for a friend's child but was careful to note that this friend knew she was a lesbian. While she received no direct acknowledgment of her lesbian existence from the Catholic Church or its religious leaders, together with her child's godmother, Eileen was able to take part in a religious ritual and make a commitment before God to help rear her godchild on a religious path.

Or take the example of Carmen and Cassandra, who baptized their daughter in a Catholic church before a priest who never acknowledged their status as comothers. The visibility for this couple stems from their belief that the Catholic Church is God's home and, thus, there among their family and friends, they can have their daughter absolved of her original sin, despite the limitations of organized Catholicism. In this space, this couple believes they are seen and validated not by religious leaders or organized religion but by God. In all of these instances, one sees the respondents' efforts to engage with God in a meaningful way as lesbian, bisexual, and queer women. It was this goal of visibility that the study participants sought while on their spiritual and sexual journeys.

Regardless of whether or not the participants were active in the church, most were troubled by the perception that their same-sex relationships were condemned by God. Even among those participants who refused to attend church services and who spoke most vehemently against the church, there was a need to redefine what the church proclaims to be God's stance on homosexuality. The participants were willing to distance themselves from organized religion but not from God, and thus they redefined God's perception of them. They affirmed their identities by reminding themselves that God created, loved, and saw them for who they were. Those who could not obtain visibility from the church found comfort in knowing that God saw and validated them even if organized religion did not.

Finding One's Spiritual Self

The participants who reported the most success at integrating their identities had learned to separate organized religious teachings from their own spirituality and individual beliefs in God. As Wilcox (2002) notes, the flexibility stemming from religious individualism is essential for allowing LGBTQ individuals to integrate their identities. This does not have to mean moving away from organized religion altogether, but it involves learning how to establish one's own connection with God and to remain affirming of one's sexual identity despite the stance of many organized religious institutions. Religious individualism requires one to separate God's love from the religious institutions available in everyday life as disseminators of God's word. Achieving this separation was a learned process for the participants. Learning to maintain a separate relationship with God that is independent of organized religion is part of the identity integration process.

Identity integration is always a process that LGBTQ individuals negotiate throughout the course of their lives (E. Rodriguez 2010; Shallenberger 1996). It is rarely finished and can involve different stages where an individual is angry with religion, God, or the self. Moving beyond negative feelings and toward a loving and healthy outlook of one's sexuality and one's relationship with God requires work. In this passage, Sara describes her experiences with this process. Her words indicate the incompleteness of her journey: her move away from the Pentecostal Church, her anger with its rejection, and her renewed connection with God, separate from organized religion:

> I haven't actually attended a Pentecostal church in years. In large part, I think that I'm at a point in my life where I'm seeking, I'm trying to find a connectivity between my spirituality and my sexuality. My church at home doesn't permit these to coexist. I came back home one time on vacation, and I went to church with my mother and I ended up leaving, walking out of one of the sermons at the church because the pastor at the time was preaching against homosexuality, and I just disagreed with a lot of his politics. I've always disagreed with a

lot of his politics. So I actually ended up, like, leaving and walking out. And
that was a huge argument that my mother and I got into in the car because she
asked me why did I leave, and I told her, "Mom, that's like someone sitting up
there telling you that being Puerto Rican is a sin." So I was trying to find a way
to make her understand why I felt uncomfortable. But now I've kind of found
peace with myself, having to deal with this. So I feel now more than ever more
connected to God than I did before, even though I haven't been as active and
involved in the church.

Sara's deeper connection with God comes in part from her ability to block out
the disaffirming aspects of religion from her daily life. Deepening her personal
relationship with God has helped to strengthen her sense of self. In this passage,
Sara is also describing the work of teaching as an emotion work strategy. Sara tries
to explain why she feels alienated from the Pentecostal Church in a way she knows
will resonate with her mother. In doing so, she teaches her mother that she cannot
sit in the church and hear the pastor berate gay people and take comfort in the fact
that he is not condemning her directly. She is teaching her mother that visibility is
important to her. The example she gives her mother is deliberate in that she hopes
it will help her mother understand that the pastor's words injured an essential part
of who she is. Sara's decision to develop a more individual relationship with God
stems in part from her desire to protect herself from the lack of acceptance and
visibility she has experienced within the Pentecostal Church.

The separation between religion and spirituality can take on multiple forms.
Distancing oneself from organized religion and deepening one's personal relationship with God is one manifestation of this process. However, González-
López (2007) notes a slightly different kind of separation that helps heterosexual
Mexican women understand the contradictions between their religious faith and
their sexual lives. González-López finds that these women favor redefining the
church's responsibility as only to promote faith and spiritual growth and not
to provide believers with guidance on how to live their sexual lives. By separating sex, sexuality, and the body from religion, González-López notes that these
women are better able to sift through the parts of Catholicism that are beneficial
to them and exclude those parts that are not in line with their social and economic needs. The participants in this study engage in this strategy often, sifting
through the parts of religion that work for them and ignoring the parts that do
not. In doing so, they are better able to live with the contradictions.

Conclusion

As their words suggest, the respondents were all at different places in their journeys toward identity integration. Their words were a testament to their resiliency
as they retold the hurtful rejections they experienced from the two institutions
(religion and family) that otherwise would have been their stabilizing forces. I

have attempted in this chapter to highlight the ways these women navigated the contradiction between their sexuality and their religion. Whether they left the church, established more tangential relationships with the church, or switched churches altogether, the study participants had to learn to reconcile conflict in their lives and to come to terms with their many marginalities. These women's spiritual journeys provide a glimpse into their resiliency and the creative ways through which they resisted being caged. In Anzaldúa's (1999) writings, she creates an analogy with the Shadow-Beast, the part of the self that refuses to be caged. It is the part of the self that does not conform. The marginalized find the strength to resist their oppression in part by confronting the Shadow-Beast within, which I read to be the sexually nonconforming self, the rebel within that resists constraints.[4] Erika Aigner-Varoz offers that Anzaldúa's Shadow-Beast and her concept of *la facultad* are weapons that coexist to help the oppressed resist oppression (2000, 59). In learning to see the Shadow-Beast as an ally and in achieving la facultad, one is better equipped to resist being caged by the patriarchal institutions that constrain one's life. In Anzaldúa's case, the Shadow-Beast is caged by culture, the family, religion, or men. The Shadow-Beast is the part of the self that pushes to the surface as mestizas embrace the complexities of their sexualities and the consequences that arise on account of it. There were many cages in the study participants' lives. For some, organized religion became a cage; so many participants reported feeling their identities being fragmented within organized religion. Their attempts to break free from this cage were part of their spiritual journey. By resisting religious ideologies that condemn their sexualities and by redefining their relationships with God to be more in line with other parts of the self, these women are freeing their Shadow-Beast and strengthening la facultad within themselves. They are in the process of finding ways to make themselves whole.

Much of Anzaldúa's writings embody a strong spiritual dimension and provide a glimpse into her emotional journey toward a deeper understanding of herself and others. In an interview with Christine Welland in 1983, Anzaldúa spoke about spirituality as a means of protection for oppressed people (Keating 2000). In a later interview with AnaLouise Keating, Anzaldúa shared her growth in learning to understand the oppressive attitudes of others, their *desconocimientos,* or "narrow-mindedness" (Keating 2000, 287). She notes that through a stronger connection with both the material and spiritual world she has come to understand not only herself but also the fear that exists in others and leads them to become complicit in oppressing one another. She spoke of learning to heal wounds and letting go of the anger and disappointment that we hold for others when they reject us. In a way, these interviews mark stages along Anzaldúa's (2002) journey, a journey that she later called "the path to *conocimiento,*" a "deeper knowledge." Achieving conocimiento enables us "to negotiate racial contradictions, survive the stresses and traumas of daily life, and develop a spiritual-imaginal-political vision together" (Anzaldúa 2002, 571). The study participants in *Amigas y Amantes* were all at different stages on this path of conocimiento, and their experiences highlighted in this chapter document their many shifts negotiating religion, sexuality, and family: their inner struggles, the ways they reconcile the limits of the material world and make sense of their faiths within it.

The study participants strengthen la facultad along their paths to cono-cimiento. Living in nepantla aids them in this process as it provides them with a physical or imaginary space to work on identity integration and cultivate whole-ness. All of these processes are part of the emotion work LBQ Latinas do to help themselves cope with the stresses of contradiction. This is the work these women do to develop more positive, self-affirming ideologies about themselves. This emotion work helps the study participants take on another task: helping their families of origin and choice reach understanding. In the next few chapters, I will shift the focus away from the work the respondents do on themselves and onto the work they do for others.

CHAPTER 3

DOING FAMILY FROM WITHIN INTERRACIAL/ INTERETHNIC RELATIONSHIPS

As I write this chapter, there have been ongoing developments across the country regarding the rights of same-sex couples to marry. On October 10, 2008, Connecticut became the third state to allow same-sex couples to legally marry. Sylvia, a Connecticut resident in her early fifties and an immigrant from Cuba, took advantage of these developments and legally married her life partner of over fifteen years. Elena and Marta both married their partners several years earlier when Massachusetts made history as the first state to extend the institution of marriage to same-sex couples. When I interviewed Luisa, also a resident of Massachusetts, she was planning her wedding, which was scheduled for the summer of 2009. In 2011, New York also started allowing same-sex couples to marry, opening up the option for even more participants in this study. At the time of the data collection, all of the Latinas who were married or in the process of getting married were in relationships with white women. Thus, in deciding to marry, they are transcending heteronormative laws that have restricted marriage as only between a man and a woman, and they have joined heterosexual couples in transcending miscegenation laws that historically prohibited interracial couples from marrying. These women are among the many I interviewed who have crossed racial and sexual boundaries in their relationships.[1] The participants had various partnership arrangements: some were legally married, some were in civil unions, and others have chosen to not involve the state in any aspect of their relationships, either by choice or because their undocumented status will not permit it. Despite differences in the formality of their relationships, these women shared a struggle to connect intimately with their partners on account of racial, ethnic, and cultural differences.

In choosing to form interracial/interethnic unions, the sexually nonconforming Latinas in this study were tasked with finding ways to move past the racial and sexual boundaries at both the interpersonal and the familial level. At an interpersonal level, they struggled to maintain a strong emotional connection with their partners on account of the cultural clashes, the language incompatibilities, and the power imbalances stemming from different immigration statuses. These women were also simultaneously contending with multiple societal and familial disapprovals. They reported tensions from families of origin and their race/ethnic support systems on account of their unions. These challenges led study participants to make extraordinary efforts to diminish the disapprovals of others and shaped the ways in which they do family.

The scholarship on interracial relationships has overwhelmingly focused on heterosexual couples and mostly addressed the complications that arise between African American and white interracial couples (Chito-Childs 2005). The relative overrepresentation of African American–white interracial couples in scholarship is particularly interesting, given that Asians and Latina/os have been found to have significantly higher rates of intermarriage with whites than do African Americans (Qian and Lichter 2007). The focus on African American–white couples can obfuscate the complexities associated with other interracial/interethnic couples. In particular, the language incompatibilities and immigration status issues, which emerge most frequently in relationships where one partner is born in the United States and the other is not, are overlooked. However, in analyzing sexually nonconforming Latinas' interracial/interethnic relationships, these unique complications were very present in their descriptions of the struggles they faced doing family. They struggled to establish an intimate, emotional connection on account of racial/ethnic and cultural barriers. However, the study participants not only experienced an intimate disconnect when in relationships with white Americans, but also reported similar disconnects in relationships with other minority women as well. The tensions that exist in relationships consisting of two minority groups have received even less attention in academic scholarship. Thus, the findings on sexually nonconforming Latinas' interracial/interethnic relationships can add to several existing gaps in scholarship and flesh out some of the nuances of these relationships.

Within a heterosexual context, interethnic couples have been found to have fewer support groups and to be at greater risk for divorce or separation (Hohmann-Marriot and Amato 2008). Furthermore, patterns of interracial dating, cohabiting, and marriage differ along gender lines. Men are more likely to date interracially than are women, and women in particular report familial disapproval as a deterrent from transgressing racial boundaries (Clark-Ibañez and Felmlee 2004). Thus, we know that gender matters in the experiences of interracial/interethnic couples. What we don't know is whether or not the familial barriers expressed by women in heterosexual interracial relationships apply to women in interracial/interethnic same-sex relationships. How much does familial disapproval influence same-sex interracial/interethnic couples in particular? When I started interviewing sexually nonconforming Latinas about their experiences negotiating racial/ethnic and cultural boundaries in their partnerships, their responses were loud and unambiguous. The frustrations they described to me in these relationships were shaped by the lack of support they received from their families of origin. In addition to their struggles to create intimate emotional connections at an interpersonal level, the study participants were also tasked with negotiating familial support for their unions. Their successes and failures at these negotiations have contributed to the distinct strategies which these women use when doing family.

Why Interracial/Interethnic Relationships?

The complexities in racial identity formation for Latina/o groups make it particularly difficult to understand the interracial/interethnic relationships they build. These complexities have historically served as obstacles for scholars like myself who see the Latina/o immigrant experience in the United States in racialized terms. Thus, in writing about sexually nonconforming Latinas in relationships with women who do not share their ethnicity, I employ both the term "interracial" and the term "interethnic." This is because at times their experiences are very much attributable to cultural differences, and at other times their experiences are clearly about race. Take, for example, the reflections of one study participant, Marta, a white Puerto Rican woman, who is married to a US-born white non-Latina woman named Rachel:

> Yo me identifico como latina pero yo siempre he sido puertorriqueña primero. Yo estoy en contra de decir que soy una mujer de color. Yo no me siento como una mujer de color. Mi pareja y yo no nos sentimos que estamos en una relación interracial. Podíamos decir bicultural, pero eso de interracial es una idea absurda porque yo me crié siendo una mujer blanca en Puerto Rico.

> (I identify as a Latina, but I've always been Puerto Rican first. I'm against saying that I'm a woman of color. I don't feel like a woman of color. My partner and I don't feel like we're in an interracial relationship. Bicultural, we might say, but that whole interracial thing is an absurd idea because I was raised as a white woman in Puerto Rico.)

Interpreting her relationship as an interracial one is difficult for Marta, given her racial identification as white in Puerto Rico. While her experiences as a well-educated, middle-class woman growing up in Puerto Rico afforded her white privilege, she is not white in the rest of the United States. She does not hold white privilege outside of Puerto Rico, and in spite of her protests, others will categorize her as a racialized other. Consider her description of an encounter she had with a white man shortly after arriving in the United States. She describes it this way: "When I first left Puerto Rico, I met this guy in school. He told me he was white, and I was Latin. I told this guy, 'Excuse me, you are white/Caucasian, but I am white/Latina,' and he said, 'No, you are just Latin.' I said, 'No, I am white.' But then with time, reality set in because I realized, yes, he was right: I was a Latina woman. I was just a woman of color, and I was very angry. I am still angry." Marta's experience is indicative of many first-generation Latina immigrants and migrants from Puerto Rico. She has had to learn through experience that she does not hold the same social position in a US racial hierarchy as does her partner Rachel. Others will look at their relationship as a transgression of racial boundaries because, outside of Puerto Rico, her Latina identity is a racialized one. Examples like this one create a challenge for me as a researcher. In trying to analyze the experiences of Latinas in relationships with other women who do not share their race or ethnicity, I have differentiated between how the participants interpret their own relationships and how their relationships are interpreted by members of the dominant society. In the United States, these individuals are othered, and therefore their experiences in relationships with members of the dominant group, as well as with other marginalized groups, are going to be riddled with racial and cultural tensions. For these reasons, I have chosen to use the term "interracial/interethnic" to describe these unions and employ an analytic lens that accounts for racial, ethnic, and cultural tensions.

Barriers to Intimacy for Interracial/Interethnic Couples

The study participants pointed to racial, ethnic, and cultural differences when describing the barriers to intimacy in their relationships. They share many of these concerns with African American and white interracial couples. However, because many of the study participants had been raised in a Latin American or Spanish-speaking Caribbean country, their experiences in these relationships were complicated by issues of language incompatibility and immigration status. The participants repeatedly pointed to differences in language and immigration status as being obstacles to intimacy. Furthermore, these differences often led to power imbalances in their relationships.

Lost in Translation

Language creates intimacy. It provides a comfortable way to share feelings and emotions; however, these sentiments cannot always be translated from one language to another. Particularly for the immigrant and migrant Latinas, speaking in Spanish among themselves was a way of creating comfort. Thus, for those women in interracial/interethnic relationships, a certain comfort is lost if the non-Latina partner is not bilingual. They reported lacking a closeness with their partners that comes from sharing language and culture. They felt their partners could only come to know and love a part of them. Elena is a Puerto Rican migrant who is married to a white woman named June. Below she describes what is missing in their relationship:

> Just the other day we were talking and I was telling her [June], "I have this whole other life. I have this whole Puerto Rican life where everything is in Spanish, and you're not in it. I'm sorry, but I can't be translating: 'This is cilantro. This is recao.'"[2] I think that when you are in a relationship with somebody who is in a different culture, at least for me, I get divided in two. I don't know how to flow easily, like when I hang out with my Puerto Rican friends: we all speak Spanish. I don't have to translate. We don't speak English to each other, even though we all speak perfect English. It's not like to make a political statement about our language or culture. It's just being relaxed talking to each other and not worrying about translating.

Here Elena expresses regret for not being able to reach a heightened level of intimacy with June. She laments the work involved in teaching June things she has come to take for granted, like the differences between cilantro and recao. She struggles with wanting June to understand the taken-for-granted, day-to-day things that are a part of who she is. Although she is very happy in her relationship, the language differences make Elena feel further apart emotionally from June than she'd like to be.

Language as a barrier to intimacy was particularly acute in relationships where one partner was not fluent in English. In these instances, not only did language create an obstacle to the couple establishing a deeper emotional connection, it also created a power imbalance. For example, Maritza is a Peruvian immigrant who was in a relationship with a US-born white woman named Lynn. When they first met, Maritza spoke very limited English, and Lynn spoke no Spanish. This presented a difficulty for the couple not only in communicating with one another but also in socializing within each other's social groups. Maritza's networks, much like Elena's, consisted of other Latina lesbian migrants, most of whom could speak English but who preferred Spanish. Lynn's social circle consisted predominantly of other white lesbians who were English dominant. Maritza describes the early phases of her relationship with Lynn in this way:

> En el principio no nos entendíamos. Yo no hablaba mucho inglés. Cuando ella me llamaba, una amiga mía o alguien que hablara inglés hablaba con ella y me decía a donde encontrarnos. Y nos encontrábamos. Yo no entendía lo que me decía por teléfono. . . . Yo tenía un conocimiento de inglés desde Perú. Entonces, poco a poco nos comunicábamos. Cuando alguien te gusta, uno hace el esfuerzo . . . y ella también aprendió un poquito de español. Ella aprendió el español y yo aprendí el inglés. Ella tenía mucha paciencia también. . . . Ella se llevó bien con mis grupos de amistades Latinas porque ellas hablaban inglés. Pero yo también me llevé bien con unas amigas de ella, pero por el idioma era

difícil. . . . Hubo un tiempo que no salíamos. No éramos mucho de salir a bailar de todos modos. Pero hubo un tiempo que no salíamos.

(In the beginning we didn't understand each other. I didn't speak very much English. When she would call me, a friend of mine or someone who could speak English would talk to her and would tell me where we were meeting. And we would meet. I didn't understand what she said to me over the phone. . . . I had some understanding of English from Peru. So, little by little, we communicated. When you like someone you make the effort. . . . And she also learned a little Spanish. She learned Spanish, and I learned English. She had a lot of patience. . . . She got along well with my group of Latina friends because they spoke English. I also got along with some of her friends, but the language issues made it hard. There was a period when we didn't go out. We were never big into going out dancing. But there was a time we didn't go out at all.)

The early phases of their relationship were spent in isolation because of the language barriers they experienced. The language barrier fostered for Maritza a strong dependence on Lynn for basic things. In many ways, the early dependencies that Maritza had on Lynn created additional challenges for their relationship long after she had learned to communicate in English. As the language concerns became less of an obstacle, the couple began socializing with Lynn's group of friends. As Maritza started spending the majority of her time within Lynn's social circle, her connection to her own Latina lesbian social group suffered. Social spaces for sexually nonconforming women are often segregated along race and class lines. This is particularly the case in major cities like New York, where the social scenes for sexually nonconforming individuals are large enough to foster these divisions. Since these two women belong to different racial and ethnic groups in the United States, their social circles are completely different. Their respective social groups gather at different clubs, listen to different music, and speak different languages among friends. This creates a situation where socializing with friends becomes a matter of choosing whose friends to socialize with. These decisions can often come down to which partner is a better advocate for herself. Maritza's relationship with Lynn already had dimensions of codependency on account of the initial language barriers, compromising her ability to advocate for herself.

While Maritza enjoyed spending time in the US lesbian bar scene, her connection to this space was completely dependent on her relationship with Lynn. The race and class boundaries dividing social spaces for sexually nonconforming women in New York City are permeable enough to allow Maritza access to Lynn's social group. However, when the couple later split up, Maritza no longer felt comfortable continuing to participate in this white, English-dominant social scene without Lynn. In this way, crossing racial/ethnic boundaries to be in a relationship with Lynn left Maritza vulnerable to losing her connection to her own

Latina social group as well as to the US-born white social group, in which she participated as a partner in an interracial/interethnic relationship.

The language barriers between Maritza and Lynn had bigger implications than those faced by Elena and her partner June. As was the case with Elena and June, language incompatibilities initially affected Maritza and Lynn's emotional connections to one another. However, as it involved an immigrant to the United States who was not fluent in English, the language incompatibility issue had greater consequences for the success of Maritza and Lynn's relationship. It led Maritza to become dependent on Lynn in a way that was eventually harmful to the success of the relationship. The language barrier created a dynamic where one partner held a significant relative privilege over the other. Power imbalances emerge for Latinas like Maritza who are not fluent in English and who are in relationships with women who are. These power imbalances influenced how these couples interacted with one another and how they advocated for their own needs in these relationships.

Undoubtedly, these power imbalances shaped how the study participants connected with one another on an interpersonal level. Because of their multiple marginalities, the study participants were more likely to compromise their needs for those of their partners. Maritza's case demonstrates these compromises as she lost a connection to her own Latina lesbian social group when she entered a relationship with Lynn. She found herself socializing predominantly with a group of US-born white lesbians with whom she struggled to communicate verbally. Still, she made an effort to connect with them in order to make her lover feel less fragmented. Had the couple been able to split time more evenly with friends, both might have had a chance to retain their social group.

Immigration Status

The power imbalances created by language incompatibilities were sometimes exacerbated by the participants' immigration status. More often than not, those study participants who struggled most with English fluency either were undocumented or had fallen out of legal status in the United States. For these women, yet another layer of complexity was added to the issue of power imbalances in their interracial/interethnic relationships. Like the participants who were not fluent in English, those Latinas who were undocumented immigrants also faced issues of dependency in their interracial/interethnic relationships. Their vulnerable status in this country impeded their quality of life and often frustrated their partners, many of whom had taken their own citizenship for granted. Vanessa is a thirty-six-year-old undocumented immigrant from Colombia. At the time of our interview she had just gotten out of a difficult relationship with a woman named Emily. She described the relationship in the following way:

> Ella era blanca americana. Ella ganaba más dinero que yo. Entonces ella tenía
> su apartamento, mientras yo no tenía. Entonces siento que ella tenía una

situación de poder. Pues, me parecía que me abusaba mucho. O sea, como entre un hombre y una mujer. Me hacía mucho abuso emocional. Siempre como que trató de subir como haciéndome sentir mal. Pero yo podía ver esas cosas. Ella trataba de decirme, "Ni me acuerdo porque tampoco me interesé en ti. Acuérdame." Pero nunca la dejé. Ella trataba de hacerme cosas. Pero yo no dejaba que me afectara.

(She was a white American woman. She earned more money than me. So she had her own apartment, and I didn't. I felt like she was in a position of power over me. I felt like she abused me a lot. Kind of like between a man and a woman. She would abuse me emotionally a lot. She always tried to build herself up by making me feel bad. But I could see those things. She would try to say to me, "I can't remember why I was ever interested in you. Remind me." But I never left her. She tried to do things to me. But I wouldn't let that affect me.)

Vanessa has been living in the United States for less than five years. She came with a tourist visa. She has since remained in the United States on education visas but is no longer able to do so because the cost of schooling is too great, and thus she has fallen out of status. She has been unable to find an employer to sponsor her stay. Her hurdles with immigration have impeded her economic mobility in this country, despite the fact that she is proficient in English. Vanessa does data entry work for a children's resource center. Her earnings are consumed by lawyers and the fees involved in filing immigration documents. These struggles have made her vulnerable to an arduous relationship with Emily. The power differentials between her and Emily on account of race, class, and immigration status resulted in a less than egalitarian relationship. Even though it was evident that Vanessa was in a less than ideal relationship, her lack of independence made it difficult for her to leave. In entering a relationship with another woman, she had idealistically expected to find an equal partner to build a future with. However, her experiences are indicative of how multiple disadvantages in the United States have left her vulnerable in romantic partnerships. Although they are both women, they are not equal: they do not share the same oppression or history. Emily is a member of the dominant group in the United States. She enjoys the privilege of citizenship and of her native language being the recognized language of this country. Vanessa's social position in the United States leaves her a marginalized platform from which to command respect and equality in her relationship with Emily.

In the case of the Latinas in this study, citizenship was a major determiner of one's position vis-à-vis her partner on a status hierarchy. While this presented a problem for women like Vanessa in relationships with white women, the issue of citizenship persisted even for those undocumented Latinas in relationships with another woman of a racially or ethnically underrepresented group. Lucy is an undocumented Mexican immigrant in a relationship with Cecilia, a US-born Dominican woman. Lucy struggles with English, and while she obtained a professional degree in her country of origin, in the United States, she has mostly worked in the service sector. Cecilia is fluent in English, has a college degree from a city university in New York, and is working on a master's degree. She holds a leadership position for an organization that works for LGBTQ rights. Cecilia's citizenship status, higher income, and education afford her advantages in navigating opportunities in New York City that are unavailable to Lucy. Lucy works much longer and less structured hours. Her work is more physically taxing. When asked about the level of satisfaction in her current relationship, Lucy reports struggling to find the time and energy to nurture the relationship. The disadvantages she faces in the United States as an undocumented immigrant are not conducive to nurturing a family. This is a tension the couple has consistently juggled, and because it is Lucy's schedule that impinges on the couple's time, she does the work of advocating for a more family-friendly work schedule. Lucy takes on the task of budgeting time for their relationship, explaining:

> Ella tiene un trabajo más normal. De lunes a viernes. De la mañana a las cinco de la tarde. Es difícil pero hemos logrado más o menos superar, porque afortunadamente yo he peleado para tener los sábados libre. Entonces eso como que nos salva. Y en la semana procuro igual que me den el horario temprano en la mañana. Y en la tarde nos podemos ir al cine, a cenar, o encontrarnos aquí en casa para convivir. Y durante el día, tenemos la bendición del teléfono celular y así nos podemos mantener en contacto.

> (She has a more normal job. Monday to Friday. Morning until 5:00 p.m. It's difficult, but we've more or less managed to overcome it because, fortunately, I've fought to have Saturdays off. So that sort of saves us. And during the week, I also make sure that they give me the early-morning schedule. And in the afternoon, we can go to the movies, to dinner, or we can meet here in the house to spend time together. And during the day, thankfully, we have the cell phone and that way we can stay in touch.)

While Lucy and Cecilia share language, they do not share citizenship status, which puts Lucy at a major disadvantage in the relationship. They are both Latinas, but their experiences could not be more distinct. Lucy was raised in Mexico, and Cecilia was raised in New York City. Cecilia earns more money and has her own apartment, while Lucy does not. Furthermore, Lucy relies on Cecilia a great deal to help her through the process of getting her educational credentials translated so that she can earn some credits toward a college degree in the United States. Her reliance on Cecilia for these things creates a dependency in their relationship, which parallels those reported by study participants like Vanessa and Maritza, who are in relationships with US-born white women. Like white privilege, the privilege of citizenship can create power imbalances in a couple's relationship because it has direct implications for an individual's job prospects and quality of life. Thus, even for someone in a relationship with another Latina woman, issues of power and dependency can emerge on account of citizenship.

Despite the obvious differences found between them, both Lucy and Vanessa took on most of the burden of trying to preserve their relationships. Vanessa, like Lucy, worked long hours and was trying to juggle school while in a relationship with Emily. She found herself making extraordinary efforts to find time for her partner and still keep up with her obligations to her job and to school:

> Bueno, yo venía desde New Jersey hasta Queens todos los fines de semana. Yo tenía que hacer tarea, exámenes y papeles. Pues, yo trataba de sacarle el tiempo. Cuando no había clase a mí me encantaba, porque no andaba tan apurada. Pero el último año ella quería comprarse una casa. Entonces íbamos a mirar casas.

> (Well, I would come from New Jersey to Queens every weekend. I would have to do homework, tests, and papers. So I tried to carve out time for her. When there weren't classes, I loved it because I wasn't running around in a hurry. But the last year, she wanted to buy a house. And so we would go look at houses.)

Here Vanessa describes how she juggles her job, educational, and relationship demands simultaneously. She travels more than an hour every weekend to spend time with her partner but must also carve time out during these weekends to complete homework assignments and study for tests. In an effort to be a supportive partner, Vanessa adds house hunting with Emily to the list of responsibilities she juggles during the weekends. What's most important about Vanessa's description is that she does not complain about the sacrifices she makes for her relationship. She does not describe the juggling of her multiple obligations as in any way being a form of labor. She does not even point to these negotiations as a possible strain in her relationship with Emily. Instead, Vanessa describes these tasks as an inconsequential aspect of her role as a supportive partner. In doing so, Vanessa minimizes the efforts she makes not only to physically find time to nurture her relationship with Emily but also to make peace with the obligation of having to sacrifice this time in the first place.

In both Lucy's and Vanessa's relationships, the burden of overcoming the barriers to intimacy falls upon them because they hold less power and autonomy in the relationship. Interestingly, in neither relationship was language incompatibility an issue. Vanessa spoke very good English, which she learned at an American school in Colombia, and Lucy's partner, Cecilia, grew up speaking Spanish in a Dominican household. Therefore, the common issue of language incompatibility that often plagues interracial/interethnic couples was not a concern for either of these women. Citizenship became the major inhibitor in these relationships because it constrained the amount of time, the quality of the time, and the financial resources they had for romantic partnerships. Being aware of this limitation caused both women to overengage in the labor involved in making their relationships work. This they took on in addition to their already overextended loads.

These participants' experiences highlight some of the obstacles women face when they hold multiple, marginalized statuses simultaneously. Oftentimes, the scholarship on same-sex couples focuses on the ways in which these relationships are not recognized by the state and the mechanisms couples use to protect their unions without state recognition. The research on women's same-sex relationships has specifically focused on motherhood and creating family. However, while these issues are ever present in the lives of the women in this study, they were not the most immediate concerns for the majority. The participants in this study were more consumed with the everyday struggles of doing family. The tensions emerging from their interracial/interethnic unions in terms of language and citizenship had a more immediate effect on their daily lives.

Latinas in Relationships with Other Racial Minorities

As Lucy and Cecilia's experiences demonstrate, the respondents didn't just report difficulties arising from incompatibilities in language and citizenship while in relationships with white women. They experienced many of these same concerns and others when in relationships with other racially or ethnically marginalized women. The tensions faced by same-sex couples where both partners are racial or ethnic minorities can be easily overlooked. One might assume that a shared status as racialized others and as women would create common ground for these couples; however, this was not always the case. The respondents' experiences in relationships with other racial minorities were shaped by where each stood relative to her partner in the racial/ethnic status hierarchy in the United States. Their experiences in these rarely studied types of interracial/interethnic relationships provide us a glimpse into the realities and complexities of romantic unions where both partners are marginalized by the dominant society.

Racial and ethnic boundaries were just as strong among couples where both partners were members of underrepresented groups as they were for couples where one partner was a member of the dominant group. Study participants who were in relationships with other racially or ethnically marginalized women reported many of the same barriers to intimacy expressed by those who were in relationships with white women. In both relationship types, respondents reported a disconnect on account of racial, ethnic, and/or cultural differences. Also, in both relationship types, power imbalances were evident due to the participants' different social positions along a status hierarchy.

Do You See Me?

Diana and Corinne met in college and have been together for two years. Diana is Afro-Dominican, and Corinne is African American. For Diana, as for many second-generation immigrants, college has been a time for strengthening her ethnic identity. She attended a predominately white boarding high school and is now glad to be back in New York City on a college campus with other Latinas. Being in this space has helped her learn how to produce *Latinidad*, a collective Latina/o identity or affinity that can be formed in a given ethnic enclave or social space.[3] She has devoted a lot of her energy to nurturing the Latina self in college, which has created some emotional distance between herself and Corinne:

> I'm in a Latina sorority, and I'm very Latina central. In the past four years, I really have been trying to get my roots in the forefront. This is who I am. These are my people. This is my language. This is my culture. This is my food. I really embrace that because it's really important. And I don't ever want to lose it. For her [Corinne] it's not like that. And it's definitely a problem. There are things that she doesn't understand. She wishes she could understand. There are always little errors in translation. I wish that she could have more desire to find out about her own culture. I don't wish she would find out about my culture. But I wish that she would be more inclined to find out who she is, or what her people are about.

Corinne has not felt the need to negotiate ethnicity in the way that Diana has. Corinne's social group consists mostly of white college students. Diana, on the other hand, is putting much of her emotional energy into her Latina sorority. She spends much of her time with other sisters, and Corinne feels she doesn't belong within this network, which creates a distance between them. Much like Maritza and Lynn, Diana and Corinne have completely different friendship circles. When Corinne tries to participate in events that Diana's hermanas hold, Diana feels she cannot appreciate them in the way another Latina woman would because Corinne doesn't share the culture or language. In this way, Diana's frustrations resemble those expressed by Elena earlier in this chapter. When Diana participates in Corinne's friendship circle, she is frustrated by the assumptions made by others in this group who erase her Latina identity and presume she is African American like Corinne. Diana provides the following example: "Some individuals who don't know me call me black. Whatever . . . they don't know. You can't even be mad at people like that because you just feel sorry for them." To Corinne's white friends there is no racial difference between her and Diana. In these predominantly white circles, both women are presumed to be African American. Despite sharing a racial position in the United States with Corinne, Diana feels her ethnicity and cultural traditions are erased by others who do not see her as a Latina or a Dominican. Diana shares this frustration with the Latinas in this study who were in relationships with white women. Diana's desire for Corinne to learn about her roots stems in part from her frustration with Corinne's affiliation with people who she deems culturally insensitive. Furthermore, Diana's desire for Corinne to become more involved in learning about her ethnicity is rooted in her own feelings that the two are moving in very different directions.

While Diana embarks on a journey to construct an ethnic self, Corinne, she feels, is distancing herself from her roots as an African American woman. These differences have contributed to Diana feeling emotionally disconnected from Corinne. The barriers to intimacy she expresses parallel those expressed by Elena. Interestingly, despite their similarities, Elena expressed the emotional disconnect as being related to language incompatibilities and cultural differences. Diana frames the disconnect in her relationship as being more about race/ethnicity. She feels misunderstood and invalidated by Corinne and her group of friends. For Diana it becomes a matter of wanting to be seen and validated as a black woman of Dominican descent and wanting to surround herself with others who understand the nuances of what this racial and ethnic identity means to her. The end result for both couples is the same: Elena and Diana struggle with feeling fragmented and emotionally disconnected from their partners. When looked at together, their experiences complicate how we understand the challenges inherent in interracial/interethnic relationships. At an interpersonal level, these examples illustrate the parallel difficulties that emerge when Latinas enter relationships with white women versus when they enter relationships with African American women.

The issue of not feeling seen or understood was a very common concern for interracial/interethnic couples in this sample. Particularly, this was the case for the study participants in their twenties who were at the height of their self-exploration and identity building. Because these women were so new in their journeys to explore their ethnic self, it was particularly important that their partners see them as racial and ethnic beings. This task was a challenge and a barrier to intimacy for many of the interracial/interethnic couples in this study. Like Diana and Corinne, Yanet and Gisela also met in college. Yanet is of Mexican descent and Gisela is Afro-Dominican. Yanet is a very fair-skinned Chicana who was raised in a part of California with a large Mexican population. Her parents are Mexican activists and community workers who taught all of their children to be prideful of their Chicana identities. However, her strong identity as a Chicana did not make it easier for her to connect with Gisela. The couple struggled early on in their relationship to connect on account of their different ethnic identities and experiences. Yanet describes it in the following way:

> I think she was getting shit from around her for having a biracial relationship or interracial relationship. And she just started projecting on me that I didn't understand her life as an Afro-Latina woman. And I didn't know how I didn't understand. Except that I knew that, yeah, I didn't know everything about Africans in the Dominican Republic or slavery. I think that I know what most people know, but I don't have the full value. But it would hurt my feelings that she would say that because I didn't know how to remedy that issue. I think she was having her own personal racial struggle internally and so a lot of that got projected onto me.

Like Diana, Gisela was using college as a time to explore her Afro-Latina self. Most of her friends were straight women of color who criticized her for transgressing racial boundaries by entering a relationship with Yanet. Despite the fact that both women are second-generation Latinas in the United States, Gisela's friends did not read Yanet as being part of their racial group. Despite sharing a Latina identity, Gisela and Yanet are worlds apart on a US racial hierarchy. Gisela is still read as black because of her dark skin, while Yanet is read as white on account of her fair-skinned complexion. These differences between the two served as a barrier to intimacy. It created tensions at an interpersonal level between them as Gisela grew frustrated of being in a relationship with a woman who she felt could not understand her blackness. Yanet, on the other hand, felt helpless to connect with her partner on this level.

For both couples, a major barrier to intimacy is feeling unseen. The work necessary to prevent both Gisela and Diana from a feeling of ethnic invisibility is not being effectively carried out in their respective relationships. In both relationships, it is clear that despite the fact that both partners are members of racially or ethnically underrepresented groups, there are no automatic connections between them on racial or ethnic terms. These couples still have to work just as hard as do couples where one partner is Latina and the other is a member of the racially privileged dominant group in the United States. This work is crucial in order to better understand one's partner's ethnicity and what her racial identity means to her. Those couples who succeeded at overcoming the barriers to intimacy inherent in their relationships were better able to validate one another as ethnic and racial beings than were those couples who were unable to penetrate the racial/ethnic divides as needed to make their partners feel supported.

Gisela and Yanet were able to strengthen their relationship after Gisela became the victim of a horrendous hate crime on her college campus. She came home one day to find that her roommates' boyfriends had painted racist and homophobic remarks all over her bedroom door. Yanet describes this experience in the following way:

> I get to her apartment and it's all taped off with police tape. So as soon as I walk in there are cops everywhere. No one was hurt—it wasn't a violent crime. All I could see was the whole entryway to the apartment, and only her door was painted on. They put an upside-down purple triangle on her door. They wrote "Bitch, die." There were swastikas everywhere. It was a lot of really fucked–up, mostly homophobic, and racist stuff. Gisela got there in the morning, and they [the perpetrators] were trying to paint over it. They were shirtless and both of them have tattoos on their backs with iron crosses and swastikas. They admitted they did it by trying to paint over it. They were kind of laughing when she got there. And her roommates thought it was funny.

Yanet immediately mobilized her LGBTQ community in support of Gisela. While Yanet was not the direct target of the incident, her ability to help mobilize support for Gisela solidified a support network for the two as an interracial/ interethnic same-sex couple. Yanet describes the incident in this way: "I didn't feel that unsafe because I knew I had this community of people who would immediately mobilize with me and make me feel safe. I think she [Gisela] was a little more afraid because she didn't have the same community except through me. And then I think that fortified our relationship and her joining my friend circle." The fact that Gisela fell victim to this crime, and Yanet did not, is in itself indicative of Yanet's privilege. Her racial phenotype does not immediately mark her as a racialized other to members of the dominant group. It is this fact that made it easier for Yanet to transgress racial boundaries and become active in a predominantly white LGBTQ college community. Ultimately, Yanet's relatively privileged position was instrumental in creating a safer environment for both women and paved the way for Gisela to become more active in this community. As was the case for other couples like them, Yanet and Gisela's experiences parallel those described by Latinas who were in relationships with white women. Despite the fact that both women are Latina, one still holds racial privilege over the other, creating inequalities for this couple. Thus, Yanet and Gisela are left to grapple with power imbalances similar to those reported by study participants who were in relationships with women who are part of the racially privileged dominant group in the United States.

The experiences of these couples illustrate the complexities that emerge in relationships involving two members of racially oppressed groups. Latinas in relationships with other racial/ethnic minorities did not necessarily report stronger connections with their partners than did those Latinas who were in relationships with racially privileged white women. Even while in relationships with other racial or ethnic minorities, study participants continued to clash on account of their distinct racial, ethnic, and cultural identities. The one exception to this came from those participants who were in relationships with someone of their same nationality. Those women who shared a national origin with their partners had fewer transgressions to overcome with both families of choice and origin.

Conflicts with Families of Origin

In addition to the tensions I've noted above that have strained the study participants' success at doing family in their relationships, their relationships are also strained by problems arising with families of origin. These women face conflict stemming from their family of origins' reactions to their same-sex relationships. They simultaneously negotiate the disapproval from their family of origin on account of their racial and sexual transgressions. Thus, the familial stressors on their relationships are twofold. The study participants' experiences illustrate the ways in which their racial and sexual transgressions intersect to simultaneously get in the way of familial approval.

Analyzing how interracial/interethnic same-sex couples manage members of
their family of origin illustrates the different strategies that sexually nonconforming Latinas and their families of origin and choice employ to gain acceptance. Inocencia is a Puerto Rican migrant. She works as a schoolteacher and
is in a cohabiting relationship with Elizabeth, a US-born white Jewish woman.
Both Inocencia's and Elizabeth's families had a very hard time with them being
in a relationship with another woman. However, once Inocencia's family came to
terms with her being a lesbian, they sought to make Elizabeth feel welcomed in
their home. In doing so, they learned about Jewish holiday traditions and incor-
porated some of these into their own Puerto Rican rituals:

> Two years ago, we celebrated Hanukah in Puerto Rico because Hanukah and
> Christmas fell around the same time. And it was introducing the family to
> Elizabeth's culture and religion and giving Elizabeth part of her holiday with
> the new family. To this day she will say, "I have not had a better Hanukah in my
> life." And the whole family worked on that. I wanted to be sure, so I sent a note
> to Grandma. "Grandma, I would like to do this. It is not Christian but would
> you consider . . ." and she was like, "It's good to know about all religions."
> So we did the whole Hanukah festivity with the candles, with the readings in
> Hebrew, with the singing, and the dreidel. It was a great Hanukah. It's funny
> the kids still remember it. I went in June because my mother had cancer, and I
> went to be with her. And my nieces were like, "Titi, you're coming in Navidad
> [Christmas], right?" I was like, "Yup." "Are we playing with the dreidel again?"

Inocencia was proactive in trying to make the visit back to Puerto Rico a success for
both herself and Elizabeth. She communicated Elizabeth's needs to her family of
origin. However, she did so carefully, so as to not upset her Christian grandmother.
She appealed to her grandmother's respect for all things religious so that her
request to celebrate Hanukah was not threatening. In this way, Inocencia managed
the emotional needs of both her partner and her grandmother simultaneously,
finding a way to have both Christmas and Hanukah together and to introduce her
family of origin to Judaism. In saying the "whole family worked on that," Inocencia
highlighted the labor involved in this process, as everyone worked to evoke a warm,
welcoming feeling for Elizabeth and a pleasant holiday for one another.

Reaching the point where a holiday like this was possible was part of a gradual
process of doing emotion work. It started with Inocencia helping her parents and
grandparents to overcome their discomfort over her relationship with a woman.
This process alone took a great deal of time and energy on Inocencia's part. She
wrote letters, sent informational materials to her family, answered all of their
questions, and gave them the necessary time to come to acceptance. Upon overcoming the sexual transgression, Inocencia was tasked with assisting her family
of origin in overcoming the racial/ethnic barriers. Inocencia must help her family grapple with the fact that Elizabeth is a white woman who is not Latina, does

not speak Spanish, and is not Christian. On their first visit as a couple to Puerto Rico, Inocencia and Elizabeth stayed in a hotel, something Inocencia had never done when visiting family. However, on that trip, it was necessary to create some distance so that everyone could become comfortable with one another on their own terms. She describes the experience in this way: "So when I went I took her. We stayed in San Juan in a hotel. So there was that distance. It went okay: my grandparents loved her. She spoke a little bit of Spanish. Even if she said, 'Hola, buenos días abuelo,' my grandfather was ear to ear because the gringa was speaking Spanish. It went well. The only thing I kept seeing was my family is very close, and everybody was like on top of us because we were there just for ten days. For her that was overwhelming. I was in heaven, and she felt in hell. As loving as it was, she was like, 'Why are these people so huggy-huggy?'" All of these steps that Inocencia took were part of her process of bringing her family of origin to the point of accepting her new relationship. She made a concerted effort to make everyone feel comfortable, respected, and validated. In this way, Inocencia eased her family of origin into accepting her partner as a member of the family and into accepting her partner's different religious beliefs.

Elizabeth has not had the same kind of success with her family of origin that Inocencia has experienced.[4] They have faced a great deal of familial ignorance from members of Elizabeth's family of origin, who lack exposure to members of different racial/ethnic or cultural groups. During our interview, Inocencia described the ignorance she experienced from Elizabeth's family members, who made assumptions about her citizenship status based on her Puerto Rican identity. She described one such instance:

> I remember one of the cousins that came from California. He said to me, "Are you Hispanic?" [I said,] "Yeah, from Puerto Rico." "Are you with Elizabeth for the papers? You know, because people get together for papers." [I said,] "I am a US citizen. I was born a US citizen. You need to get your facts straight, and I take offense to that." People think that because you are Hispanic, you just need the green card or the citizenship stuff. They think, "She must be with Elizabeth because she wants the green card."

This example not only demonstrates this cousin's ignorance regarding the social position of Puerto Ricans in the United States as well as the inability for an American citizen to sponsor his or her same-sex partner for immigration under current US law, but also implies that he interpreted their relationship as one based on manipulation or deceit rather than love. Getting others to recognize their relationships as legitimate and based on love is something that many same-sex couples face. When issues of race, ethnicity, citizenship, and immigration status complicate these relationships, extended families can be even more suspicious about the couple's intentions. Those suspicions fuel family members to invalidate their loved one's relationships.

While in the case of Inocencia and Elizabeth, it was the non-Latina partner's family who did most of the rejecting, this was not always the case. The study participants didn't just experience rejection from their white partner's families. Their own families often engaged in the same kind of rejection when they introduced partners who did not share their race/ethnicity. Even at times when families had grown comfortable with their loved one's preference for same-sex partners, they would object to those same-sex unions crossing racial or ethnic boundaries. In these instances, race was the factor that created the most conflict. Consider Laura's description of her family's reaction to her first black female partner, named Monique:

> I think that the hardest thing for my family, which brought up a lot of issues, is that she's not Mexican, she's not Spanish speaking, and she's black. I think that a lot of internalized racism came up, which is really horrible. And we had to have a lot of intense conversations that were really uncomfortable and that were really a strain on my relationship with my family. While they were fine with her being in my life as a female, she is as proud of being Senegalese and black as I am of being Mexican. But that didn't really translate when my family would get together in all Spanish. Or that didn't translate when her cultural norms weren't equivalent to our cultural norms. Why wasn't she doing this or why wasn't she doing that? It was perceived as her not being respectful, when, in fact, it's just not part of her cultural norms, and we were not being respectful. I think that got complicated, and it was much more difficult and stressful.

Laura's family had already learned to accept her queer existence and had accepted her partners in the past. However, when she introduced them to a woman of a different racial group, things changed. It is clear then for this family that Laura's racial transgressions superseded the sexual transgressions. Laura's mother's and sister's concern that her new partner would not be respectful of their cultural values created a barrier in their obligation to welcome Laura's new partner into the family. Their hesitation stemmed from a lack of adequate interactions with black immigrant groups in the United States, discomfort for the unknown traditions and values of another group, and preference to remain well inside the racial boundaries they had grown accustomed to. Laura's approach to her family's discomfort was also interesting. She had to first allow herself to believe that her family's reservations were based on racist beliefs as opposed to the more innocuous way in which it was being framed (as a concern for cultural incompatibility). However, once she came to this realization, Laura held her family accountable for their ignorance. She describes this process:

> I didn't know what they were doing was racist. I knew something was off, but I didn't know what the term was, and I think a lot of it was because it was coming from my family. And finally when I was able to own that that's what it was, then it made more sense. Then I had to have those uncomfortable

conversations with my family. And it put a lot of shame on my family because this is something new to them, and they didn't know what was going on. But I needed to call them out on it. I needed to let them know this is what you're doing. And I told my sister, "I don't allow people in my community to talk or act this way, so I need to create an environment where my family doesn't do that either. Because that's not okay."

As a person involved in antiracist work, Laura was well equipped to address this issue honestly and directly with her family of origin. This is something that many of the other study participants were not able to do. Interestingly, once her family was confronted with the reality of their racism, they were ashamed. The fact that Laura is Mexican and her family knows firsthand the realities of discrimination and racial oppression in the United States forced them to consider the ways in which their own actions could be perceived as racist. Ruth Frankenberg (1993) places familial acceptance of interracial relationships on a continuum, noting that acceptance is complicated by factors having nothing to do with the couple in question. She points out that we assume interracial couples and their families will be culturally different from one another, but that is only the case when one is referring to a homogenous family structure. Families that are already culturally heterogeneous are more likely to not see interracial relationships as much of a transgression. In addition, I would argue that families like Laura's who are themselves racially oppressed have a greater potential for acceptance of interracial/interethnic relationships because they have experienced racial oppression firsthand. It is this knowledge that creates the shame Laura describes above.

The participants who reported the least amount of difficulty negotiating acceptance from their families were those in relationships with someone of their same nationality. These participants reported strikingly different levels of support and acceptance from their families of origin and a deep sense of belonging among their partners' families of origin. Consider Angelica, a Dominican woman raised in Santo Domingo who is in a relationship with Miguelina, also a Dominican from New York:

> Yo conozco a toda su familia. Nadie tiene problema conmigo. Cuando yo vine a vivir para acá, yo vivía con su familia. Con ella en la casa de su familia. Después decidimos mudarnos solas. Ahora, yo voy a la casa de su mamá. El primer trabajo que yo tuve acá me lo consiguió su mamá. Y era con su mamá que yo trabajaba. Son gente que me aceptan. Yo digo que es mi otra familia. Es la única familia que yo tengo aquí. Si vamos a ir a una reunión familiar, todo el mundo va a llegar con su novia o con su novio o con su esposa, yo voy a llegar con ella.

> (I know her whole family. Nobody has a problem with me. When I came here to live, I lived with her family, with her in her family's house. Later we decided to move out by ourselves. Now, I go to her mother's house. Her mother found me the first job I had here. And it was with her mother that I worked. They're

people that accept me. I say they're my other family. It's the only family that I
have here. If we're going to go to a family reunion, everyone will show up with
their girlfriend or their boyfriend or their wife. I'll come with her.)

Angelica not only reports having Miguelina's family's acceptance but also reports
seeing them as her own family. Several important circumstances helped to make
this type of connection possible. Miguelina's family of origin came to terms long
ago with her lesbian existence, and bringing Angelica into the family did not con-
stitute any further transgressions for them. Furthermore, Angelica does not have
any biological family living in the United States, which makes it easier for her to
envision herself as part of her partner's family. However, both of these statements
are true about Inocencia's relationship with Elizabeth and Laura's relationship
with Monique. Neither Inocencia nor Monique have members of their family of
origin within close proximity, which theoretically could have made both women
more apt to adopt their partner's family of origin as their own.

Furthermore, both Elizabeth and Laura had disclosed a lesbian existence to
their families before entering their present relationships, theoretically making
the process of introducing a new partner to their extended families less shocking.
Despite these similarities, Inocencia and Laura reported vastly different experiences with families of origin than did Angelica. I attribute this difference in part
to the fact that Miguelina and Angelica are both Dominican. The connection of
national origin that they share eliminates some of the barriers faced by the other
interracial/interethnic couples in this sample. The absence of these national barriers has drastically shaped the possibilities available to this couple in merging
families of choice and origin.

The study participants' experiences highlighted in this chapter indicate that
responses of families of origin to their loved ones' relationships are shaped by
racial hierarchies in the United States. For sexually nonconforming Latinas who
are in relationships with white women who are not Latinas, the strongest disapproval most often comes from the white partner's family. In these instances, Latinas are rejected by individuals who stand higher up on a racial hierarchy than
they do. However, for Latinas who are in relationships with African American or
black immigrant women, the disapproval and rejection comes from their own
families of origin, as Laura's example illustrates. In these instances, it is the Latina
families who do the rejecting and distancing from the racialized other, whose
social position is perceived to be below them on the racial hierarchy. Same-sex
couples who share a nationality are less likely to report disapproval from family-
of-origin members. This is to be expected, given the pattern set by the other couples in this study. Couples who share a nationality are more likely to be similarly
positioned on a racial hierarchy, making familial rejection unnecessary.

Since the data used in this study are based on a very small and specific sample, it is difficult to assess if this pattern would persist among other interracial/
interethnic couples and their families. This is particularly the case because this

analysis is based only on how members of these partnerships perceived their family-of-origin members' behaviors and reactions. No formal interviews were conducted with family-of-origin members directly. Nonetheless, this analysis provides us with a starting point from which to better understand the conditions under which racial transgressions are accepted or rejected for interracial/interethnic same-sex couples.

CONCLUSION

The examples of participants in relationships with other racial/ethnic minorities illustrate that while marginalized women may have a mestiza consciousness in common, they do not automatically come to inhabit the same borderland spaces. Borderland spaces are meant to be a home and safe space for those with conflicting identities. But racial hierarchies, class differences, and differences in immigration status create heterogeneous experiences of marginality and result in mestizas having different needs from their borderlands. How the racial and class differences, as well as the differences in immigration status among the participants, lead to more heterogeneous borderland spaces becomes even more apparent in the next chapter on parenting. While the study participants share a mestiza consciousness and a resilient spirit, their abilities to reconcile the contradictions in their lives are not homogenous. Their borderlands are as diverse as the participants themselves.

All the interracial/interethnic couples struggled at an interpersonal and familial level in order to overcome the barriers to intimacy created by their multiple marginalities. They went to extraordinary efforts to help preserve ties with families of choice and origin. Their racial and sexual transgressions made doing this work a necessary part of doing family. In some ways, their experiences doing family strongly resemble those of heterosexual women who prioritize caring for their and their families' needs. Much as the research on heterosexual nuclear families notes, the study participants were concerned with supporting their partners and creating emotional intimacy. While the study participants did not automatically face gender inequality in their relationships, they did face power imbalances on account of citizenship status, language incompatibilities, and racial hierarchies. The participants still needed to negotiate white privilege and the privilege of citizenship at every interaction with their partners. Thus, while it may be tempting to assume that, due to a lack of patriarchal male figures, these relationships are somehow more egalitarian, the experiences of these study participants show us the opposite. Caring for their and their families' emotional and physical needs is still a significant part of how these women do family, even if the process associated with this work changes.

While the emotion work that the study participants do holds many commonalities with that of heterosexual women, in other respects it is decidedly different.

The participants in this study began the process of doing family from a place of nonconformity. Their alternative sexualities created the first barrier they had to overcome with their families of origin. Racial/ethnic transgressions were compounded on top of the existing sexual transgressions, creating an additional level at which visibility and invisibility must be negotiated. The added complexities inherent for those participants who wanted their families of origin to make both transgressions visible meant that these women had to change the way they did family and resulted in their investing additional time and energy into making that visibility possible. At times, this difference led participants to be strategic and intentional in managing their families of origins' feelings so as to help them reach a place of acceptance. This strategy can be seen in both Laura's and Inocencia's cases. However, there were many instances when study participants did not fight for visibility from their families of origin, instead finding ways to navigate invisibility. In these instances, participants were committed to redeeming their sexual transgression in the eyes of their families of origin and sacrificed some of their visibility in order to gain an alternative form of validation. This strategy becomes more apparent in chapter 5.

CHAPTER 4

PARENTING AMONG FAMILIES OF CHOICE

Early on in the data collection process I met Carla, a middle-aged Dominican woman, and her partner, Dolores, at a small gathering that took place at the home of a mutual acquaintance.[1] Carla and Dolores had been in a relationship for more than ten years and lived in a small immigrant community just outside New York City. Carla had never had any relationships with men, but Dolores had two children from a previous relationship with a man in Puerto Rico, her place of birth. The children were now teenagers and had lived with Carla and Dolores for more than ten years. The oldest was about to begin her last year in high school:

> CARLA: We are very happy together, Dolores, the kids, and I. We have one room and the kids have another. Our relationship is stable but the kids don't know about it.
> KATIE: What do you mean they don't know?
> CARLA: We never told them anything.
> KATIE: Really?
> CARLA: When they were younger we didn't want to confuse them, and we didn't want problems with their father. And when they got older we left it like that.

Carla's family represents a common family form for sexually nonconforming women with children. Same-sex families raising children from previous heterosexual relationships must often find ways to negotiate the biological fathers of the children in their lives, considering the potential legal implications that their sexualities can have on their families. These concerns can affect their level of openness about their relationships with their children and families of origin. Sometimes, these families prefer to minimize the visibility of their sexual nonconformity and present to the larger world as *amigas*, or "friends." The term "amigas" can provide protection and much-needed anonymity. These families raise many questions about the challenges of coparenting under such circumstances, most of which the existing scholarship is only just beginning to uncover.

Carlos Decena's (2011) concept of *sujecto tacito* (tacit subject) is most useful here as it names the unspoken understandings that families like Carla's negotiate. As sixteen- and eighteen-year-old young women who share a home with this couple, one would imagine that Dolores's daughters must have some understanding that they are more than friends. When Carla says, "They don't know about our relationship," she means that the children have never directly been told. Still, while the nature of their relationship has never been discussed, these women do see themselves as a family, and they see Dolores's children as a part of that family.

Very little research exists that explicitly focuses on sexually nonconforming women who bring children from previous heterosexual relationships with them into new families of choice with other women.[2] This absence in research is interesting given that the majority of sexually nonconforming women who are mothers became so through previous heterosexual relationships and/or marriages or by becoming "stepmothers" to their partners' children from previous heterosexual relationships (Lewin 1993; Moore 2011). In particular, lesbians who are also racial or ethnic minorities are more likely to have entered relationships with other women after having had children in previous heterosexual relationships (van Dam 2004). Lesbian stepfamilies, as these unions are often called, are more likely to earn less money than do lesbian mothers who had children within a same-sex relationship and receive less support from their families of origin (van Dam 2004, 457).

While research on stepparent households among sexually nonconforming women is sparse, the existing research on lesbian mothers is less so. This work has focused on women who choose to have children through assisted reproductive technologies or adoption within the context of their same-sex relationships (Reimann 1997; Ryan and Berkowitz 2009; Sullivan 2004).[3] Although it is undeniably important that scholars bring this type of information to light in academia, research on women who start their families using these means tends to emphasize the experiences of lesbian coparents who are predominantly white and middle class. These studies are limited in that they are only one of many types of comother family forms. The experiences of sexually nonconforming mothers who are also racial minorities, single, poor, and/or undocumented look very different from those described in previous works.

The parenting experiences of the participants highlighted in this chapter provide a glimpse into the unique realities that LBQ Latinas face raising their or their partners' children within the confines of their working-class and immigration statuses. While many of the participants in the overall study were middle class, most of the mothers and those planning to become mothers were not.[4] In addition to their economic limitations, three of these participants (Cassandra,

Maritza, and Angelica) were not legal citizens. As the examples in this chapter will illustrate, these women's limited economic resources and immigration status shaped how they chose to expand their families of choice. However, while these women's limited economic and legal resources narrowed the options available to them in choosing to become mothers and raise their children, these limitations did not keep them from becoming mothers. As Ellen Lewin (1993) found, while working-class lesbian mothers would prefer a more adequate household income, they do not see it as essential to their having children. Instead, Lewin found that having children without the privileges of a stable income merely meant that these mothers relied more on their families of origin to provide support through childcare and small monetary loans. In this study, raising children within their families of choice, as in other aspects of their lives, allowed respondents to continue navigating the boundaries of visibility and invisibility with their families of origin. In some instances, this allowed for more visibility as the arrival of children signaled to families of origin that their same-sex relationships were not a phase, and other times this created more invisibility of their sexual nonconformity as children served to reinforce the presumption of heterosexuality.

This chapter provides a glimpse into the lives of LBQ Latina mothers, stepparents, and mothers-to-be whose parenting struggles involved negotiating visibility and protection both with their families of origin and in the legal realm. These women's experiences highlight the ways multiple forms of oppression can operate simultaneously to create the most vulnerable and invisible same-sex families—those who, in addition to being sexually nonconforming, are working-class, racial or ethnic minorities, and/or undocumented. Four of the women highlighted in this chapter, Desiree, Margot, Carmen, and Cassandra, are already raising children, either within their same-sex relationships or as single mothers.[5] Both Margot and Desiree have experienced raising their children in stepparent households. All four of these mothers are working class, and their class status (and in some instances their or their partners' immigration status) has contributed to their inability or unwillingness to create legal protections for their families. In addition to negotiating gendered scripts and power dynamics within their families, these women are also preoccupied with the needs for safety, shelter, health insurance, and education for themselves and their children. Two additional study participants, Luisa and Angelica, are actively planning to become mothers with their respective partners in the near future. These women have distinct life circumstances and thus different options available to them in making decisions for when and how to expand their families of choice. Luisa is solidly middle class and planning to have a baby within a relationship with her partner, Courtney, who is a US citizen. Angelica is working class and not a US citizen. She is partnered with Miguelina, who was born in the United States. Comparing the experiences of these two women allows us to address how poverty as well as immigration status hamper the choices of poor lesbians who desire to expand their families. In addition, this chapter also offers the experience of Maritza, whose former partner Lynn has one child from a previous heterosexual relationship. Her experiences highlight the difficulties that same-sex couples experience within their relationships when those relationships involve children from previous heterosexual relationships.

SEXUALLY NONCONFORMING LATINAS STRUGGLE
TO BUILD STEPPARENT HOUSEHOLDS

It is less common among lesbian stepfamilies for the nonbiological mother to have a legal tie to the children than it is for a lesbian couple who chose to have children within their relationships (van Dam 2004). Stepfathers in heterosexual relationships may also often lack a legal tie to the children they raise alongside their wives; however, heterosexual privilege affords these men a legal connection within these families through marriage that nonbiological, sexually nonconforming stepmothers do not automatically have. Presumably, a child being raised in a heterosexual stepparent relationship can have access to a nonbiological parent's health insurance and other employer-provided benefits such as tuition remission at schools. In addition to these formal benefits, there may also be a wealth of informal advantages that heterosexual stepparent households enjoy over same-sex stepparent households. For example, it is likely that heteronormativity makes it so that many people do not automatically question the legality of heterosexual stepparent households upon first encounter if they do not already have a reason to question biology. In other words, unless a heterosexual stepparent family is interracial or their differing last names become apparent to an outsider, said family's legal legitimacy will likely go unquestioned because others will likely presume legal and biological connections. Legal and biological ties in a heterosexual stepparent household may not be immediately visible to an outside individual, which would make their experiences different from those of same-sex stepparents. My personal experiences in a same-sex stepparent family have made me aware of the ways in which my family is publicly visible (always the family that stands out at a school event) and legally invisible to the larger society. Outside individuals presume that both my partner and I are not biologically connected to our son and thus are more likely to question the legalities of our family. For us this has been most evident in school settings and doctors' offices, where we are likely to be questioned by administrators who presume that we do not both have a legal and biological connection to our son and are unsure how to effectively incorporate us both into their respective environments. In this way, my family's experiences stand apart from both those of same-sex couples who have children within their relationships and heterosexual stepparent households. In addition to adjusting to the many difficulties of coparenting within a stepfamily arrangement, the participants in this study also had to learn to navigate visibility and invisibility both among their families of origin and, separately, in addressing public visibility and legal invisibility within state institutions.

Margot is thirty-six years old and of Puerto Rican descent. At age nineteen, she had a daughter, Stephanie, and remained in a relationship with Stephanie's father for five years thereafter. However, the couple's relationship was riddled with problems from the start. Shortly after Stephanie was born, Margot's boyfriend was shot in the streets and suffered a long rehabilitation process. Margot became the main caretaker for all three. Margot struggled to provide her family with suitable housing and to maintain a relationship with a man who physically abused her and who had developed a drug problem. In the end, their relationship dissolved, and Margot was forced to go back to living with her parents. It wasn't until years later, when she finally became independent enough to live on her own and held a stable job, that Margot finally acknowledged her feelings for other women. At that point, she met her partner Jade, with whom she cohabited and coparented ten-year-old Stephanie for three years. She describes their relationship in the following way:

> To this day it's like, wow, I never felt like that before. She just kind of stole me. . . . She adored me; she was always with me. Her mom didn't know she was gay, so we had to keep it a secret. We were raising Stephanie, but then Stephanie went to live with her dad for a year. And Jade wanted to break up with me. She wanted to get back with her ex-fiancé because she wanted to have a baby. And I was like, "If that's what you want, by all means, you have my blessings. Just go." She and I parted ways. She got pregnant. But she was still in love with me, and I was still in love with her. And even when she was pregnant, she would come see me. She was just driving me crazy. When she got pregnant, it killed me. She was beautiful when she was pregnant. She was amazingly gorgeous. My daughter came back that summer. And she was like, "What happened to Jade?" And I was like, "Jade didn't want me anymore." She was like, "That's not true, Mommy. She always wanted you; she loved you." And I was like, "I know, but she's with somebody else, and I got to get over it."

Despite the intense emotional connection that Margot and Jade shared, their relationship suffered from the invisibility which they maintained with both their families of origin, as well as from a lack of positive models to help guide them through the process of comothering. As working-class individuals, dealing with the realities of trying to stay above the poverty line, this family did not have the economic resources or the leisure time to seek out affirmative role models, such as through participation in same-sex parenting groups. Heterosexual families (even stepfamilies) less often lack the positive scripts to guide them through the task of coparenting in healthy ways because these scripts are more readily available in mainstream media outlets. However, Margot and Jade would have had to make an intentional effort to seek out support groups for same-sex stepparents as well as support groups designed to assist same-sex couples interested in getting pregnant. Without the assistance necessary from such groups and without the scripts on how to parent successfully in this alternative family, Margot and Jade had to navigate their parenting roles for Stephanie on their own—a task with which they particularly struggled as two women. Under the circumstances, it was difficult for Jade to establish an identity as mother to Stephanie because Margot already served that role. Jade didn't have a frame of reference for how other families consisting of two mothers shared this role. Jade also had never discussed her relationship with Margot with her family of origin and therefore lacked the potential visibility as a coparent that families of origin can sometimes provide for these couples. Furthermore, Stephanie was ten years old when Jade and Margot initiated their relationship. Jade had already missed many of the formative years in Stephanie's life. These missing years would likely have been difficult to overcome for any stepparent family, regardless of sexuality. Therefore, Jade continued to long for the experience of full motherhood and felt she could not find this experience from the family she had built with Margot.

This lack of references inhibited Jade from developing a strong sense of personal, relational, and public motherhood (Reimann 1997). Renate Reimann (1997) argues that strengthening these three dimensions of motherhood is important in helping comothers develop their own parenting identity. She notes that when comothers feel insecure about their ability to connect with the children they are raising alongside their partners, it can challenge their gender identity. As women, they are socialized to mother, and part of that mothering involves protecting, nurturing, and feeding a child. When legal, social, and physical barriers stand in the way of one's ability to mother in this way, it can lead to feelings of insecurity and inadequacy. Even though Jade loved Stephanie very much, she couldn't find her role as mother, or stepmother, in Stephanie's life. Furthermore, she couldn't envision herself having a child with another woman. It is evident, however, by the fact that long after the two had separated, Jade continued to return to Margot even after she was pregnant with another man's child, leading one to believe that Jade did not want to end her relationship with Margot. Rather, it appears, she struggled to reconcile her desire to be in a relationship with another woman with her desire to mother. These two things may have felt incompatible to her at the time. As a couple with limited economic resources, Jade and Margot would have had a difficult time navigating the medical and legal bureaucracies necessary to make it possible for them to share a legal and biological connection to a child of their own. All of these limitations undoubtedly factored into Jade's decision to end her relationship with Margot and enter a heterosexual marriage.

Margot and Jade's relationship is indicative of the difficulties which can arise in same-sex stepparent households. Since Jade did not have any legal connection to Stephanie and since she had not parented her since birth, Jade did not feel she held adequate parental say in decisions regarding Stephanie's care. As

Mignon Moore (2011) notes, biological mothers tend to have more family power in these relationships to decide how much, if any, authority the stepparent will have.[6] The power that biological mothers have in stepparent families is likely similar for both same- and opposite-sex couples. However, this dynamic may be more complicated for same-sex couples because both the nonbiological step-parent and the child can have a hard time figuring out their roles. Children who are familiar with a heterosexual family model and are later introduced to a new same-sex stepparent family model may struggle to find a place for their new families within a heteronormative society. Furthermore, these children may struggle alongside their nonbiological same-sex stepparents to develop connections with one another, given that said children may already have both a mother and a father. These arrangements can leave the stepparent unable to develop her own identity as mother and can inhibit her from developing her own relationships with children in the home.

LBQ couples who choose to have children within the context of their relationship used a variety of different strategies to help strengthen the relational, public, and personal motherhood experiences of both partners. These strategies include enacting a second-parent adoption, having the child take the last name of the comother as opposed to the birth mother, and equally dividing the time they spend with the children so that one parent does not automatically become the primary parent. However, while these strategies may be effective for LBQ couples who have children within the context of their relationships, they may not always be possible in stepparent households (irrespective of sexuality). This fact, coupled with the fact that some LBQ stepparent families live their lives within a heteronormative society that renders them publicly visible and legally invisible, may make it difficult for the participants to gain validation and legitimacy for their families from dominant society or even to envision themselves as a legitimate alternative family unit.

The stresses that arise from sexually nonconforming Latinas' stepparenting arrangements can have devastating impacts on the couples' relationships with one another. At times, the complications can keep a relationship from flourishing to its full potential. Maritza (first introduced in chapter 1) had been in a relationship with Lynn for four years before they separated. When I asked what contributed to the demise of the relationship, Maritza began to explain that their relationship reached a standstill when Lynn's fifteen-year-old son, who was not comfortable with their relationship, moved into the home. The child had previously lived mostly with his father, visiting his mom occasionally when he had time off from school. However, when circumstances changed and the child came to live full time in the home, Maritza's relationship with Lynn began to buckle under the pressure:

MARITZA: Cuando yo la conocí, él tenía trece años. Al inicio era todo ché-vere porque él vivía más con el papá. Pero parece que está muy rebelde y el papá quiere que viva ahora con la mamá. Los primeros años felices. Si ella extrañaba mucho a su hijo, pues él se iba a quedar una temporada y luego regresaba a la casa con el papá.

KATIE: ¿De dónde venían los problemas con el niño?

MARITZA: Un día entra y estábamos durmiendo juntas. Y él nos encontró. Él nos vio y se fue a su cuarto. Ahí se jodió. Ella se levantó y se puso estresada. Se puso a llorar. Yo me cambié y me fui a mi casa. . . . Él no quería que ella sea gay. Después de tres años juntas, yo quería vivir con ella. Yo estaba pensando en eso. Y ella que no, que su hijo, y "mi hijo, mi hijo . . ."

KATIE: Cuando ustedes hablaban sobre los problemas, ¿qué te decía ella?

MARITZA: No, que él tiene que entender, que él va a entender porque él quiere que ella sea feliz. Que le dé tiempo porque es su único hijo. Ella lo sobreprotege demasiado. Otras cosas que habíamos planeado hacer, él la llamaba, y ella iba corriendo a donde él. Yo también lo entiendo porque es su único hijo.

MARITZA: When I met her, he was thirteen. At the beginning, everything was great because he lived more with his dad. But I guess he is too rebellious, and so the father wants him to live with his mother now. The first few years were great. If she missed her son too much, he would go stay with her for a while and then would go back to his dad's house.

KATIE: Where did the problems with the little boy stem from?

MARITZA: One day he comes in, and we were asleep together, and he found us. He saw us and he went to his room. That's when things got fucked up. She got up and got stressed and started to cry. I got dressed and went to my house. . . . He doesn't want her to be gay. After three years together, I wanted to live with her. I was thinking about that. And she was like no, her son, and "my son, my son . . ."

KATIE: When you would talk about the problems, what would she say to you?

MARITZA: No, that he has to understand, that he is going to understand because he wants her to be happy. That I should give him time because he's her only son. She's overprotective of him. Other things that we had planned to do, he would call her and she would go running. But I understand because he's her only son.

Based on Maritza's description, it appears that their relationship suffered from many of the common stepparent-child tensions that also plague heterosexual households, including the problem of the biological parent (in this case, Lynn) being caught in between her partner's needs and those of her child. However, for same-sex couples like this, these tensions can be complicated as the children involved must confront how their parents' sexual nonconformity may potentially impact their lives. In this way, same-sex stepparents stand to face a different set of problems from those faced by heterosexual stepparent households or same-sex households where couples have children within an existing partnership. In several instances, Maritza's comments indicate that she has been unsuccessful in finding a role for herself as part of this family. This is most apparent as she describes getting up and leaving after Lynn's son walks in on them asleep in bed. In this instance, despite Lynn being visibly upset and crying after her son has witnessed something for which he may have been unprepared, Maritza leaves, rather than staying to help Lynn address this difficult issue with her son. Furthermore, Maritza's description also implies that she feels discarded as Lynn, consistently in her eyes, chooses her son's needs over her own. This is apparent in her explanation for why they had never moved in with one another, as she states, "And she was like no, her son, and 'my son, my son,'" or in her statement, "Other things that we had planned to do, he would call her and she would go running to him." These statements indicate that Maritza struggled with her feelings that Lynn prioritized her son's needs and wants over her partner's on a consistent basis. However, while this may be a common concern in stepparent households irrespective of sexuality, it may be more pronounced in the homes of sexually nonconforming women because every member of the family must face the children's potential resistance to their mothers' alternative sexualities, as Maritza notes in her statement, "He doesn't want her to be gay." Lynn's son's resistance to his mother's sexuality creates an added complexity for this stepparent family to navigate, one that both women appear ill prepared to handle. Like Margot and Jade, Maritza and Lynn lacked models and support groups from which to seek advice. These support groups are harder for them to find as a same-sex couple within the context of their limited socioeconomic means and Maritza's undocumented status.

Susan Dalton and Denise Bielby (2000) write about lesbian mothers as agentic beings who, by nature of their relationships, reconstruct the institution of family, rewrite societal discourses around parenting roles, and expand upon the notion of mother. However, this phenomenon may be more prevalent in families of choice who have children together as a way of expanding their family and less so among LBQ stepparent households in which women become mothers first and later enter same-sex relationships.[7] It appears that in the cases of both Lynn and Margot, an element of these separate identities prevails. In neither case did the biological mother do the work of helping to integrate her partner as a legitimate parental figure in the family. Especially in the case of Maritza and Lynn, it is clear that the success of their relationship was contingent upon Lynn's son living mostly with his dad. In this case, the effort made to try to integrate Lynn's dual identities as both a sexually nonconforming woman and a mother seems to disrupt the larger dominant system of conformity within which she operates. Contrary to Dalton and Bielby's findings, the LBQ stepparent households in this study seem not to challenge dominant structures but find ways in which to be validated as good mothers from within these structures. This, I argue, contributes to the tension between public visibility and legal invisibility, which I will address in the following section.

LEGAL INVISIBILITY

Possibly, one of the biggest stressors for LBQ stepparent households is the invisibility they face under US family law. Legal and policy debates surrounding same-sex marriage or the legal recognition of lesbian and gay families often presume that children being raised in these households have always lived in these family structures and oversimplify the potential sexual variance that can exist in these homes (Patterson 2009). Thus, laws and policy debates have centered around and privileged improving the legal conditions for same-sex couples who have children together within their relationships either through birth or adoption. Legal advancements to protect these families are imperative to a larger goal of equality for same-sex families. However, these policies do little to protect two-parent, same-sex stepparent households. Children born within a heterosexual relationship who are later raised in a two-parent, same-sex stepparent household remain particularly vulnerable and invisible within our current US legal structure.

The potential legal risk that two-parent, same-sex stepfamilies may face did not arise for Margot and Jade. However, these legal issues did arise for Desiree, her partner Elisha, and their two children. At the time of the interview, Desiree was a twenty-six-year-old Nicaraguan woman. Her son, Max, was born when she was twenty years old and in her sophomore year of college. Desiree has struggled ever since to finish her bachelor's degree while working two jobs and parenting her son. When her relationship with Max's father did not work out, she started to explore her romantic interest in women. Desiree and Elisha were in a relationship for more than three years. Like Desiree, Elisha also had one child from a previous heterosexual relationship. They, together with their children, Max and Violet, lived in an apartment in Staten Island. The happiness of their relationship was interrupted when Elisha suffered a mental breakdown. Elisha reached a point where she had to be hospitalized indefinitely because her doctors felt she posed a threat to herself as well as to the children. With Elisha in the hospital, Violet was sent to live with her father and the children were separated. Desiree, having no legal connection to Violet, could not fight the separation, and overnight the family was divided.

Desiree stood by Elisha while she was in the hospital for months; however, upon her release, Elisha was no longer the same person. Violet continued to live with her dad, and Elisha moved back in with Desiree and Max. However, the medications she was taking made her aggressive, jealous, and possessive. As Elisha's moods began to fluctuate, Desiree became more and more afraid that her outbursts would become violent. During one fight, Elisha became destructive, breaking things in the house and trying to disconnect Desiree from the outside world. Desiree decided to end the relationship. For months Elisha continued to pursue her, finding her at the homes of friends were she was staying, going to her job, and calling her incessantly. It was during this extended and very painful breakup that Desiree first sought legal intervention, as she explains:

I got in touch with a counselor from the antiviolence project, and I was just telling her about the stuff that had gone on. Even though Elisha hadn't been very physical with me in the past, the way she was acting, she was overly jealous; she wanted to know everything. It wasn't a healthy relationship and I had to leave. I filed a report against her. It's hard to get an order of protection for a domestic violence issue involving a same-sex couple because you can't get the order through family court. You aren't really seen as a family. So you have to get it through criminal court, and in order to get it through criminal court, Elisha would have to be arrested, which she wasn't. I went to the precinct. I had the misfortune of dealing with an officer who was really homophobic or something. She was so mean to me that eventually I started crying. . . . Luckily, my counselor became an advocate.

Desiree's experience using the legal system to protect the needs of her family was riddled with problems. She waited until after she had already moved out of the home she shared with Elisha before seeking counseling or legal protection despite the fact that she had experienced extreme and increasing stress ever since Elisha had first been hospitalized.[8] She had not previously sought counseling for herself or her son despite the turmoil they experienced from having their family so abruptly divided. Desiree only sought support when she had reached a point of fearing for her own and for Max's safety. Desiree interprets the advocacy she received from her domestic violence counselor as lucky, implying that she did not necessarily expect to receive this kind of support and saw it more as an exception than the norm. Unfortunately, when Desiree finally did seek the help she needed, she encountered a legal system riddled with homophobia and heteronormativity. In addition to being met with hostility from the police officer taking her report, Desiree faced numerous hurdles in obtaining the order of protection she needed because, as she recounted, family court didn't recognize her relationship with Elisha. Desiree was therefore forced to attempt navigating the criminal court system for an intimate partner violence case that would most likely have, in the case of a heterosexual couple, been dealt with in family court. Her inability to get the legal system to protect her and Max from a situation no longer under her control ultimately led her to enter the shelter system. Doing so allowed her to be in an anonymous place where Elisha could not find her, and only after taking this step was she able to end this unhealthy relationship.

The difficulties that Desiree faced in ending an unhealthy relationship with Elisha are indicative of one of the many ways in which the US legal system fails to protect same-sex couples and their children. The fact that both of these women are mothers and have coparenting relationships with the biological fathers of their children further complicates the legal opportunities available to them, both within their relationship and after its dissolution. For example, even though Desiree and Elisha had been living together with their children for two years, Desiree had no legal rights to play an advocacy role for Elisha's daughter,

Violet, or vice versa. Desiree and Elisha's inability to create a power of attorney or other legal documentation to protect the interests of the children they were raising within their same-sex stepparent family of choice is complicated by the fact that Elisha was still legally married to Violet's father. Despite her cohabiting relationship with Desiree, Elisha remained married to her estranged husband for immigration purposes. At the time of her breakdown, Elisha was not yet a US citizen and had made an agreement with Violet's dad that they would not legally separate until the immigration process was complete. While the agreement Elisha made with Violet's dad protected her pending citizenship case, it did not allow Elisha and her estranged husband to lay out the terms and conditions of their separation or the custody of their daughter. These circumstances made it particularly difficult for Desiree to play any kind of advocacy role for Violet while her biological mother was hospitalized. If this couple had been able to take legal precautions to protect their same-sex stepparent family, Desiree might have been able to work with Violet's biological father in creating an arrangement that could best suit the child's needs. This couple's decision to not enact such legal protections was not an isolated incident and, in part, was driven by this couple's suspicion of allowing US formal institutions to interfere in their familial affairs, a suspicion held by several other couples in this study.

A heterosexual stepparent family may face similar obstacles if dealing with a situation like that of Desiree and Elisha. However, heterosexual stepparent families may not suffer from the same kinds of legal invisibilities. By entering a heterosexual marriage, they create a legal tie that is recognized in the eyes of US courts and may serve to protect stepparents who are raising their stepchildren in the event of an extenuating circumstance such as this one. Desiree's legal invisibility as a coparent in Violet's life and her inability to legally marry Elisha made it impossible for her to access these protections. While the circumstances leading to this family's misfortune may appear out of the ordinary, it, in fact, is not implausible that a biological mother could fall ill and temporarily be unable to care for her children. If said biological mother were in a same-sex stepparent relationship, that family could face many of the hardships Desiree and Elisha experienced. Furthermore, seeing as many of the women in this sample were not born in the United States, their immigration status has constrained their choices in similar ways.

Desiree and Elisha's difficulties in trying to get the US legal system to serve their familial needs was not a problem confined only to sexually nonconforming mothers in stepparent households. These same concerns arose for Carmen and Cassandra, the only couple in the study who were already raising a child conceived within their relationship during the time I was collecting data. Theoretically, this couple should be eligible for a second-parent adoption. However, on account of multiple complications, including Cassandra's undocumented status and the couple's mistrust of US legal systems, they have not obtained a second-parent adoption for their daughter. This is constantly a point of tension for Carmen, who recognizes her own vulnerability in exercising rights for her daughter. Carmen's legal invisibility as a parent was apparent from the day of her daughter's birth in the hospital. A series of complications resulted in Cassandra having an emergency C-section and the baby being born almost three months premature. The baby was immediately moved to the neonatal intensive care unit, and Cassandra, who had suffered serious complications in childbirth, had to undergo several other serious medical procedures. Carmen recalls the anxiety that this experience produced for her: "I was really worried for both of them [Cassandra and the baby] because it was such a hard delivery. In the hospital, the nurses kept asking me who I was whenever I asked questions about the baby. They put them [Cassandra and the baby] in two separate rooms, so I had to keep explaining to everybody that I was the baby's "other" mother. And they all looked at me strange. I couldn't wait for us to be able to leave the hospital, so I wouldn't have to deal with those people treating me like I didn't belong there, like Analisa wasn't my daughter too." In the hospital, Cassandra and Carmen filled out a birth certificate for Analisa. They gave her Carmen's last name. However, Carmen could not help getting frustrated as they filled out the application for the birth certificate: "The stupid form, it has two spaces, one for mother and one for father. So obviously there is no space for me. It seems like such a minor thing. Why not just have two lines, one for each parent?" In theory, if the birth certificate application did have one line for each parent instead of one line for mother and another for father, comothers like Carmen could gain legal recognition as parents immediately after the child's birth. Theoretically, this could be even more simplified if the comothers were legally married and lived in a state that recognized their union. But under current US policies, same-sex marriage does not automatically create a legal connection to the children for both mothers.[9] Instead, even same-sex couples who are married are advised to obtain a second-parent adoption. Thus, they have to wait until after the baby is born, retain a lawyer, and await a court date in order to adopt their children. But Carmen and Cassandra did not live in a state that recognized same-sex marriage at the time I interviewed them. Nor were they legally married in another state, in part because of their mistrust of US legal systems. This process can be very daunting for a family like this one in which one mother is undocumented. The family is afraid to engage the legal system in order to obtain a second-parent adoption for fear that it may arouse suspicion about Cassandra's citizenship status. Carmen recalls a phone consultation she had with a lawyer about this issue: "I got the number to this lawyer guy, and I called him and explained to him the situation. This was when Analisa was nine months old. I told him that I wanted to adopt her, and he was so stupid. He just kept asking me all these stupid questions. Finally, he asked me why I wanted to adopt her. Can you believe that! I'm over here; this is my daughter; why wouldn't I want to adopt her? I just said forget it, because I don't want these lawyers to take all my money and not do anything like they did when we tried to see a lawyer to fix Cassandra's immigration problem." Carmen and Cassandra's previous negative experience with lawyers has made them particularly skeptical to use them in executing a second-parent adoption. However, their distrust is about more than just money. These women recognize that the complexities of their family are greater than laws like second-parent adoption are designed to protect. The fact that Cassandra is undocumented and that they chose to conceive their child without using a sperm bank, choosing instead to make an informal verbal agreement with an acquaintance, complicates this case. However, it's precisely these reasons that make this family among the most vulnerable in the study. Roberta Villalón (2010) writes about the formal and informal barriers that get in the way of immigrants receiving the benefits to which they are entitled by law. She notes that the formal and informal constraints created by gender-, sexual-, racial-, ethnic-, and class-based parameters can shape an individual's agency. She points to cost, required documentation, and mistrust for government officials as some of the formal constraints keeping eligible immigrants from obtaining the benefits they are entitled to and the lack of cultural capital needed to present oneself as responsible and compliant to be one of the informal constraints creating the barrier. While Villalón is referring specifically to the constraints created by immigration policies, the same can be said for other legal services that immigrants and the poor attempt to access. In this case, Carmen and Cassandra's failure to document that the sperm donor was willing to relinquish his parental rights, coupled with their inability to document Cassandra's legal right to live in the United States, deterred this couple from pursuing the legal protections to which they are entitled. What's more, their overall mistrust of lawyers and governmental bureaucracies has made them less likely to advocate for their familial needs.

Knowing of Carmen and Cassandra's legal concerns, I invited them to attend a health fair with me in the Washington Heights neighborhood of New York City. The Gay and Lesbian Dominican Empowerment Organization (GALDE) has sponsored this event annually since its inception fifteen years ago. While this event is put on by a gay and lesbian organization focusing on the needs of Dominicans, it attracts people of all Latina/o nationalities from throughout the city. The event took place in a park on a beautiful Sunday afternoon with food, music, and lots of people sitting on picnic blankets on the grass. A bike path cut through the center of the park, and bikers, runners, and Rollerblade skaters stopped as they passed to look on with curiosity. The space was full of tables and tents to accommodate the different LGBTQ organizations in the city, each promoting their mission, handing out information booklets, and offering free health screenings. I attended this event with Carmen, Cassandra, their baby, and my son. As we walked around gathering information from the different groups, we stopped at a table to read pamphlets from a gay legal advocacy organization. The woman behind the table started asking Carmen questions about her family:

NONPROFIT ORGANIZATION WORKER: Your daughter is so cute. How old is she?

CARMEN: [Smiles] Thank you. She's two years old.

CASSANDRA: [To their daughter] Analisa, say hi to the lady.

CARMEN: [To the worker] We wanted to know about second-parent adoption.

NONPROFIT ORGANIZATION WORKER: Call us. We can refer you to a lawyer who can help because it's really important.

CARMEN: Yeah, I spoke to a lawyer before but it's expensive, and they were asking all kinds of complicated stuff.

NONPROFIT ORGANIZATION WORKER: You need to start saving money for a second-parent adoption. Money will always be tight, and you need to just figure it out because tomorrow, if something happens to the birth mom, what will happen to the baby? No, no, no, you just have to do it.

Carmen smiled politely and walked away. A key point in this interaction came when Carmen said she had spoken with a lawyer "and they were asking all kinds of complicated stuff." In doing so, Carmen was assenting that the complexities of her family made second-parent adoption unattainable for them. Their distrust of government bureaucracy and their experiences of being unable to fit the constraints these bureaucracies place on them has resulted in their commitment to keep their household outside of the purview of the law. This distrust was not much different from that of Desiree. Despite the fact that Desiree's experiences and familial needs were very different from Carmen and Cassandra's, they share a hesitance to seek legal intervention and/or counseling for their families. Their desires to manage their intimate problems informally among themselves and other members in their communities stands in contrast to the dominant discourse used in the fight for legal protections for same-sex families. These discourses are framed on the importance of public recognition, legal visibility, acceptance, and protection. However, these values were not driving the families highlighted in this chapter. They mostly seemed to find ways around bureaucratic systems. Thus, while I write about the public visibility and legal invisibility that the participants described experiencing in this chapter, it is important to note that these women were sometimes complicit in their legal invisibilities. They made choices to circumvent legal systems because of their distrust for these institutions. Given this distrust, the public visibility they would experience if they presented as same-sex families of choice to the larger society would yield unwanted scrutiny and surveillance into their personal lives and the informal arrangements under which they operate. Thus, this public visibility is also something the participants did not welcome and at times labored to mitigate. The recognition, visibility, acceptance, and protection these women sought came from families of origin and their immigrant communities, not from US legal structures or the larger public society. These women were much like those Ellen Lewin (1993) interviewed for her work on lesbian motherhood in that they sought out connection with their families of origin in order to foster a sense of legitimacy for their alternative family forms. In this way, their experiences are very different from those frequently highlighted in public debates for same-sex marriage or gay and lesbian familial recognition.

For various reasons some of the parents highlighted in this chapter were reluctant to navigate the US legal system. Carmen and Cassandra were motivated by distrust. Desiree's reluctance seemed to be related to her apprehension of homophobia. Margot's inability to create these legal ties may be attributed to a lack of knowledge or desire. Regardless of the reasoning, these women's inability to engage with the legal system made it so that their families are legally invisible and unprotected. Despite this, LBQ Latina mothers are building families without the recognition of the state. They are raising children within a heteronormative world and in the absence of validating examples of alternative families. Their experiences are significantly different from those of white, middle-class lesbian mothers and other mothers who generally create families through assisted reproductive technologies or adoption. As all sexually nonconforming mothers do, they contend with deciding what the children should call each mother and dividing care responsibilities in a way that won't result in the child favoring one mother over the other. However, the mothers in this study do all of this without many of the legal protections that white, middle-class, same-sex couples enjoy and under extreme economic constraints.

Parenting as an Avenue for (In)visibility with Families of Origin

In addition to Carmen and Cassandra, two other study participants were actively planning to have children within their same-sex relationships at the time of the interview. Their experiences provide us with insight into how they negotiated planning to have children with their families of origin. For one couple, having a child within their relationship would help cement their partnership in the eyes of their families of origin. However, for the other couple, having a child would simply serve to further cement the illusion of heterosexuality. Planning the conception of their children became one of the ways that the study participants used to navigate visibility and invisibility with their families of origin. While scholarship points to the ways in which having children can create a bridge for familial acceptance (Sullivan 2004) or can lead lesbian and gay parents to develop stronger connections with families of origin than they do with families of choice (Carrington 1999), I find that the mothers must themselves actively create a platform for that "acceptance" in order to achieve it.[10] If they do not, as one of the participants discussed below did not, same-sex parenting gets added to the list of tacit subjects that family members do not mention.

Luisa (first introduced in chapter 1) is a corporate employee in the finance district. She was born in Ecuador but raised in a suburb outside New York. She and her partner, Courtney, were in the midst of planning their wedding in Massachusetts, a step they had decided to take because they were ready to have children. It is important to note that Luisa and Courtney are the only couple in this chapter who reported feeling the need to get married before having children and are the only ones who turned to the legal system to legitimize their relationship. I attribute this difference to the fact that they are the only participants highlighted in this chapter with professional class statuses and did not face the same immigration hurdles that plagued some other participants. At the time of the interview, the couple had decided to use alternative insemination and to have Courtney be the birth mother. They had first considered asking Luisa's brother to be the sperm donor so that the child could have a biological connection to both partners. Initially, it was important to Luisa that the baby have a biological connection to her in part because her mother had distanced herself from their plans by arguing that the child would not be her grandchild since Courtney would be the biological mother. At this point, the couple had decided against this plan because they were concerned that Luisa's brother might become too attached to the baby. They are now considering an anonymous donor and Luisa explained:

> I'm ready. I've been ready. We've just been trying to give everybody else time to be ready. Initially, both my parents said they don't think it's right for us to have a baby. They think it's selfish because we are going to be bringing a child into the world who wouldn't have a dad. And who's going to be the child's role model? We are also bringing a child into the world who is going to be made fun of and disadvantaged. And those are just their concerns about kids. That's not addressing that they think we are in an unnatural relationship. I think it's hard for my mom because she likes my partner. It would be easier to condemn the relationship if she didn't like her. She sees that my partner is nurturing, and she knows I'm nurturing. They see two people who could be great parents in a relationship they don't agree with. At first they were like, "Well, if your partner has a child, that's her child; that has nothing to do with me." So we thought it might be smart to have my brother be the sperm donor for my partner. My brother is certainly on board. Then the child would look like me and Courtney. It would work in theory. My mom flipped out. I don't know if we will go that route. . . . It really muddies the waters . . . but we thought about it for a long while. My mother couldn't come up with a solid reason for why it would be bad. It would fix our problems. She wouldn't be able to say that it wouldn't have any relation to me.

Luisa and Courtney delayed getting married because Luisa's parents were not supportive of their relationship. However, the couple now feels they have delayed expanding their family long enough. Despite Luisa's parents' concerns, they are moving forward with their plans to get married and have a baby. Luisa and Courtney's initial desire to use Luisa's brother as the donor was motivated by their desire to gain visibility within and legitimacy from Luisa's family of origin. Luisa wanted to increase her family of origin's connection to the baby by creating a biological link through her younger brother.

The importance of biological lineage can be a common point of tension for sexually nonconforming women who have children in the context of their same-sex relationships. This issue is particularly important because biological lineage can shape how families of origin react to the same-sex couple and to the children they have together (Sullivan 2004). As Maureen Sullivan (2004) finds in her work, families of origin of nonbirth parents are more likely to not accept the child as a member of the family. However, because of homogeneity in terms of race and class in Sullivan's sample, it is unclear if these findings would be consistent for racial minorities and/or working-class families. Furthermore, Abbie Goldberg (2006) found that both biological and nonbiological mothers reported receiving more support from their families of origin after the birth of their baby. At first glance, Luisa's mother's reaction supports the idea that biology is important irrespective of race or ethnicity. However, her mother's reservations regarding Courtney being the birth mother for their baby may also be attributed to racial differences between the two. Since Courtney is white and the donor has not yet been chosen, it is possible that Luisa's mother feels a disconnect from this future child because she presumes it will not share her Ecuadorian lineage. However, since Luisa's mother did not become any more accepting of the couple's plans to make Luisa's brother the donor, it is possible that her resistance had little to do with the biology or racial makeup of the unborn baby and more to do with her overall disapproval of homosexuality, two women in a relationship with one another, and even more so with a child being raised without a father in the home. It is further possible that Luisa's mother has romanticized the importance of biology as a way of managing the image that the extended family of origin receives regarding Luisa's sexuality. This would certainly fall in line with this mother's previous concern (as seen in chapter 1) that Luisa wear a dress on her wedding day so as to solidify her womanhood. Following that logic, it is possible that Luisa's mother prefers that she be the birth mother as a way of revalidating her womanhood for the extended family of origin.

Luisa's description of her mother's reaction to her plans to have a child with Courtney is distinct from how Carmen and Cassandra describe their families of origin responding to the birth of their daughter. Cassandra has no family of origin in the United States. Her relationship with Carmen, even after more than fifteen years, is a tacit subject among her kin; and because she is undocumented, she has been unable to return to the Dominican Republic to visit her family since she arrived in the United States in the mid-1990s. She speaks to her family weekly, and they know that she lives with Carmen and they have watched Analisa grow up through pictures and phone conversations. However, Cassandra has never verbalized her relationship with Carmen to her family of origin. Cassandra's family understands that she is raising Analisa with Carmen, but they have never asked any questions about the circumstances that led to her pregnancy or their coparenting. Carmen's family of origin also initially rendered their relationship a tacit subject. However, in Carmen's case, many members of her family of origin do live in the United States. Her parents do not, but they visit the United States often and stay in Carmen's home with her partner when they do. In both cases, rendering their relationship a tacit subject makes it easier for these families of origin to connect, bond, and support one another. In this way, Carmen's family of origin has come to "accept" her relationship with Cassandra.[11] When Analisa was born, many members of Carmen's family of origin shifted to more actively accepting their relationship. Analisa, while not biologically related to Carmen, has been integrated in the extended family-of-origin network, as are all of the other children within this family. This is particularly interesting considering that not only is Analisa not biologically tied to Carmen, but Carmen doesn't have a legal connection to this child—making Analisa's involvement with Carmen's family of origin contingent upon her relationship with Cassandra. Still, in spite of these vulnerabilities, by all accounts, Carmen's family of origin has accepted Analisa unequivocally. The juxtaposition of Luisa and Courtney's experiences with Carmen and Cassandra's points to the complexities inherent in how families of origin react to their LBQ kin's relationships and their biological or non-biological children. These examples indicate that biology may be only one in a myriad factors, including class, religion, race/ethnicity, and legality, that shape how families of origin respond to sexually nonconforming women's families of choice. Furthermore, the juxtaposition of these two families points to the importance of individual agency in shaping acceptance and visibility. Carmen and Cassandra made choices not to push their families of origin to acknowledge the tacit subjects that hold their relationships together. If they had, they might have experienced much of the initial turmoil and grief to which Luisa's family of origin subjected her. Instead, Carmen and Cassandra chose to avoid familial rifts and negotiate a space for their family of choice that allows them to maintain connections with their families of origin. For Carmen and Cassandra, having a child did not eradicate the tacit subjects that preserve their bonds with their families of origin.

Carmen's experience suggests that children can help strengthen acceptance with families of origin regardless of whether or not there is a biological or legal connection. The findings show that the same kind of support is also possible among two-parent stepfamilies as well. Milagros, who during our interview described a previous relationship with a woman who had a child, received more support from her mother because the relationship involved a child. In this particular case, Milagros's mother had wanted to be a grandmother, and since

Milagros is an only child her mother relied on her to provide one. Her previous relationship with a woman who was also a mother, therefore, was very appealing to Milagros's mother:

> Milagros: Ella [mi mamá] quiere un hijo. Yo le dije, "Mamá, yo lo adopto pero yo no me veo embarazada. Yo no me veo en el proceso de embarazo. Quizás de aquí en un par de años me vea en ese proceso. Puedo cambiar. Yo no me limito. Pero mi primera opción en este momento sería adoptar."
>
> Katie: Y ¿tú nunca has tenido parejas que tienen hijos?
>
> Milagros: Yo tenía una pareja que tiene una hija de trece años. A la cual mi mamá le encantaba esa idea de que yo estuviera con una mujer con una hija. Porque así ella podía conectar con mi pareja. Porque ellas tenían algo en común.

> Milagros: She [my mother] wants a child. I told her, "Mom, I'll adopt one, but I don't see myself pregnant. I don't envision myself going through the process of pregnancy. Maybe in a few years I'll envision myself in the process. I can change. I don't limit myself. But my first choice right now would be to adopt."
>
> Katie: And have you never had a partner who has children?
>
> Milagros: I had a partner who had a thirteen-year-old daughter. My mother loved the idea of me being in a relationship with a woman who has a daughter. Because that way she could connect with my partner because they had something in common.

For Milagros's mother it appears that the issue of biology is less salient than her desire to be a grandmother. Interestingly, Milagros notes that her mother liked her previous partner because, as both were mothers, she could relate to her in a way that was not possible with some of Milagros's other partners. Motherhood provided a point of commonality that helped Milagros's mother connect with her daughter's partner.

While in Carmen's case the birth of Analisa has allowed her family of origin to become more meaningfully involved in her support network, children do not always serve this purpose. By incorporating Analisa as a member of their familial circle, Carmen's family of origin is acknowledging her relationship with Cassandra while simultaneously leaving the issue a tacit subject. This provides the couple with a certain sense of visibility as lesbian comothers. However, sometimes having children can help steer families of origin away from making their same-sex partnerships visible and toward more stably creating the illusion of heterosexuality. Consider the case of Angelica. At the time of the interview, Angelica had lived in the United States for two years. She came by entering a marriage of convenience with her gay male friend, Darío, whom she has known since college. At the time, Angelica was eager to live in the United States because she had been in a long-distance relationship with her partner Miguelina for several years.

Angelica and Darío's marriage served two purposes: it gave Angelica the opportunity to come live in the United States with a path to citizenship, and it allowed Darío's family to stop pressuring him about settling down and starting a family.[12] Given these two goals, Angelica and Darío never told their parents that their marriage was a contractual arrangement rather than romantic, nor did they discuss their plan for Darío to become the sperm donor so that Angelica could get pregnant and fulfill her desire to become a mother.

After Angelica immigrated to the United States, she went to live with her partner Miguelina. After living in the United States together for two years, Angelica and Miguelina agreed to soon begin trying to conceive. Angelica recounts:

> Nosotros [Darío y yo] siempre habíamos hecho el plan de que íbamos a tener un hijo. Entonces, cuando comenzamos a hablar de nuevo, él me dijo, "Mira— ¿qué vamos a hacer? Ya mi mamá me está preguntando por el hijo de nuevo. Yo tengo treinta y pico de años. Ya es tiempo." En su caso, supuestamente su mamá no sabe que él es gay. En mi caso, también. Entonces nos casamos y ellos fueron felices. Este año, yo creo que vamos a tener un hijo. . . . Mi pareja está de acuerdo. Desde el principio que comenzamos a tener una relación estable, yo siempre le hablé de mi intención de tener un hijo. Es algo que está en mí. No es que yo quiero hacer felices a mis padres. No es eso. Es algo en mí.

> (We [Darío and I] always had a plan that we were going to have a child. So when we started to talk again, he said to me, "Look, what are we going to do? My mother is already asking me about children again. I am in my mid thirties. It's time." In his case, supposedly his mother doesn't know he's gay. In my case, too, though. And so we got married, and they were happy. This year I think we're going to have a child. . . . My partner agrees. From the beginning, when we started to have a stable relationship, I always talked to her about my intention to have a child. It is something that's in me. It isn't that I want to make my parents happy. It isn't that. It's something in me.)

Angelica, Miguelina, and Darío have informally agreed that Darío would remain involved in the child's life but would not be responsible for any of its financial needs. Many of the plans for Angelica to get pregnant were sketched out before Angelica and Miguelina even met. Angelica has always felt an intense desire to mother, and Darío, being a good friend and someone she had known previously as her "boyfriend," was always her choice in donor. Miguelina came later, and thus her involvement as a coparent in this child's life is something that appears to not yet be worked out. Angelica's comment that her "partner is in agreement" indicates that Miguelina may not be an active participant in this process, and thus it is unclear what role she will play in the life of this child. Even if Miguelina has a strong desire to be a comother to this child, there are some legal concerns that may complicate matters. Miguelina may not be able to adopt the child because Angelica is legally married to Darío and must remain so for the purpose of immigration. If Darío did not legally claim this child as his, it would raise a red flag for immigration regarding the legitimacy of their marriage. If Miguelina and Angelica obtained a second-parent adoption in order to create a legal connection between Miguelina and the baby, it could expose Angelica's marriage to Darío as fraudulent and result in a denial of her citizenship application. Thus, given their immigration hurdles, much as was the case with Desiree and Elisha as well as Carmen and Cassandra, the formation of this family is entirely dependent upon informal agreements and understandings. Their familial arrangements, much like those of most of the other families discussed in this chapter, exist completely outside the purview of the state.

CONCLUSION

The experiences of the participants highlighted in this chapter support the previous findings that children can help the family of origin accept the relationship as legitimate and stable as opposed to a phase. Families of origin may come to create greater visibility for the same-sex couple after the birth of a child. This can occur even among families who render these relationships tacit subjects. In these instances study participants can, through their children, be successful at integrating their families of choice and origin. This was the case for Carmen and Cassandra. However, as the example of Angelica and Miguelina portrays, having children can also serve to make sexual nonconformity less visible in the eyes of families of origin. It can allow people to appear to fit into a heteronormative paradigm within which these women were already confined on account of their families of origin and against which they consistently measured themselves. This is not to say that LBQ Latinas have children for the sole purpose of pretending to be heterosexual to their families of origin. Rather, in families like Angelica's, who treated her relationships with other women as a tacit subject, creating the outward illusion of heterosexuality may go a long way in helping them carve out an in-between space within which to build sexually nonconforming families of choice. In the next chapter, I will further explore how the study participants' families of choice lived in a state of "nepantla," or an in-between space, in order to facilitate integration with families of origin. I will further illustrate how study participants navigated visibility and invisibility among their families of origin while being in a state of nepantla.

CHAPTER 5

INTEGRATING FAMILIES OF
CHOICE AND ORIGIN

GAINING VISIBILITY THROUGH CARE WORK

I interviewed Aurelia at a restaurant in downtown Boston. We had corresponded through email a few times but had no mutual acquaintances. Aurelia is Nicaraguan, college educated, and holds a professional job. She identifies as a lesbian, and at age twenty-seven she has had one serious long-term relationship with another Nicaraguan woman named Pamela, whom she met when she was twenty-one. Their relationship blossomed very quickly, and within a year the couple was living together. Aurelia's family had a difficult time accepting their relationship. Her father chose to ignore it, her brother was openly hostile in his disapproval, leaving the two estranged, and her mother was inquisitive but also visibly uncomfortable. The lack of support she received from her family of origin meant that Aurelia was forced to distance herself from them significantly after moving in with Pamela. Pamela, on the other hand, was very close to her family of origin, and when her sister and niece needed a place to live, Pamela and Aurelia allowed them to stay in their apartment. Aurelia's relationship with Pamela lasted six years, during which time the couple was very isolated from a larger LGBTQ community. They interacted very infrequently with Aurelia's family of origin, and thus what little support they did have came from Pamela's family of origin, who depended on her a great deal for financial resources. In return for the financial sacrifices they made, Aurelia and Pamela received visibility for their relationship and a great deal of emotional support, which they relied on because of the scarcity of other social ties.[1] As one can imagine, the strain of Pamela's familial obligations and the lack of support from Aurelia's family eventually took a toll on such a young couple. By the time of the interview they had ended their relationship and dissolved the domestic partnership they had created with one another years earlier.

In their research on care work among siblings, Shelley Eriksen and Naomi Gerstel (2002) note that while often ignored in academic scholarship, care work among siblings is not a rare occurrence, particularly among younger individuals and those who are single. Siblings, Eriksen and Gerstel find, can serve as an important safety net for one another. These ties are most common when parents are alive, as parents tend to serve as coordinators for these care relationships. This was certainly the case for Aurelia and Pamela, who supported Pamela's sister and allowed her to live with them; however, they were not the exception in this study. This couple, like so many other women in this study who often spoke of their devotion to their families of origin with pride, rarely hinted at the sacrifices they had to make in order to carry out these duties. On the surface, the participants often presented an infallible image as they emphasized their love, dedication, and devotion for their mothers, grandparents, and siblings. They carefully managed the impressions they gave of the work they did to support their or their partners' families of origin.[2] However, I was less interested in this carefully cultivated presentation of self. I wanted to know about the tensions associated with the care work they were doing and how their relationships with their partners were affected by this work. Following Arlie Hochschild (1979), I wanted to look beyond the impression management occurring at the surface to the deep acting or emotion work that occurs in the core of the social actor.[3] Anita Garey (2011) writes about the "maternal visibility" that working mothers perform to emphasize their commitment to motherhood and dispel the myth that they are inferior to stay-at-home mothers. Working mothers, Garey notes, strive to make the difficulties involved in juggling employment and parenting appear effortless despite the toll it takes on them emotionally. I found a similar phenomenon with the LBQ Latinas in this study. They took pride in recounting all of the different ways they supported their families of origin and choice but were more reluctant to share the ways in which this care work undoubtedly weighed on their lives as well, thus making a personal choice to focus on the optimistic rather than the troublesome aspects of their lives. Through more frequent interactions with the respondents, participation in their family events, and conversations with their partners, I came to piece together the complexities involved in the care work arrangements they maintained. Although not always the focus of their narration, these care arrangements created emotional baggage not just for the participants but also for their partners; however, they often undertook this labor as a way of expressing their support and becoming integrated in each other's family. Mothers, I found, also managed their emotions about their daughters' sexual nonconformity in strategic ways: finding ways to show their disapproval but continuing to support their daughters when they were in need.

While there seems to be a polarization in the academic scholarship, whereby those writing about families of choice predominantly focus on white LGBTQ individuals and those writing about fictive kin building focus on black and Latino families, all of whose members are presumed to be heterosexuals (Bennett and Battle 2001), these divisions did not exist in this study. The findings show that most study participants maintained support and care networks that centered on both their families of origin and families of choice. Their experiences with these expanded support networks led them to desire synergistic connections between their families of choice and origin. Incorporating their partners, friends, and other members of their LGBTQ communities into these familial networks was a natural next step for these women to take as adults. They desired this integration because of the visibility it created for their families of choice, albeit a visibility filled with tension and struggle in addition to positive gains.

The kinds of familial responsibilities that the participants in this study describe have at times been attributed to the cultural values of Latina/o families, often referred to as the values of *familismo* (Baca-Zinn 1982; Vega 1995). However, the concept of familismo has the potential to reduce the values that make up close-knit familial ties to one ethnic group without consideration for the social conditions, such as immigration, racism, and poverty, that may foster the need for familial solidarity as a mechanism for survival (Baca-Zinn 1998).[4] In part, the social, legal, and economic needs of the LBQ Latinas in this study and their families of origin influenced the kinds of relationship patterns they formed as adults. However, so did the participants' sexualities and how their families of origin responded to those sexualities. These findings suggest several questions: How do the care work arrangements the study participants maintain shape their social position within their families of origin? What kinds of tensions emerge as the study participants and their partners attempt to gain visibility through care work arrangements?

Caring and Making Sexuality Visible While Living in Nepantla

Caring for and supporting one's family of origin most often involved the study participants' efforts to meet the needs of their mothers. For some older participants, caring for their ailing mothers meant tending mainly to their physical needs. In her study of women who care for their elderly parents, Emily Abel (1991) notes that sometimes when daughters serve in a care-giving capacity for their mothers, they bring with them old feelings of rejection and hurt. In caring for their mothers, daughters may be simultaneously hoping to heal such old wounds. At times, the care work LBQ Latinas performed for their mothers served a similar purpose. It helped to redeem them as good daughters despite their sexualities and thus helped the participants heal from previous feelings of rejection.

Wendy was in her fifties when I first met her. She has been married to a man for almost thirty years and raised two children with him. Wendy describes their marriage as one of convenience. They have separate bedrooms and different friends, and they spend very little time together. Although Wendy feels unable to divorce him because she relies on his financial support, she does not see her life attached to his in other ways. Wendy's marital arrangement shows a vague resemblance to what some scholars have called mixed orientation marriages, or "MOMs" (Wolkomir 2009), in that, despite being married, Wendy identifies as a lesbian and her husband identifies as heterosexual. The resemblance is further supported by the fact that Wendy maintains a romantic relationship with another woman outside of her marriage.[5] For the past six years, Wendy has been in a relationship with María, with whom she does share a strong emotional connection. Wendy served as the primary caretaker for her mother in the final months of her life. When I interviewed her, it had been less than a year since her mother's passing. She described the time she spent caring for her mother: "When I was working I had to do everything, like helping her in the bathroom, calling up social workers, and she always counted on me. We went shopping for clothing and things; she depended on me and, you know, that was a priority in my life, taking care of my mom. I felt like I aged so much and so quickly during that time. Everything went so fast." Initially, Wendy tried to juggle working for pay and caring for her mom. However, as her mother got sicker, this was no longer possible, and Wendy quit her job. She visited her mother every morning, tended to her physical needs, and provided her with companionship. While her mother's illness progressed, so did Wendy's relationship with María. Within the context of this care work arrangement, Wendy started to bring María with her to visit her mother on occasion. María came to be known among Wendy's family of origin as her *amiga*. María developed her own bond with Wendy's mother and other family members. Under the guise of friendship, these two women were originally able to create a space for themselves among Wendy's familial circle that allowed Wendy to care for her mother and to include her partner María in this intimate setting. Wendy recounts, "She [María] used to go to all the family events with me, birthday parties, holidays, everything. She would go to see Mami. Yes, she would meet me there. She loved my mother a lot. My mother liked her, too. And she connected with her. My father even said, 'Oh, we love you, we love you.' I used to think, 'My God, you're lucky to have that. In the life, you don't see families like that.'" Despite the fact that most of Wendy's family of origin did not know or acknowledge them as a couple, the two found power in the in-between space they created. In-between spaces exist at the juncture of in versus out of the closet. I recognize that the metaphor of the closet is limiting as an analytical tool. The notion of the closet implies that it is possible for individuals to neatly fit into being either in the closet or out and proud. This simple dichotomization does an injustice to the arrangement Wendy and María maintained with Wendy's family of origin. Furthermore, this dichotomization does not fit with the experiences of many of the other participants in this study. Their experiences are more adequately expressed by a concept that is flexible and malleable. For this reason, I use Gloria Anzaldúa's (1999) term "nepantla" to describe the in-between spaces where participants live. Nepantla is the space one inhabits when one is in transition. It can be a physical space or a state of being that one inhabits as one moves through the different stages in life. While nepantla is a space of uncertainty and change, it can also help connect us to other people. I use nepantla here to describe a space that sexually nonconforming Latinas inhabit with their families of origin and choice, a space that affords these women power and agency as they negotiate visibility and invisibility, silence and validation.[6] Wendy's and María's ability to create this space made it easier for them to juggle the needs of their relationship with those of Wendy's sick mother. Being the main caretaker for her mother was a full-time job for Wendy. She cooked for her, took her to doctors' appointments, refilled her prescriptions, and tended to all of her basic bodily needs. These duties left little time for her relationship with María. Integrating the two in an in-between space or nepantla allowed Wendy to gain some visibility of her relationship with María from her mother and other members of her family of origin. In this way, Wendy's arrangement with her families of choice and origin held an element of reciprocity. Karen Pyke (1999) notes that care work creates a reciprocal relationship, where the provider is receiving something in return for his or her services beyond the satisfaction of fulfilling his or her familial obligations.[7] For the LBQ Latinas in this study, fulfilling care work obligations seemed to allow for acceptance, tolerance, or visibility of their nonconforming relationships. The work Wendy and others do is in part in exchange for tacit compliance or visibility of their same-sex relationships.

Wendy and María's success at integrating their two families was interrupted with the death of Wendy's mother and the familial disputes that ensued. The family disagreed over the best course of action to care for her mother in her dying days. These disagreements led to some harsh exchanges between Wendy and her siblings and, ultimately, to an irreparable rift between Wendy and her sister. These circumstances completely disrupted nepantla for Wendy and changed her family's reaction to her relationship with María:

> Well, my sister and I had a fight. She called me a fucking lesbian or something. She said all these horrible things to me about how I fuck men and women. My mother was dying in the hospital. And the family was pretty upset when Mami died, and she said some mean things to me. She got into everything that I had done; told me that I don't know if I want men or women or what. So I don't want to bring María around my family no more. It's just not the same anymore. . . . And I feel like I don't want to expose my family to the other half of me because I think it's just too confusing to them, too much trauma I think. If it ever comes out, I don't know what would happen. . . . And I feel a lot of times in the life, when people come out, a lot of times they lose their family or you don't have connection. I have girlfriends that are not connected to their mamis because their mothers just don't want to talk about it.

By allowing her relationship with María to remain tacit and by allowing her relationship to live in nepantla in order to negotiate her families of choice and origin,

Wendy created a vulnerability for herself that her sister was later able to exploit under the extreme anguish of losing a parent. Because Wendy had never verbally disclosed the romantic nature of her relationship with María to her family of origin, her sister was able to use this tacit relationship against her during a time of despair. Their argument did violence to the tacit arrangement Wendy had maintained with her two families for years. This disruption changed Wendy's ability to integrate her relationship with María into her family of origin. During our interview, she lamented that she has completely separated these two worlds in order to avoid further trauma to her family members. However, her words insinuate that this is only half the story. She fears the potential rejection from her family if they were forced to make her romantic relationship with María visible as opposed to incorporating them into the larger familial network as friends. Thus, her decision to keep her family of choice separate from her family of origin is also about protecting herself and her partner from any more emotional trauma.

Although most of the participants did not completely separate their families of choice and origin, many of the study participants reported the tensions that arose when trying to integrate their partners into their families of origin. These tensions were particularly difficult when the efforts to integrate were made at a time when families of origin had strong care needs. Under such circumstances, many heterosexual couples would also likely experience difficulties with integration; however, this obstacle is complicated for the study participants by the fact that they are in relationships with other women. This is particularly the case for those whose families of origin do not recognize or make their same-sex partnerships visible. Most research on women as caregivers for their ailing parents assumes a heterosexual carer and thus ignores the unique difficulties that sexual nonconformity can place on the caregiving arrangements that families must make (Manthorpe 2003).[8] Sexually nonconforming women and their families of choice may experience an additional layer of emotional baggage: fulfilling their care work obligations for their families of origin who do not acknowledge, recognize, or make visible their obligations to their families of choice.

When I first met Scarlet, a Puerto Rican woman in her fifties, she had been laid off from work and had decided to return to school to get a master's degree. Scarlet was in a relationship with Rocío, a Puerto Rican woman in her thirties. Present on Scarlet's mind during our initial interview were the disagreements she'd been having with Rocío. The couple was under a great deal of stress because Rocío's mother was terminally ill and Rocío was doing her best to care for her mother at home, where her mother felt most comfortable. Rocío had moved in with her mother to manage her daily needs. These arrangements put an inordinate amount of stress on Rocío, whose responsibility it became to juggle medical prescriptions, meals, and doctor visits. Because Rocío was also juggling a job, Rocío's aunt came from another state to stay with the family and help them through this time of crisis. The problem arose for Scarlet when Rocío's aunt began to verbally express disapproval of their relationship. Scarlet described their encounters in the following way: "My partner is caring for her mom in the house. Her mom is really ill. And the sister, her mom's sister, was helping her with the care. When I started dating her, I would stay over in her room, and the aunt started having issues, telling her that I was disrespecting her mother. And then the aunt started to disrespect me. I have decided not to live with her yet. I'm not ready to live with her. My relationship is important, but moving in with her and the way her life is structured in her home, it's a big responsibility for her, so I don't know."

The relative newness of Scarlet and Rocío's relationship occurred at the same time that Rocío's family of origin was undergoing a crisis. This crisis presented an opportunity for Rocío to care for her terminally ill mother, but it also created Rocío's last opportunity to get her mother to make her relationship with Scarlet visible. Her desire to care for her mother and gain this visibility are at odds with one another because she is attempting to integrate her families of choice and origin during a very stressful time. However, while this may be a very stressful time for Rocío and Scarlet to work on integration, it is also the time when this couple needs this integration the most. This couple learned the hard way that confronting homophobia from the family can be one of the biggest risks that sexually nonconforming women face when caring for their parents (Price 2011). Price (2011) notes that in some instances the emotionally charged situation may bring sexually nonconforming women closer to their families of origin as they share care work responsibilities and mourn their loss together. Other times, however, these emotionally charged situations can fall short of creating more visibility for sexually nonconforming Latinas or integrating families of choice and origin. The latter was ultimately the case for Rocío and Wendy. However, irrespective of the outcome, caring for families of origin requires everyone to renegotiate the parameters of their relationships that sexually nonconforming women challenge on account of their sexuality (Price 2011).

The fact that Rocío's aunt's disapproval is grounded in issues of respect may be particularly hurtful because it implies that Rocío is not honoring her mother. Thus, in the eyes of Rocío's aunt, the sacrifices she makes to live with and care for her mother both physically and financially are mitigated by the fact that she is trying to openly love another woman in her mother's home. The study participants often reported feeling torn under these circumstances. While the most rewarding part of caregiving for Latinas can be fulfilling their role as the "good daughter" (Jolicoeur and Madden 2002), this very reward was jeopardized for Rocío as her aunt expressed disapproval of her efforts to integrate her relationship with Scarlet into this family unit. As their status as good daughters fell into question, the participants tried to compensate for this perceived shortcoming in one of two ways: by overextending themselves while giving care work in hopes of gaining visibility, or, if that situation did not work, by making their romantic partnerships less visible to their families of origin with the objective of gaining approval. The latter strategy occurred much less frequently and created much anguish for the participants, as demonstrated by Wendy's experience.

Participants engaged in care work often lived in a state of nepantla or a liminal space even when families of origin did not live in the same country as they did. Consider, for example, Aracely's story (first mentioned in chapter 2). Aracely was an undocumented Peruvian woman in her late twenties when I interviewed her. Her parents sent her to the United States by herself after a scandal broke out in her hometown. Aracely had been in a romantic relationship with Ana Julia for two years. Aracely's parents knew Ana Julia to be their daughter's amiga but had no knowledge of the romantic nature of their relationship. As time progressed, however, the intricacies of this relationship became increasingly evident. Ana Julia's family tried to send her to live with family in a rural part of Peru in order to separate the two. Afraid of being separated from one another, the two ran away. Aracely stole money from her parents' business and left the city with Ana Julia. After several months, they had to return as they had no means by which to start a life together. Aracely describes their return this way:

Cuando yo regresé a Lima, yo no pude ni siquiera verle la cara a mi mamá. Yo nada más andaba con los ojos abajo. No quería mirarle la cara a mi mamá porque me sentí tan mal después de lo que había hecho y el problema que yo le había causado a mi familia. Mis padres me hicieron la pregunta, "Queremos saber ¿qué es lo que está pasando aquí?" Yo empecé a llorar y dije, "Bueno, ya no les voy a mentir más. Yo les voy a decir la verdad. Ana Julia es mi pareja. Yo la amo. Yo quiero estar con ella. Nosotros queremos crear una vida junta. Yo no se lo quería decir porque tenía miedo de que ustedes iban a rechazarme, que ustedes no me iban a querer, que ustedes me iban a botar de la casa." Yo lloré, mis padres lloraron. Mis padres dijeron, "No te preocupes, hijita. Tú eres nuestra hija, tú siempre vas a ser nuestra hija. No importa lo que tú hayas hecho. Tú eres la reina de esta casa y nosotros te aceptamos como tú eres." Mi mamá dijo, "Yo sólo quería oírlo de tu propia boca."

(When I returned to Lima, I couldn't even look my mother in the face. I walked around with my eyes down. I didn't want to look my mother in the face because I felt so bad about what I had done and the problems I had caused my family. My parents said to me, "We want to know what's going on here." I started to cry and said, "OK, I'm not going to lie to you anymore. I'm going to tell you the truth. Ana Julia is my partner. I love her. I want to be with her. We want to create a life together. I didn't want to tell you because I was afraid you'd reject me, that you wouldn't love me, that you'd throw me out of the house." I cried, my parents cried. My parents said, "Don't worry, sweetie. You're our daughter; you're always going to be our daughter. It doesn't matter what you've done. You are the queen of this house, and we accept you the way you are." My mother said, "I just wanted to hear it from your own mouth.")

Aracely's mother wanted to hear from her what had already been rumored for months in their town. While Aracely's parents forgave her for abusing their trust and accepted her lesbian existence, they ultimately arranged with a coyote to send her to the United States. Her parents made this decision after months of observing Aracely's relationship with Ana Julia and growing concerned that this relationship was emotionally unhealthy for their daughter. Aracely described her relationship with Ana Julia as often volatile and obsessive. Aracely's parents feared the scandal that had broken out in the community regarding their relationship, but even more they feared the intensity of the women's relationship and were concerned that Aracely had allowed this relationship to derail her plans for a stable and successful future. Given the circumstance, her parents sent her to the United States to live with a brother. She describes her current relationship with them in the following way:

> Después que yo le dije que soy lesbiana, mi relación con ellos ha mejorado bastante. Ahora puedo hablar con mi mamá sobre de cualquier cosa. Algo que no era posible antes. Yo puedo hablar con mi mamá sobre de lo que pasa con mis parejas. Ahora confiamos más una con la otra y tenemos una relación más saludable.

> (After I told them that I'm a lesbian, my relationship with them has improved a lot. Now I can talk to my mother about anything. That wasn't possible before. I can talk to my mom about what happens with my partners. Now we confide more in one another and have a much healthier relationship.)

While Aracely describes her current relationship with her parents to be a healthy one, she continues to feel guilty for the problems she caused them in her early twenties. Even as she recounted the events to me (the theft and the lying), the sadness was evident in her demeanor as her voice grew faint and her eyes stared at the floor. Since moving to the United States, she has repaid them for the money she took and also for the money they had to borrow to pay the coyote to help her cross the border safely. Nonetheless, it is clear that the work Aracely feels she must do to redeem herself in the eyes of her parents remains unfinished. One of the things she does to help redeem herself is to care for her alcoholic brother in the United States. While her brother is a functioning alcoholic, his drinking problems and battles with depression are of great concern for Aracely's parents in Peru. One of the things that Aracely does to recompense for her previous wrongdoings is to help her parents feel more secure about both of their children living so far away. Caring for her brother allows Aracely to regain and maintain the position of good daughter within her family of origin.

Since immigrating to the United States, Aracely has lived in a state of nepantla. She is able to gain visibility for her relationships with women in the United States through communication with her family of origin in Peru. In this way, her parents can support her relationships, offer her advice, and make her feelings visible, without ever meeting her partners or sharing a physical space with them as a couple. While her relationship with Ana Julia also left her in a state of nepantla in Peru, it is clear that their current stage of transition is much more desirable. In Peru, Aracely's parents knew her partner Ana Julia to be her friend. As friends, the couple enjoyed the privilege to sleep at each other's houses and go out together unsupervised, but that in-between space was ultimately based on lies and deceit. Aracely's current relationship with her parents is now healthier, though it has come with time and with her diligent efforts to redeem herself in their eyes for her previous wrongdoing.

Some of the study participants were not as forthcoming as Aracely was with her family of origin about their sexualities or their relationships. These women also lived in a state of nepantla and found ways to achieve visibility through the in-between spaces they inhabited together with their families of choice and origin. Even when leaving tacit that which is evident, the study participants could be successful at integrating their same-sex relationships into their extended families of origin. Take, for example, Minerva, who is a woman in her fifties of Mexican and Nicaraguan descent. She enjoyed a life partnership with Daniela, who recently died of cancer. When I asked Minerva about their relationship with her mother, she responded in the following way:

> With my mother, I never came out to her. And there was always this she knew and she didn't know kind of situation. But what I used to tell myself was that I didn't want to lose my mom. How realistic that fear was, I don't really know, but that's what I told myself. And so I never came out to my mom. But, my mom adored Daniela and would cook for her. When she found out that Daniela liked lamb, she started making lamb; when she found out that Daniela didn't eat pork, she switched and started making all of her traditional dishes with turkey and chicken. They had a very, very warm connection to one another even though they didn't speak the same language. My mom loved Daniela, and Daniela enjoyed her. She appreciated her for who she was, and that came through despite the language barrier.

While Minerva never verbally articulated her sexual nonconformity to her mother, it is clear that she believes her relationship with Daniela was visible. Minerva's mother has passed away, and thus, she will never know if her mother really saw them as a couple; however, that is less important than the fact that Daniela was loved and accepted as a member of the family. Minerva's words, "she appreciated her for who she was," are very telling because they leave ambiguous by whom the appreciating was actually being done—Daniela or Minerva's mother. Presumably, Minerva would say both appreciated one another this way. How then can one make sense of this mother's appreciation for Daniela if she does not acknowledge Daniela as her daughter's life partner? The answer to this question lies in the in-between space Minerva inhabited with her partner and her mother—Minerva's relationship with

Daniela resided in nepantla and thus remained tacit but not unseen. As a woman living in nepantla, Minerva uses seemingly contradictory language to describe how she negotiates visibility with her mother, "she knew and she didn't know." Those are perhaps the only words that could capture the in-between nature of their relationship, a relationship without words but with deep understanding.

Caring for their mothers within in-between spaces occurred sometimes in curious ways. While living in a state of nepantla, the participants' romantic relationships were made visible while still remaining tacit subjects. The participants found ways to care for their mothers' emotional needs and their mothers found ways to care for their daughters' emotional needs even while their same-sex relationships remained a tacit subject. Even at times when the emotional loss for the participants was great, their resilience and determination to continue caring for their mothers' feelings were apparent. Consider Minerva's experience as she lost both her partner of nineteen years and her mother within the same year. Minerva discusses her experience of losing these two important women in her life in the following exchange:

> MINERVA: One of the things that I've always been thankful for is that my mom died before Daniela did. It would have been very hard for my mom to see Daniela die. So that would have been very difficult. So I'm glad for that, that she died before Daniela did.
>
> KATIE: And how did Daniela die, if I can ask?
>
> MINERVA: She had breast cancer. When she was diagnosed, she immediately had a bilateral mastectomy. Threw everything she could think of at it and then some. It was in remission for about nine months, and when the cancer came back, it came back. You know, it came back hard and strong, and she wasn't able to beat it. She lived with breast cancer for about three years total, from the time of the diagnosis to the time of her death. The last month of her life we lived in the hospital. So it was very tragic and a very difficult thing to live through, but, you know, life happens.

Minerva shares with me a concern that her mother not have to experience the loss of Daniela, while saying very little about how this death affected her as an individual. Her statement, "It was very tragic and a very difficult thing to live through, but life happens," points to her own struggle with this double loss, a struggle perhaps too difficult to continue articulating, but beyond these words her description focuses on how Daniela's death would impact another. In this way, focusing on her mother's feelings even after death helped Minerva cope with her own grief.

DAUGHTERS CARING BY MAKING SEXUAL NONCONFORMITY INVISIBLE

Much as Carolyn Mendez-Luck and colleagues (2009) find in their work on familial care work in Mexico City, the study participants believed it to be their job to protect the emotional health of their families and not cause them undue stress. Some of the study participants did this by not pushing their families of origin to acknowledge their partnerships with other women. In deciding when and if to disclose their sexual nonconformity to their families, the study participants considered the stress this would cause their mothers and grandmothers.[9] They lamented the potential stigmatization this would cause their families of origin and obsessed over how to protect them from distress. Sometimes, the study participants focused on the emotional care needs of their families even to the point of compromising their own. However, the care work in which these women engaged cannot be reduced to a narrative of simply sacrificing their own emotional needs for their families. While this is certainly part of the story, it does not present a full picture of the kinds of negotiations these women do. LBQ Latinas came to define their own happiness and emotional stability in part based on that of their families of origin. Thus, if making their same-sex partnerships invisible helped ease familial stress, these women often found ways to do so because, by keeping their families of origin content, they were ridding themselves of potential stress and frustration.

Consider Julie, a Puerto Rican bisexual woman in her late twenties. Julie was one of the few participants in the study who was in a monogamous relationship with a man at the time of the interview. She contacted me after I placed a call for participants on a queer Listserv to which she subscribed. I had never seen Julie at any community events, nor did she hold a connection to any of the other women who participated in the study. When I interviewed Julie, I was struck by the way in which she spoke about her previous relationships with women. They had been by and large secretive encounters and short-term relationships with women with whom she seemed to hold strong emotional connections but whom she was unwilling to share with others she loved. In contrast, her description of her current relationship with a man was unenthusiastic and practical. She did not describe an emotional connection to her current partner. Not knowing how to read her description, I questioned her further:

KATIE: Are you happy?

JULIE: Not necessarily.

KATIE: So why do it?

JULIE: A lot of it has to do with heterosexuality. You have to get acceptance from your family. And I think that's why a lot of bisexuals who are in heterosexual relationships probably do it—because of the ease and the stability, too. It's hard to meet people. It's hard to meet other women, especially if you aren't part of that community. I think a lot of the reason why I stay in a hetero relationship is because my little sister is a lesbian. So we already have the one lesbian in the family, and I don't want to mention the fact that we have one bisexual, too. It would be upsetting to my mom.... During the time that my sister came out to her, I was in college and I was the middle person, saying, "You know, Mom, just give her some time." It's just ironic because I'm the middle person but I'm also in between homosexuality and heterosexuality.

In this quote, Julie articulates her position as a nepantlera. As a woman living in nepantla, it is Julie's job to navigate the difficult conflicts that arise from her opposing worlds. She is a mediator who must make herself vulnerable in order to create healing within her family of origin. She is the one who supports her mother in her struggle regarding her younger sister's lesbian existence. Her decision to not discuss her bisexuality with her mother and to not openly pursue a same-sex relationship stems from her desire to not create more turmoil in her mother's life. In this part of her framing, Julie's motivations for nondisclosure are to a certain degree altruistic. However, there is also an emotional gain for Julie. She enjoys being the stable, supportive daughter in the eyes of her mother while her sister is the challenging daughter. By playing this supportive role Julie is both compromising and nourishing her own emotional needs. She compromises in that she settles for a heterosexual relationship that is unfulfilling to her and nourishes herself in that she receives the approval of her mother, for which so many other participants in this study longed.[10]

Mothers Caring by Making Sexual Nonconformity Visible

Sometimes the participants sacrificed greater visibility of their alternative sexualities through nondisclosure to their families of origin, as was the case with Julie and Wendy. But other participants did attempt to gain visibility through disclosure, as is ultimately the case with Aracely. In some of these instances, while initial disclosure can result in rejection, mothers may eventually come to provide emotional support, visibility, and protection for sexually nonconforming Latinas. Gloria is a bisexual college graduate in her early twenties. In college she had been engaged to a long-term boyfriend, though they did not marry, in part because of her unresolved feelings for a woman. At the time of the interview, she was in a relationship with a woman named Nicole. As in Julie's case, Gloria's sister is also a lesbian. Unlike Julie, at the time of our interview Gloria had disclosed her bisexuality to her mother. This open communication, however, resulted in Gloria's mother pressuring her to fulfill her familial obligations by not dating women. Gloria provides an account of a fight she had with her mother:

> And I told her, "If I fall in love with a woman and decide to marry a woman, that's going to be it, Mom. You're going to have to deal with it." And she said, "You're still welcome in this family, but she will not be." . . . So I said, "You are pushing me away, and I don't understand how you can push someone who is going to be such a big part of my life away from you, too. You essentially will be prohibiting me from interacting with my siblings. And you wouldn't interact

with my children." And that's when she told me, "You're being selfish; you don't want to sacrifice yourself for your family." And I told her, "No, I don't want to do that. I want to live my life. I don't think that's fair." And so I told her, "Also recognize that you aren't willing to sacrifice yourself, either, to keep the family together." She said, "Okay, I'll recognize that." So I said, "All right, fine. We're both selfish, and that's how we're going to live our life, and we just won't talk about it then."

Gloria and her mother had developed an avoidance after disclosure strategy to manage their relationship (Acosta 2010). They had agreed to disagree on the issue of Gloria's bisexuality and to develop a relationship where her partnerships with other women would not be discussed. In this case, Gloria's bisexuality made it more difficult for her mother to accept her sexuality, in part, it appears, because her mother sees it as Gloria's familial obligation to "sacrifice herself for her family" by marrying a man rather than a woman. In effect, she asks Gloria to limit her relationship options to those that will not stigmatize the family of origin. Her mother creates the conditions under which she is willing to accept Gloria's future family of choice in their home. Gloria, then, must learn how to juggle this stipulation in their relationship. While their current arrangement of "just not talking about it" is not the sacrifice Gloria's mother asks her to make, it is in and of itself a sacrifice. It prevents Gloria and Nicole from being able to situate their relationship in nepantla, where they could enjoy the benefits of integrating families of choice and origin. Interestingly, while this arrangement results in Gloria compromising some of her emotional needs for her mother's, it also plays an unintended role for Gloria's sister, who identifies as a lesbian and who has not verbally disclosed to their mother. Gloria describes her initial encounter disclosing her bisexuality to her mother, and her sister's reaction:

> She [Gloria's mother] said, "Are you a lesbian?" And I told her, "No. I like men, too." And then she got even more pissed: "That's just plain disgusting. You're a freak. How could you like men and women at the same time?" And I was like, "I said I'm bisexual, not that I'm a slut." I think it was too much to handle for her. She gave me a speech of "You can't do this at home. I don't want to know anything about it." She said, "Don't tell your siblings. I don't want them to think that their sister is like that. That is disgusting." I walked into my sister's room, and my sister says, "Did what I think just happened happen? Thanks for taking one for the team." So I was like, "You owe me big time." And she was like, "I know; thanks for helping me out. Mom will be much easier next time." I'm very fortunate that my sister and I are very much each other's support group.

Both Gloria and her sister recognize that Gloria has potentially eased the situation for her sister. Gloria finds comfort in this sisterly role, despite the fact that her verbal disclosure to her mother did not initially result in the emotional support she sought. Furthermore, she finds comfort in knowing she can rely on her sister for emotional support.

Gloria's verbal disclosure solidifies her social status as a pariah within her family of origin. Her mother's reaction implies that Gloria's bisexuality is something she believes must be contained and kept at a distance so as to not contaminate others in the family. Gloria's attempts to change her mother's homophobic beliefs are part of her larger strategy to gain visibility. While Gloria had initially been unsuccessful in getting her mother to make her bisexuality visible, her mother's disapproval and lack of desire to engage in any conversation about Gloria's same-sex relationship only goes so far. When Gloria was in an unsafe relationship, her mother ultimately provided her with emotional support. The following example illustrates how both mother and daughter care for one another's emotional needs and, through their actions, create visibility of Gloria's sexuality and relieve her of feelings of isolation. Gloria recounts:

> So I started this relationship with this woman. It was a very ugly relationship. . . .
> I had brought her home as my friend. Everybody knew she wasn't just a friend, but my mom overlooked it and was willing to pretend to keep us closer. I think because she didn't trust her. There was a lot of emotional abuse during the relationship. One time this woman was at my apartment and I felt very threatened physically and I was very scared. . . . There was a point when I had a bruise on one arm and I would go home every few days and one day out of the blue my mom told me, *the woman who never wants to talk about this*, said, "I've been thinking about the kind of life that you're leading. And I've been thinking about the kind of relationships that you'll be in and they can be very isolating. Be careful not to fall in an abusive relationship. Don't abuse anybody and don't let anybody abuse you." And that was a wakeup call for me. I thought, "Shit, my mom, who never wants to talk about this, called me out." . . . It was important for me that she said that and I think it was a really important step for her too. Later, I told her, "Part of the reason why this relationship lasted this long is because I felt alone. I knew I couldn't talk to you about it. I knew you didn't want to hear it and I didn't know what to do."

Gloria's experience seeking emotional support from her mother while in an abusive relationship is very telling of the kinds of negotiations that the study participants and their mothers maintained in doing family. Initially, out of respect for her mother, Gloria did not discuss her abusive relationship and, in doing so, chose to compromise her own needs to protect her mother's. However, while Gloria's mother reacts harshly when she first discloses her bisexuality, she ultimately offers her daughter the emotional support and guidance she needs when Gloria is threatened. This example illustrates the reciprocal relationships that participants maintained with their mothers. Not only were the participants caring for their mothers' needs, but the mothers found ways to support them as well: by intervening in unsafe situations, as Gloria's mother does, or by allowing their same-sex relationships to reside in nepantla, where participants can integrate their partners as amigas, as Wendy's mother does.

Consistent with previous findings (Oswald 2002; Patterson 2000), in this study, mothers were sometimes instrumental in helping study participants move beyond verbal disclosures toward visibility in the context of families of origin. Like their daughters, these mothers also sometimes took on the role of nepantleras with the extended family of origin, defending their daughters against the rejections of others and doing so even in instances in which they themselves struggled to accept the nonconformity. Inocencia's (first mentioned in chapter 3) mother was instrumental in helping her grandparents begin to make her lesbian existence visible. However, the passage below illustrates how she did so even while still reconciling her own reservations about her daughter's sexuality. Inocencia describes the experience in the following way:

> I sent my coming-out letter and I included a booklet published by PFLAG, *Porqué Mi Hijo Es Gay? Preguntas y Repuestas para los Padres de Hijos Gay* [Why is my son or daughter gay? Questions and answers for parents of gay children]. My grandma spent a month crying because I was going to hell and she wanted me in heaven. My grandpa was infuriated . . . "How could I do that to the family?" And my mother was the angel that would always come and say something to make them shut up. Once my grandpa was saying, "Oh, I don't know, Inocencia with that girl, that is sinful." And my mother said, "Well, Vladimar is using drugs and stealing things from you to buy them. Isn't that a greater sin? How is Inocencia affecting you? Is it in the Ten Commandments that one can't be gay? Because stealing is." My grandpa didn't talk to her for two weeks after that. But Mami would always come with something to make them think about what they were saying.

Here, Inocencia introduces us to her mother, boldly challenging her own parents in an effort to defend her daughter. But there also exists a glimpse of Inocencia's mother's reservation. As she challenges her father, she does not imply that homosexuality is not sinful, but rather that stealing is a greater sin. It is clear, then, that even as she defends her daughter, Inocencia's mother continues to struggle with the issue of homosexuality as sinful. Nonetheless, in this example, the way she assists her daughter in gaining visibility from the rest of the family is clear. Inocencia's parents and grandparents ultimately grow to accept her and her partner. This is evident from the stories Inocencia recounts, in chapter 3, of bringing her partner to visit Puerto Rico. While it is Inocencia who takes the initial risk of engaging in verbal disclosure, it is her mother who later plays the instrumental role of nepantlera, making sure that this disclosure becomes visible and is not silenced by the rest of the origin family.

Study participants like Minerva, Julie, and Inocencia take very different approaches to negotiating their own and their families' emotional needs. Minerva cautiously protects her mother from having to verbally acknowledge her relationship with Daniela while still receiving the love and support she and her partner need to fortify their relationship. In this way, Minerva gains visibility while her relationship resides in nepantla. Julie chooses to protect her mother by making her bisexuality invisible. She plays the role of the good daughter who unconditionally supports her mother in coping with the difficulties of having a lesbian daughter. Inocencia gains visibility by using her mother as an ally to help mediate acceptance and visibility for her from other family members of origin. In all of these instances, irrespective of the individual strategies they employ with their mothers, these women are attempting to establish acceptance and maintain their social position within the origin family. This is crucial to the participants' desires to tend to the emotional needs of their mothers, but it is also crucial for the mother's desires to tend to the study participants' emotional needs. Ultimately, the work they do is about gaining and maintaining social acceptance through visibility and invisibility from families of origin and finding ways to integrate families of origin with families of choice.

Tensions in Integrating Families of Choice and Origin

Scholars have argued that the level of satisfaction, sense of fulfillment, and protection that one feels in one's romantic relationships is related in part to the approval and support one receives from the extended family of origin (Schmeeckle and Sprecher 2004). Unfortunately, there has been little consensus in the research on this issue with regard to same-sex couples.[11] We know very little about how support from families of origin affects same-sex couples or how the lengths to which same-sex couples go to integrate themselves into families of origin affect their relationships. In this study, the participants reported a lot of tension in their efforts to integrate their partners into their families of origin. They reported feeling stuck between caring for the needs of their families of origin and those of their families of choice. This was as much the case for participants who desperately tried to integrate their two families, despite the resistance they sometimes encountered, as it was for those few who grudgingly kept their families separate. This is because the few participants who kept their origin and choice families separated did so only after making concerted efforts to bring them together. In addition to the tension that participants reported experiencing when integrating their families, they reported their mothers' conflicts over supporting their daughters or giving in to their own discomforts. Their experiences leave one to wonder how everyone involved fares under these strained conditions. In a deeply personal, introspective autoethnography, Nancy Naples (2001), who grew up in a white working-class home, describes her journey meeting the care needs of families of choice and origin and the many ways in which she compromised her individual needs in order to meet those of the ones she loves. In it, she writes:

> The features of my own story include the ways in which religion, class differences, as well as gender and sexuality increasingly widened the emotional and physical divide that ultimately severed me from my family as a complex unitary form. The struggle to negotiate my lived experiences as a lesbian within my family has helped me differentiate among the family members, distancing me from some siblings while drawing me closer to others. In this way, I can now integrate these particular members of my childhood family as chosen members of my family of choice, creating a much more affirming and flexible relational structure. (Naples 2001, 38)

Naples shares her journey to create a family for herself that incorporates supportive members of her families of origin and choice. In doing so, she has become more comfortable distancing herself from the negativity of her homophobic siblings. But this strategy of coping with familial tensions by retaining affirming family members of origin and distancing oneself from those who are homophobic was not popular among the LBQ Latinas in this study. Very few of the participants reported choosing to permanently distance themselves from any members of their families of origin, although some were forced to at the request of the unsupportive family member. Instead, most of these women fought to gain visibility from their families of origin for their chosen families, only giving up on the occasion when they had become deeply scarred by this fight. This was the case for Wendy, who, after rejection, tried to rationalize the insensitivities of her siblings with statements like "It's just too confusing for them, too much trauma." Even in the case of Julie, who did not discuss her bisexuality with her mother, she isn't separating her choice and origin families; rather, she is choosing to not enter relationships with women so as to not force her mother to face the emotional difficulty of integration. But the study participants by and large didn't make conscious decisions to construct affirming families of choice by distancing themselves from unsupportive family members of origin. Instead, these women focused on finding ways to redeem themselves in the eyes of unsupportive family members in the hopes of eventually gaining visibility and integrating their two families. For nonwhite families in the United States, families of origin can be the primary social unit for emotional and material support, particularly when combating racism and other forms of inequality (Greene 2000). Thus, while it may be difficult for the study participants to obtain full acceptance from their families of origin, the larger role this family plays in combating racism and anti-immigrant sentiment makes families of origin an indispensable unit for many LBQ Latinas. While they don't always gain support for their families of choice, they continue to try by negotiating the care needs of their origin families because the benefits in retaining this family unit outweigh the freedoms of relinquishing them.

In a study on gay and lesbian couples and their perceptions of familial support, Sharon Rostosky and colleagues (2004) found that very few couples perceived that a lack of support from their families of origin had no effect on their relationships. Instead, they found that most couples felt that support from their families of origin strengthened their relationships; and when it was absent, they tried to create either narratives of resistance or boundaries to protect their relationships. The LBQ Latinas in this study used both of these strategies and several others in their efforts to protect their relationships when their attempts at integration did not go smoothly. They promoted narratives of how their relationships were overcoming the lack of support. They described the strategies they used to protect their lovers from the rejection of their families of origin or how they protected their families of origin from the realities of their same-sex relationships. Repeatedly, the strategies they chose to use amounted to one thing: the level of power that the support or lack thereof of their families of origin had on their happiness and on the stability of their relationships. For LBQ Latinas, support from families of origin mattered enough that they often felt incomplete when they were unsuccessful in obtaining this support. Lucy and her partner Cecilia have been together for four months. Lucy is an undocumented immigrant from Mexico, and Cecilia is of Dominican descent but was raised in the United States. All of Lucy's family is in Mexico, and her mother passed away many years ago. Cecilia's family members, on the other hand, all live in New York and do not approve of her lesbian existence or her choice of a partner. Her family has been vocal about their disapproval, leaving Cecilia conflicted by her desire to integrate her partner into her family of origin. Lucy describes the situation in the following way:

> Su madre es una loca. Ella no acepta lo nuestro. Y pues sí—la ataca. Siempre le dice cosas como para tratar de que no siga nuestra relación. Mi pareja no vive tranquila en su lesbianidad. La mamá le pide a ella que no mencione cualquier cosa relacionada con el asunto gay cuando está con la familia. Le crea problemas a mi pareja porque ella es muy familiar. Ella, sí, quiere que haya una integración entre yo y su familia. Yo la conozco a la mamá. La mamá no fue grosera conmigo en persona, pero, sí, después le dijo, "Esa señora está muy vieja para ti." Pero, bueno, afortunadamente mi pareja no se deja influenciar por eso. A veces me trato de poner en su lugar. Si mi madre estuviera cerca, yo creo que a mí también me dolería que ella tuviera ese tipo de reacción. Yo diría, "¿Qué hago? ¿Me quedo con lo que me dice mi madre, o con mi pareja?"

> (Her mother is crazy. She doesn't accept us. And so she harasses her. She always says things to her as if she's trying to ruin our relationship. My partner isn't comfortable about her lesbianism. Her mother asks her not to mention anything related to gay things when she's with the family. It creates problems for my partner because she's very family oriented. She wants there to be an

integration between her family and me. I met her mother. Her mother was not rude to me in person, but afterwards she did say, "That lady is too old for you." But, fortunately, my partner doesn't let herself be influenced by that. Sometimes I try to put myself in her place. If my mother were close, I think it would hurt me too if she had that kind of reaction. I would ask myself, "What do I do? Do I go with what my mother says or stay with my partner?")

Cecilia's mother's comment that Lucy was too old for her was a way for her to show disapproval for their relationship. However, one can deduce that her disapproval was more for Cecilia's lesbian existence than for her choice in partner, as Lucy is only four years older than Cecilia. Cecilia's failed attempt to gain more visibility and support from her mother for her relationship with Lucy has taken a toll on their relationship. Lucy tries hard to be understanding of her partner's struggles but also grows insecure about the future of their relationship given that the integration process has not yet been successful. Couples like this one, who have not gained much success with integration, do not simply acquiesce to maintaining separate family units. They continue to try to create integration, and the stress of their efforts affects the intimate relationships these women form with one another.

Women like Cecilia who place great importance on obtaining validation from their families of origin sometimes alter their behaviors and interactions with their partners when around families of origin so as to not make them feel uncomfortable. These alterations involve not showing affection for their partners in the presence of their families of origin or changing their attire so as to not wear anything that could insinuate a non-normative sexuality in the eyes of their families of origin (see chapter 1). Thus, in their efforts to make families of origin more comfortable with their relationships, participants made a conscious effort to make those relationships less visible. These alterations only became apparent to me through observing how the participants interacted with their two families simultaneously. Rarely did these behaviors come up unsolicited during an interview, in part, I argue, because many of the participants were not fully conscious of the extent to which they engaged in these behaviors. The participant observation I conducted along with the interview data became crucial for understanding the nuances of these behaviors.

Josefina and Milagros had been in a relationship for one year at the time of the interview. Milagros came out to her mother as a teenager. Following a period of erasure of nonconformity (Acosta 2010), during which her mother had tried to control Milagros into giving up a lesbian existence, her mother had ultimately become much more accepting. On the contrary, Josefina had tacit relationships with her two families, integrating all of her partners as her amigas. At one community event, Milagros introduced me to her mother. My field notes of this event emphasize the way intimacy was transformed for this couple when around their families:

Josefina comes in as I sit with Milagros' mother. Josefina gives a shy hello and leaves the room. Later that evening she explains regretfully, "Today I can't dance with my wife because her mother is here." I reply, "Yeah, but Milagros' mother knows, right?" Josefina says, "Yes, but I don't know, I just don't feel comfortable." The evening continues, and Milagros dances with other girls. Josefina dances with me, but they never dance with each other. They don't hold hands or show any signs of affection toward one another. Later in the evening, I question Josefina about this, and she replies in a defensive tone, "If my wife and I divorce tomorrow, I don't want her mother to say that it's my fault, that I made her gay."

While I often saw Josefina and Milagros kiss, hold hands, or dance together in public, the presence of Milagros's mother stifled this affection in a way that I had not before witnessed. I had known this couple to be very open about their relationship, but I had never observed their interactions around their families of origin. The presence of Milagros's mother changed the dynamic completely. Both women seemed on edge, and Josefina rebuffed every effort Milagros made to connect with her that evening. Repeatedly, Josefina explained, "No me llevo bien con las suegras" (I don't get along well with mothers-in-law). Josefina's bigger concern, however, seemed to be with being read by her partner's mother as the pariah that corrupted Milagros and led her away from a life of heterosexuality. Josefina's own preoccupation with resisting this image created a barrier to intimacy between the couple.

Milagros, on the other hand, had a different preoccupation on her mind that evening. She has been an active member of Las Chulas, a Latina lesbian organization, for more than five years and has dedicated much of her spare time to organizing Chulas' events. She has dedicated so much of her time and energy to the community that it has created friction with her mother, who struggles to accept her daughter's commitment to lesbian activism:

> Mi mamá sigue dejando saber de que ella es la que está enojada. Yo la dejo. Pero, hasta ahora, ella me apoya hasta con mi trabajo en la comunidad. A veces no está de acuerdo porque yo he tenido que faltar a cosas familiares. A veces no le dedico a ella el tiempo. Pero yo trato de manejar eso. Tengo que balancear las dos cosas. A veces, a la comunidad tengo que darle un poquito más tiempo, y ella se enoja.

> (My mother continues to let me know that she's the one who's upset. I let her talk. But even to this point she supports me even with my work in the community. Sometimes she doesn't agree because I've had to miss family events. Sometimes I don't spend time with her. But I try to manage this. I have to balance the two things. Sometimes I have to give a little more time to the community, and she gets upset.)

Milagros invited her mom to the community event described previously because she longs for her mother to share in her accomplishments with this LGBTQ organization. The members of this community are part of Milagros's chosen family, and it was important to her that her mother share in this event as a way of offering visibility and support for her chosen family. Milagros's mother's discontent in attending this event was apparent to me immediately, when we were first introduced at this event. After we exchanged greetings and chatted about the success of the community event, Milagros's mother informed me that her daughter could have been a doctor, that she spent years in school studying medicine just to turn around and do community work. She continued in a resigned voice, "This is what she likes, and I must learn to accept it because working with the community makes her happy." I reminded her of the importance of supporting her daughter, as this is something that is very important to Milagros. Her mother agreed. She then smiled and said, "Milagros is going back to school to get a master's degree in public health. At least she is doing that."

The apathy of Milagros's mother toward her daughter's devotion to doing LGBTQ community work stands in contrast to the fact that she attended this particular event in support of her daughter. Her mother, motivated by the fact that she missed her daughter and a desire to help her integrate her two families, put aside her feelings of discomfort and attended this event anyway. However, her words were very telling: "This is what she likes to do, and I must learn to accept it." In these words I sensed resignation from a mother who wishes her daughter had pursued a different path, but I also sensed the unconditional love she holds for her daughter and her unwillingness to compromise her level of support for her daughter in this endeavor. Her own feelings of conflict are also apparent in this encounter as she ends with "Milagros is going back to school to get a master's degree in public health. At least she is doing that." To me, her words indicated a mother's hope for a more secure and financially stable life for her daughter, whose commitment to community health work in LGBTQ communities she is slowly coming to accept.

Fears like Josefina's, that Milagros's mother might eventually blame her for corrupting her daughter into a life of sexual nonconformity, are not uncommon for the participants. This creates great tensions for the couples, as one partner is able to maintain a good relationship with her family of origin while her partner becomes the scapegoat for the family's anger and resentment. This is the case for Mariela and Jasmin (first introduced in chapter 1). They have been in a relationship for several years. They met in college and recently bought a home together. Both families are aware of their relationship and have had difficulty accepting their daughters' lesbian existences. Jasmin's parents have come around to integrating Mariela into family events. This compromise is important because Jasmin's parents insist that she visit at least twice a week. Jasmin describes the current relationship between her mother and Mariela as a positive one:

> When I go home, most of the time Mariela will come with me. At first I used to ask my parents, you know, like, out of respect, "Can I bring Mariela home

with me?" And they would say yes, and then after a while they said, "You don't have to ask to bring her home." And my mother accepts the situation, but I guess she knows that if she wants to see me as often as she wants to see me, not that I won't go home if Mariela can't come, but I'm not going to come as often. My parents are really good to her. At Christmas my mom bought her a present. Valentine's Day my mom got her a present. I'm graduating this year and my mom already talked to her about what they're going to do, and graduation plans, I guess.

Jasmin's relationship with her family of origin is similar to that of the collectivist families that Pyke (1999) describes in her exchange principles argument. Pyke notes that collectivist families develop a trade-off between assistance and power, whereby adult children who tend to care needs for their parents gain a certain power over them in exchange for the care they provide. Pyke notes that collectivist elders strove to be compliant around their children and to avoid intruding on their own lives in order to facilitate the continuity of their care relationship.[12] While Jasmin's mother does not require physical care, she does require emotional support and attention from her daughter. This need gives Jasmin some leverage in setting the parameters of how to integrate her families of choice and origin. Jasmin has made it clear that if her mom wants to spend as much time with her as she does, she needs to be accepting of her partner Mariela. Otherwise, Jasmin's visits home would decrease significantly. Thus, in this family arrangement, Jasmin is able to exercise power over her mother because of her mother's commitment to maintaining collectivist familial ties. However, while Jasmin believes her mother to be growing more comfortable with her relationship with Mariela, Mariela's experiences at these family events are very different. She describes them as being anxiety producing for her:

> It was strenuous when I first met them [Jasmin's parents]. At first I felt very comfortable. But after hanging out with her mom a few times, her mom started questioning me. She would say, "You know I love you as a person, but I hate the fact that you're with my daughter. I know this isn't the lifestyle for my daughter. My daughter is just on the wrong side. She just needs to find God, and then this will all change." That is one of the first "gay" talks I had with Jasmin's mom. It was a very uncomfortable situation for me. I didn't know what to reply to her mom. So I said, "I'm sorry you feel that way." And that was all I said. I didn't want to create any sort of confrontation. But she would do it tactfully. She would always make sure that she and I were the only people in the room. I talked to Jasmin, so now when we do see them, my girlfriend makes sure to always stay around so that we don't have those types of talks anymore.

In an effort to try and keep peace, Mariela subjects herself to Jasmin's mother's rejection. This creates tension and resentment between Mariela and Jasmin. Interestingly, Jasmin never mentioned her mother's reservations about Mariela during our interview; instead, she emphasized the thoughtful gestures that her mother makes toward Mariela and downplayed the fact that her mother continues to struggle with their union. Jasmin points to the fact that her mother likes Mariela as an indication of her approval of their relationship. However, as Mariela's private experiences with Jasmin's mother point out, liking Mariela as a person and approving of their union are two distinct things. Jasmin's mom, therefore, faces two contradictory desires, to outwardly welcome Mariela into the family, so as to support her daughter, and to make her discontent for their relationship known in more private settings. This couple's strategy of dealing with the contradiction is tenuous at best. Jasmin, caught between her mother's needs and those of her partner, tries to meet the needs of both by providing a physical barrier (herself) in order to integrate her two families effectively. Mariela, who has had severe difficulties with her own parents, is resentful that in addition to pacifying her parents, she must also appease Jasmin's family. Jasmin struggles with wanting to continue the tradition of making frequent visits to her family but also wanting her lover to enjoy these visits as well.

Recurring in many of these examples are the constant contradictions that mothers, daughters, and partners face when doing the work of integrating families of choice and origin. Mothers like Jasmin's, Inocencia's, and Milagros's were among the more accepting of those of the study participants. They outwardly supported their daughters in public and made their relationships with other women visible. However, despite this support, these mothers also seem conflicted about their daughters' partnerships with other women. These mothers are doing the work of reshaping their personal dissatisfaction with their daughters' relationships in order to maintain a collective family unit. The daughters strive to meet their obligations to their families of origin while not compromising the needs of their partners. Their desires for integration lead them to try to reconcile what sometimes appear to be impossible contradictions. They make these efforts because of their desire to be good daughters, but, equally important, they are driven by a desire to gain visibility from their families of origin. Thus, in caring for the physical and emotional needs of their families of origin, the study participants hope to be made visible in return, even if this visibility only occurs in nepantla. In this way, these women attempt to mobilize reciprocity in their arrangements of care. They need their families of origin to accept them so they can utilize these families to overcome the adversities they experience from the larger, dominant society. However, in order to do this, even the most accepting of the mothers described in this book must first overcome their own homophobias and compulsory heterosexuality before they can become resources for their daughters. Their relationships, then, are always a work in progress.

Conclusion

In analyzing the strategic arrangements that sexually nonconforming Latinas created with their families of origin, their movement in and out of visibility becomes evident. The participants included in this study made interesting use of space, visibility, and silence as tools to help them navigate familial relationships. They found agency in living in nepantla and in the flexibility to choose if and when to perform more or less overt expressions of their sexualities. Sexually nonconforming Latinas' experiences highlight that visibility is not merely something present or dissociated from their same-sex relationships. Rather, there are levels of visibility, in terms of their relationships, that are constantly shifting within the family. By learning how to capitalize on the visibility they obtained from families of origin and how to manipulate invisibility, the participants appeared to strategically utilize nepantla and the state of unrest present in this space to their advantage. They learned to transform the discomforts of nepantla into an asset that would help them achieve *la facultad* and develop a stronger mestiza consciousness.

Anzaldúa's writings convey an image of the mestiza as torn and frustrated by her inability to make those she loves understand her marginalities as well as by her inability to fit comfortably in any one world. She resides in nepantla as she goes through the many transitions in life. She learns to use her role as nepantlera to help heal the wounds of those she loves. Her journey aids her in reaching la facultad. These ideas resonate profoundly with the experiences of the women in this chapter. Their efforts to redeem themselves in the eyes of their families of origin are, in and of themselves, a testament of their desire to gain acceptance and visibility. We see, throughout this chapter, the strength and resistance that these women must embody in order to take on the many tensions associated with integrating families of choice and origin. We see this same strength and resistance from many of their mothers as well. The participants all find different strategies for dealing with their Shadow-Beast: some leave it caged or "push the unacceptable parts to the shadows" (Anzaldúa 1999, 42), as is the case with Julie. Others try to release the Shadow-Beast, as Gloria does, encouraging those they love to confront their marginalities and challenging others to accept them in spite of these marginalities. However, despite their different approaches, the study participants have similar end goals. They seek visibility and redemption from those they love. Finding ways to achieve this without compromising their own needs as well as those of their families of origin, their partners, or their children is their biggest obstacle.

CHAPTER 6

CONCLUSION

ARE YOU FAMILY?

In a recent conversation my partner, Hilary, shared an encounter she once had with a schoolmate she had not seen or spoken with in over ten years. She was leaving a lesbian bar with a group of friends when she was approached by a woman whom she did not recognize. The woman, it so happens, thought she recognized her from high school and called after her. As they exchanged pleasantries about current life, common friends, and such, the woman asked Hilary, "Are you family?" My partner laughed at herself as she recounted the story because when her former schoolmate had asked if she was family she did not, at first, understand the meaning behind the question. Her lack of understanding did not stem from any denial or lack of identification as a sexually nonconforming woman, but rather arose because, never having been a part of a lesbian community, she had never felt a strong sense of connection to a "gay family" and was thus, at first, unable to even decipher the meaning of the question. As my partner related this story, I thought about how truly curious the seemingly simple question is—Are you family?—and the daunting complexities of the answer one feels, gives, or chooses to give under differing circumstances. Does the experience of sharing a status as sexual minorities create familial bonds for people? Are our experiences as sexual minorities binding enough to create this type of unconditional familial tie, particularly across boundaries of race, ethnicity, class, and, in certain cases, gender? This certainly did not seem the case for the LBQ Latinas in this study. Questions like "Are you family?" or "Are you in the life?" can imply a separate and distinct gay world—a world complete with its own community members, friends, and families, and one apart from the heteronormative and unaccepting life into which many sexually nonconforming women have been born. While this experience is a reality for many, it does not accurately portray how sexually nonconforming women who are not deeply rooted in a gay community, residents of gay neighborhoods, or members of gay churches do family. For the women in this study, who by and large did not hold strong ties to gay communities, doing family looked very different. These women straddled the borderlands, creating for themselves spaces to integrate multiple families: those who raised them, their lovers, children, and friends. Their families of origin, however, always remained in the center of these spaces even if these families were less than supportive of their sexualities.

Kath Weston (1991, 116) notes that families of choice are not intended to be replacements for families of origin who reject their gay and lesbian kin, but rather families built in adulthood. Jeffrey Weeks, Brian Heaphy, and Catherine Donovan (2001) write about families of choice as idealized families that provide much of the support and assistance that families of origin are sometimes unable to provide. In both of these seminal works, there is an emphasis on how sexually nonconforming individuals are broadening the meaning of family, how they are using their own agency to create family forms that meet their needs and affirm their identities. However, these works seem to promote a model in which families of choice are separate from families of origin and fill certain gaps for sexually nonconforming individuals that families of origin are unable to accomplish. This model does not fit seamlessly with the complex familial negotiations in which the women in this study engaged.

If Weston's argument is followed, historically speaking, gays and lesbians started to refer to one another as kin after a growing dissatisfaction with the concept of community. As gays and lesbians started rejecting the notion that there is unity and sameness within their communities, it became more popular to envision one another as kin and to adhere to building individual families where one need not deny conflict or difference. However, gays and lesbians of color have always had other salient identities in their lives that are not directly related to their sexual identities. The participants in this study did not live in gay neighborhoods, nor did they surround themselves predominantly with other sexually nonconforming individuals. They lived in neighborhoods based on ethnicity. Thus, they were not insulated from the dominant society or the larger Latino community. The fact that these women did not live in predominantly "gay worlds" changed the way they built families of choice. Unlike Weston (1991) or Weeks, Heaphy, and Donovan (2001), I did not often hear sexually nonconforming Latinas refer to their gay friends as part of a separate family. By and large, these sexually nonconforming Latinas spoke of both their families of origin (including parents, siblings, grandparents, aunts and uncles, etc.) and their families of choice (including their partners, their or their partners' children, and their close friends) as combined parts of their support network. Most participants strived to integrate their chosen families with their families of origin, thus creating a rich combination of biological kin, lovers, children, and close friends.

The respondents in this study did not learn to integrate friends and lovers into their familial networks in adulthood after establishing lesbian, bisexual, or queer identities. As a matter of practice, these women grew up accustomed to seeing their closest friends as family, irrespective of their sexual identities. They were accustomed to incorporating fictive kin with whom they shared intimate support as part of their families of origin. These fictive kin included godparents, neighbors, religious leaders, and close friends. In this way, their support networks very much resembled those described in Carol Stack's (1974) work on kinship networks among poor African American communities.[1] Stack notes that African American families develop intricate webs of domestic networks in order to meet their material, financial, and care needs. These networks, she notes, are fortified by the reciprocal support that biological family, in-laws, friends, and neighbors provide one another on a daily basis. Rebecca Lopéz (1999), who studied *comadres* (the relationship between a child's birth mother and godmother) in Latina families, found a similar pattern of fictive kin building for social support among families of Latin American descent. The participants in this study relied on the support they received from their fictive kin just as much as they did on the families that raised them. There were no preferences, replacements, or exchanges. Fictive kin simply expanded their support networks.[2]

While the findings in this work offer that LBQ Latinas did not experience families of choice and origin as separate or distinct units, some research indicates that this phenomenon may not be unique to Latina families, nor to other racial minority families. Ray Pahl and Liz Spencer (2004) note that people bring together given and chosen relationships every day, developing their own personal communities in the process. They note a blurring of boundaries between families of choice and origin. Carol Smart (2007) echoes these findings in her work on the meanings of families of choice and origin for same-sex couples undertaking commitment ceremonies. She notes that given and chosen familial relationships are fluid and situational. These findings suggest that what matters most is the significance of familial relationships to an individual rather than the categorical divisions between choice and origin families. The respondents in this study mostly maintained what Pahl and Spencer (2004) have called family-dependent personal communities or partner-dependent personal communities, which place families of origin and partners at the center of the support network. Gay friends and community members often joined these families, but rarely did they shift to the center of these familial networks, nor did they exist as separate networks. LBQ Latinas in this study aimed to integrate members of their created families with their families of origin. Irrespective of whether members of their chosen families were integrated into their familial networks of origin as their gay friends, amigas, or amantes, the participants privileged the merging of their worlds and labored at every step to make these units harmonious.

The contributions in *Amigas y Amantes* occur at the intersections of family studies, sexualities studies, and Latina/o studies scholarship. Straddling these distinct areas of sociology, *Amigas y Amantes* enriches our understandings of how family is done across race, sexuality, and gender lines. The findings emphasize the lengths to which these women go to nurture the familial support networks upon which they rely. Sexually nonconforming individuals must negotiate their familial relationships and learn to strike a delicate balance between the needs of their chosen and origin families (Smart 2007). When the concept of *familismo* was developed in the 1970s and 1980s, the emphasis was on how the cohesion in Chicano families (and later Latina/o families, more generally) fosters support and rapport for the individuals within it. One of the limitations of the concept of familismo is that it implies that the solidarity and cohesion that can sometimes exist in Latino families is effortless and inherent to the ethnic families that maintain them. By paying close attention to the ways sexually nonconforming Latinas merge their chosen families with their families of origin and, by default, the tensions that arise from their efforts, *Amigas y Amantes* provides an analysis of the labor involved in creating the familial support these women enjoy in their lives. In so doing, *Amigas y Amantes* reminds us that this support should not be taken for granted as inherent to families of any particular ethnic group, so that we do not risk obfuscating the work involved in cultivating these relationships. The relationships these women have with their families of origin, close friends, partners, children, and their partners' children are a result of their own abilities and desires to create them. In this way, *Amigas y Amantes* complicates how we understand created families. We may all be given families, but the relationships we have with them are forged, and, in this way, are created. *Amigas y Amantes* offers that both choice and origin families can be created. This is true in part because, for the LBQ Latinas in this study, these families were neither distinct nor separate units, but also because the familial ties these women relied upon for support would not exist if they had not been actively forged.

One of the important themes that unfolds in the chapters of this book is that the resistance that LBQ Latinas received from their families of origin cannot be explained entirely by their sexual nonconformity. The findings suggest that families of origins' concerns are more multidimensional. As chapter 3 illustrates, even those parents who were comfortable with their daughters' alternative sexualities still expressed concerns when these daughters also crossed racial/ethnic barriers by entering interracial or interethnic relationships. Particularly, these relationships were problematic if the study participant's partner held a lower position on a racial status hierarchy. In several cases, these racial/ethnic transgressions mattered more than the sexual transgressions. Furthermore, as illustrated in chapter 1, the mothers of the study participants were more concerned with their daughters' gender conformity than they were with their sexual transgressions. One of the mothers' biggest concerns regarding their daughters' alternative sexualities was that this would change their gender presentation. In this instance, displays of dominant femininities superseded compulsory heterosexuality. The findings from both of these chapters lead to the conclusion that it is not sexual nonconformity in and of itself that made families of origin uncomfortable. It was the visible markers of racial/ethnic, sexual, and gender transgressions that families of origin tried to avoid. Consequently, at the very root of the many tensions that study participants report experiencing with their families of origin is the direct clash between these families' preferences for invisibility alongside the study participants' need and desire to be seen.

Another persistent theme present in the book is the resilient spirit of the women interviewed. These women demonstrated an acute ability to wrestle with the contradictions in their lives and to find ways to balance life's contradictory demands without compromising too much of themselves or those they love. It is in this endeavor that a mestiza consciousness becomes most beneficial to sexually nonconforming Latinas. Gloria Anzaldúa (1999) reminds us of the rebel within, the Shadow-Beast, the sexually nonconforming part of the self, which can be simultaneously empowering and terrifying. In *Amigas y Amantes,* I explore the intense emotions involved in the participants' decisions to cage the Shadow-Beast within or to let it free. The invisible labor inherent in this negotiation is part of sexually nonconforming Latinas' daily struggles, influencing their romantic relationships and their connections to families of origin as well as to their children. As the participants in this study moved throughout their lives, they learned to face their Shadow-Beast and to use its power to make gains in negotiating visibility/invisibility with their families of origin. Perhaps the most obvious example of the rebel within can be found in these women's unwillingness to give up on their mothers and other family members of origin who struggle with acceptance. In some ways, it might be easier to separate oneself from those people who are not affirming and move on with a chosen family of people who are accepting. However, the study participants never described this as an option. Instead, they drew from their resilience to find ingenious ways to be both seen and heard within their families of origin.

Like their daughters, the mothers of the study participants also learned to develop a mestiza consciousness and *la facultad*. These women were tasked with finding ways of fulfilling their role as mothers even while struggling simultaneously with their own discomfort with their daughters' sexual nonconformities. I have been brutally honest in sharing the reactions these mothers had to their daughters' verbal disclosures and the many instances of invisibility that the participants so candidly recounted. It is a risk to share these less than desirable instances of mothering, but it is also a necessary one—necessary because these honest depictions allow for a better understanding that mothers also work to maintain cohesion in their familial units. Mothers also struggle with the contradictions within themselves: their love for their daughters coupled with their insecurities for what their daughters' sexualities will mean for their safety, the social position of the family, and their relationships with God. In loving other women (and often women of different racial or ethnic backgrounds), the study participants were challenging their mothers to push beyond their comfort levels and learn to support their daughters even as they themselves embarked on endeavors with which these mothers would not otherwise agree. By exploring all of this invisible, taken-for-granted labor, *Amigas y Amantes* sheds light on this struggle and on the multiple layers of the experience.

In one of her final essays before her death, Anzaldúa (2002) traces her journey in search of *conocimiento*. This journey begins with *el arrebato*, or "rupture," which one experiences in life and that rips you out of your comfort zone and propels you on a search for personal and spiritual growth. On the path of conocimiento one must make herself vulnerable as she takes on the role of nepantlera. She must take risks, face the fear of change, and work through the feelings of in-between-ness she encounters in her interactions with others. This path is about building bridges and achieving deeper understandings through intense reflection, listening to others, and fighting for meaningful inclusive and fulfilling connections with oneself and others. *Amigas y Amantes* is a snapshot of the path of conocimiento, which Anzaldúa believes is ultimately an unending, ever-evolving transformation for us all. For the women in this study, the path of conocimiento is about learning how to deal with the struggles in life that shake them at their core and propel them on the journey toward reaching la facultad, strengthening their mestiza consciousness, and continuing to do the work of negotiating family. By sharing with me their triumphs and setbacks in negotiating visibility and invisibility with their families of origin and choice, these women enabled me to provide the reader a rough map of their journey to transformation.

Amigas y Amantes set out to present a multifaceted picture of the experiences of sexually nonconforming Latinas and to show the very real struggles of women whose experiences are often ignored. Nonetheless, much work remains undone. We still know very little about how sexually nonconforming women organize their sexual lives. Scholars, myself included, have gravitated toward work on sexually nonconforming women's families, leading to an undertheorization of the erotic. In doing so, we have risked perpetuating a stereotype of LBQ women as asexual beings. We know very little about how lesbian, bisexual, and queer Latinas over sixty, those who are disabled, and those who are single mothers build community networks. My findings on the vulnerabilities of LBQ Latina mothers and their children on account of class and immigration statuses merit further and more in-depth research. The positive changes that have been made over the past few years to grant same-sex couples the right to jointly adopt children and enter legal marriages in some states are major steps on the road to equality. However, these policies are not readily accessible to all LBQ families. Joint adoptions and assisted reproductive technologies can present formal and informal constraints, making them inaccessible to families like some of those described in chapter 4. We need to know more about how poor, sexually non-conforming women and/or sexually nonconforming women of color navigate class, immigration, and racial/ethnic barriers in their efforts to build families of choice. Such an analysis would also push us to consider some of the less visible ways that sexually nonconforming women come to experience parenthood and to incorporate their experiences into a larger discourse of same-sex parenting. Such work is particularly important given that the invisibility of such families has resulted in a lack of legal policies to protect their needs. More research that directly focuses on the parents of sexually nonconforming Latinas is needed in order to better understand the intricate balances parents maintain between their desire to accept their daughters and their apprehension regarding the struggles their daughters' sexualities may create for them in life. *Amigas y Amantes* begins to scratch the surface of this topic and will hopefully serve as a gateway for further scholarship directed toward attendant issues in the lives of sexually nonconforming Latinas.

As noted in this work, LBQ Latinas reported their mothers to be the most resistant to their sexual nonconformity. This is no coincidence. The tensions between mothers and daughters, which are repeatedly highlighted in this work, are exacerbated by societal ideas of a woman's role within the family. The study participants' mothers adhered to the belief that sacrificing for the family is women's work. This ideology directly interfered with their desires to be more accepting of their daughters. Admittedly, by highlighting how mothers and daughters navigate this balance, I have left fathers' feelings regarding their daughters' sexualities and the interpersonal relationships between LBQ Latinas and their fathers aside. This absence should not be read as a statement related to any perceived lack of involvement on the part of fathers in quotidian familial affairs.[3] As scholars begin further research on Latin American fatherhood, we will likely and hopefully see more work that directly addresses these fathers' feelings regarding their daughters' sexualities.

While *Amigas y Amantes* focuses on the experiences of Latinas, many of its findings are applicable to sexually nonconforming women of other races and ethnicities as well. Undoubtedly, some of the participants' struggles can be attributed to their immigrant status, their working-class status, and their social position on a racial hierarchy in the United States. However, in spite of these added forms of oppression, many elements of their experiences are shared by women uninhibited by these marginalities. Certainly, the contradictions these women experienced between their love for other women and their respect for religious institutions that did not affirm their sexual identities created a struggle that transcended these marginalities. Likewise, these women's negotiations between visibility and invisibility among families of origin through caring is likely not specific to Latinas. Even the findings I highlight in chapter 1 regarding how families of origin privilege gender conformity over sexual nonconformity, are likely something many LBQ white women can relate to as well. Furthermore, the prevalence of interracial and interethnic relationships in this sample indicates that even if the experiences explicated here are not directly pertinent to individuals of other racial/ethnic backgrounds, others nonetheless stand to be affected by Latinas' experiences based on how Latinas' negotiations with families of origin affect their romantic relationships. Consequently, the implications of this work, if not segmented as only pertinent to those interested in Latina/o families, will have the ability to help shape larger discourses on the intersections of race, gender, class, immigrant status, and sexualities.

APPENDIX A

PARTICIPANTS' ETHNIC BACKGROUNDS

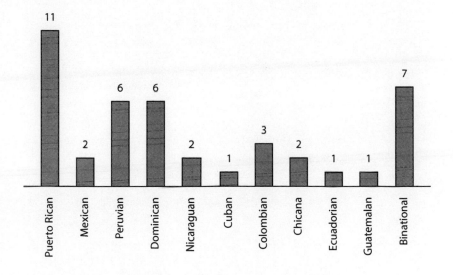

APPENDIX B

FORMALLY INTERVIEWED PARTICIPANTS

Pseudonym	Age	Sexual identity	Relationship status	Current & previous partners	Participant's nationality	Partner's nationality
Alana	29	Bisexual	Partnered	—	Cuban/ Panamanian	White non-Latina
Alexis	19	Bisexual	Partnered	Sara+	Colombian	Puerto Rican
Angelica	33	Lesbian	Partnered	Miguelina	Dominican	Dominican
Aracely	25	Lesbian	Partnered	Ana Julia*	Peruvian	Peruvian
Aurelia	27	Lesbian	Single	Pamela*	Nicaraguan	Nicaraguan
Carmen	41	Lesbian	Partnered	Cassandra+	Dominican	Dominican
Cassandra	38	Lesbian	Partnered	Carmen+	Dominican	Dominican
Cynthia	28	Lesbian	Partnered	Mallory	Peruvian	White non-Latina
Desiree	26	Lesbian	Single	Elisha*	Nicaraguan	South African
Diana	21	Queer	Partnered	Corinne	Afro-Dominican	African American
Eileen	33	Lesbian	Single	Ana*	Peruvian	Peruvian
Elena	45	Lesbian	Partnered	June	Puerto Rican	White non-Latina

(continued)

Pseudonym	Age	Sexual identity	Relationship status	Current & previous partners	Participant's nationality	Partner's nationality
Francesca	43	Lesbian	Single	—	Dominican	—
Gloria	24	Bisexual	Partnered	Nicole	Mexican/ Peruvian	—
Inocencia	41	Lesbian	Partnered	Elizabeth	Puerto Rican	White non-Latina
Isabel	21	Bisexual	Partnered with man	—	Puerto Rican/Cuban	—
Jasmin	22	Lesbian	Partnered	Mariela+	Puerto Rican	Colombian
Josefina	42	Lesbian	Partnered	Milagros+	Dominican	Peruvian
Julie	28	Bisexual	Partnered with man	—	Puerto Rican	—
Julissa	23	Lesbian	Single	—	Chicana	—
Kayla	33	Lesbian	Single	Destiny*	Puerto Rican	African American
Laura	26	Queer	Partnered	Monique	Mexican	Senegalese
Lucy	37	Lesbian	Partnered	Cecilia	Mexican	Dominican
Luisa	30	Bisexual	Partnered	Courtney	Ecuadorian	White non-Latina
Luz	30	Queer	Partnered with man	—	Cuban	—
Manuela	27	Lesbian	Partnered	—	Guatemalan	White US-born
Marcela	33	Lesbian	Partnered	—	Peruvian	Peruvian
Margot	36	Lesbian	Partnered	Stephanie	Puerto Rican	Puerto Rican
Mariela	19	Lesbian	Partnered	Jasmin+	Colombian	Puerto Rican
Maritza	30	Lesbian	Single	Lynn*	Peruvian	White non-Latina
Marta	41	Lesbian	Partnered	Rachel	Puerto Rican	White US-born
Milagros	37	Lesbian	Partnered	Josefina+	Peruvian	Dominican
Minerva	55	Lesbian	Single	Daniela*	Nicaraguan/ Mexican	White non-Latina

(continued)

Pseudonym	Age	Sexual identity	Relationship status	Current & previous partners	Participant's nationality	Partner's nationality
Sara	20	Queer	Partnered	Lydia* Alexis+	Puerto Rican	Puerto Rican Colombian
Scarlet	42	Lesbian	Partnered	Rocío	Puerto Rican	Puerto Rican
Sylvia	61	Lesbian	Partnered	Mary Beth	Cuban/ Panamanian	White non-Latina
Tanya	21	Lesbian	Single	—	Honduran/ US	—
Vanessa	36	Lesbian	Single	Emily*	Colombian	White non-Latina
Wendy	52	Lesbian	Partnered	María	Puerto Rican	Puerto Rican
Yanet	23	Queer	Partnered	Gisela	Chicana	Afro-Dominican
Yanira	35	Lesbian	Single	—	Puerto Rican	—
Yvette	22	Lesbian	Partnered	—	Puerto Rican/ Honduran	White non-Latina

*Denotes partner from previous relationship.

+Denotes partners who were also participants in the study.

APPENDIX C

METHODOLOGICAL CONSIDERATIONS

Early on in the data collection process, I learned that language would become a very important part of my interactions with the study participants. Initially, I simply thought being bilingual would be an asset to me in that it would allow me to reach participants who are not fluent English speakers. With this in mind, I gave participants the choice of being interviewed in English or Spanish. Ultimately, however, I learned that it really wasn't an either-or choice for participants. I observed the respondents switching back and forth from English to Spanish during our interviews and in conversations with one another at community events. They did this based on topic, emotions, and even setting. The maternal language is the language of emotions (DeVault 1999; Espín 1999; Gónzález-López 2005), and language can be a way to create affinity or distance with the researcher as well as with each other (Manalansan 2003). However, in collecting the data for this study, it became evident that participants switched between English and Spanish not only as a matter of preference or in creating intimacy. They also switched languages as a way of overcoming the limitations that language placed on them. Thus, when they struggled to find the words to explain their experiences, they simply switched seamlessly and effortlessly to a language that would expand their options in conveying their sentiments. When addressing issues of sexuality, the participants relied on combining Spanish and English as necessary in order to do justice to their experiences. When communicating with nonbilingual speakers, I noted the participants' frustrations at being limited to one language. As one participant, Diana, asked, "How do I explain to my mother that I'm queer? ¿Que es eso 'queer'? Los Dominicanos no usan eso." (What is that "queer"? Dominicans don't use that.) Diana's Dominican identity and her queer identity exist in different languages. Her effort to translate in the context of family an identity for which there is no Spanish word is conflicting for her. Her inability to communicate her queer identity to her monolingual mother has hurt their relationship, and Diana is limited in how much she can do to gain her mother's acceptance given the language barriers they face.

Oliva Espín (1999) found that Latinas sometimes revert to English when talking about their sexuality, although it is unclear if they do this because English allows them greater sexual expression. On the other hand, I found that participants switched from one language to the other based on which provided greater expression in any given context. Certainly, as Diana points out, the Spanish language lacks a word for "queer," making it difficult for her to convey its meaning to her Spanish-speaking mother. But there are similar limitations with the English language as well. For example, the word *amiga* in Spanish literally translates to "friend" in English, but it means so much more in the context of sexually nonconforming Latinas' lives. Participants often referred to their partners as amigas in the context of family. In these instances, the word is rich with double meanings, as everyone involved understands that these women are intimate partners. While such terminology was frequently used by study participants among their families of origin, the implicit understanding was always that amiga was a code word for lover. There is no one word in English that will encompass the complexity of the word "amiga" because its meaning shifts based on context. When the participants in this study switch back and forth from Spanish to English in their daily lives, they are developing a new vocabulary that represents their socialization in two different settings. Their sexualities evolve and grow in the dominant US culture as well as in their Latina/o cultures. Their decisions about when and if to use both languages are about communicating these simultaneous socialization processes.

Marjorie DeVault (1999) argues that there is language incongruence between standard language and the lived experiences that female subjects struggle to articulate. DeVault suggests that as the researcher it is our role to translate the experiences of our subjects into standard English. Part of the task for me in conducting this work was not only to produce a translation of my respondents' accounts, but also to translate their lived experiences into standard English, which often does not have words for these emotions. Recognizing the amount of subjectivity that can go into this process, I ultimately decided to include both the original Spanish and the English translation where appropriate. Doing so keeps the bilingual reader from being limited to my translation of the participants' words and enables these readers to form their own interpretations of what the participants intended to convey with their words. Including the Spanish ensures that the participants' original sentiments are not lost in translation and provides the bilingual reader a rare advantage over the monolingual reader to come one step closer to the participants' experiences through their original words.

APPENDIX D

PARTICIPANTS' EDUCATION LEVELS

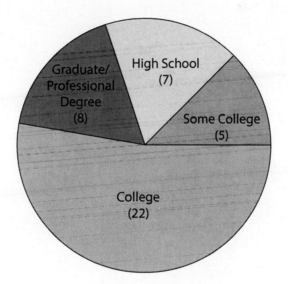

APPENDIX E

PARTICIPANTS' PARTNERSHIPS
BY RACE/ETHNIC COMPOSITION

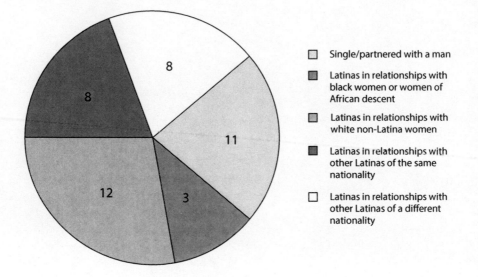

Single/partnered with a man

Latinas in relationships with black women or women of African descent

Latinas in relationships with white non-Latina women

Latinas in relationships with other Latinas of the same nationality

Latinas in relationships with other Latinas of a different nationality

NOTES

INTRODUCTION

1. The term "tacit subject" comes from Carlos Decena's (2011) work on Dominican gay men in New York. In it he describes tacit subjects as those matters that are never verbalized but always understood. Decena argues that certain subjects remain tacit around the family in order to bind people together. He notes that people are bound together by forms of connection that cannot be verbalized but that are intuited. Tacit subjects serve as these binds.

2. I use the word "queer" in this work as an analytic term. Five of the study participants identified as queer. Those who did chose to do so based on their political affinities to the term.

3. Anzaldúa advocates converting the contradictions, ambiguities, and marginality that mestizas experience on account of their plural identities into resiliency. A mestiza consciousness embodies that resiliency. It is how one is able to overcome the oppression stemming from living in contradictory worlds. The contradictions stem from living on the border of multiple cultures, where one is always a marginalized inhabitant. Contradictions also stem from the rejection one experiences within the family. Anzaldúa describes the labor involved in managing familial relationships and gaining acceptance. A mestiza consciousness, then, is a mechanism by which one can learn to tolerate the contradictions, ambiguities, and marginalization in life.

4. The LGBT Community Center in New York serves as a meeting place for over three hundred groups within the city and estimates approximately six thousand visitors per week.

5. See appendix B for a list of the participants who were formally interviewed.

6. Approximately 85 percent of all Dominican immigrants in the United States reside in the Northeast, with the largest concentration being in New York City, followed by New Jersey and Massachusetts. See the Migration Policy Institute, http://www.migration information.org/USfocus/display.cfm?id=259#3 (accessed February 26, 2013).

7. "You have a plantain on your forehead" is a literal translation of a Spanish saying that means that a person's phenotype is very typically Dominican. Since the plantain is a staple in the Dominican Republic, in saying you have one on your forehead, what is implicit in

the statement is that you cannot deny your roots because your Dominicanness is embedded in your facial characteristics.

8. In particular, I borrow heavily from five main Anzaldúan concepts. I use mestiza consciousness, which, Anzaldúa argues, helps one reconcile the contradictions one experiences on account of one's multiple, conflicting identities. Borderlands, which Anzaldúa describes as the space mestizas call home, is the space where the mestiza's contradictory identities come together. "Nepantla" is a term that Anzaldúa uses to describe a liminal state of mind and also a space with much potential for transformation. Along with this term is "nepantlera," describing those who serve as mediators and facilitators of their opposing worlds and negotiate a way for them to coexist. I also borrow the Anzaldúan term *la facultad,* meaning a deeper cognition, intuition, or an ability to dig below the surface in order to understand a deeper reality. Finally, I borrow Shadow-Beast, which Anzaldúa describes as the unacceptable part of the self that remains caged so as to not disrupt order. The Shadow-Beast can be both stifling and empowering. As you come to trust the Shadow-Beast, it can empower you when you face oppression.

9. Emotion work has been expanded beyond an understanding of how one manages his or her own feelings to how one manages the feelings of others as an act of love and care for the family. Since the task of caring for the family has been overwhelmingly relegated to women, research addressing this aspect of emotion work has focused primarily on women's roles in the home (DeVault 1991; Erickson 1993, 2005). Women feel most responsible for adhering to the care needs of others, and their emotions tend to manifest in response to the needs and emotions of others within the family (Fitness and Duffield 2004).

10. Christopher Carrington explores domesticity among "lesbigay" families, which are often stereotypically portrayed as having more egalitarian divisions of labor (1999). He offers that lesbigay couples often obfuscate the emotion work they and their partners do because of its potential to threaten the gender identities of those gay men who do it or the lesbians who do not. In another study, Carla Pfeffer looked at family units involving women in relationships with trans men (2010). She finds that, as is the case with heterosexual couples, female partners of trans men engage in a disproportionate amount of emotion work in caring for their significant other before, during, and after the transition. Her findings advance the argument that the individual responsible for emotion work in the family isn't determined by sex but by gender ideologies (Pfeffer 2010).

11. Weston (1991) defines chosen families as those that gay and lesbian individuals create to incorporate their friends, lovers, and children as kin. The existing scholarship on sexually nonconforming individuals and the family has frequently looked at families of choice in isolation, without a comprehensive analysis of the role that families of origin play in the families LGBTQ individuals create in adulthood (Carrington 1999; Moore 2011; Weston 1991). Ramona Oswald (2002) notes that for LGBTQ individuals, re-envisioning families to include nonbiological kin is about expanding one's support network and promoting resiliency for the individual or couple. In this work, I explore the relationship between choice and origin families in depth.

12. Carrington's (1999) work shows that doing family for "lesbigay" couples is linked to socioeconomic resources. Engaging in the work of building families of choice requires time, financial resources, and an adequate space in which to entertain chosen families. Carrington notes that poor, nonwhite, and lesbian couples struggle the most to do family because they have reduced access to these resources.

CHAPTER 1 — "AS LONG AS YOU WEAR A DRESS"

1. Goffman (1963) defines discredited stigmas as those that are instantly apparent to the larger world. Discreditable stigmas are not readily apparent, and thus the carrier must decide the circumstances under which to disclose discreditable stigmas.

2. The connections I make here between femininity, social mobility, and power are similar to those Gloria González-López makes in *Erotic Journeys* (2005) with the concept *capital femenino*. She uses this term to explain virginity as a social commodity among Mexican immigrant families. Her positioning of virginity as symbolic capital parallels my own use of femininity as a status marker.

3. Chapkis (1986) notes that our desire to achieve a specific beauty ideal pushes us to strive for an unattainable ideal type and fosters in us insecurities and feelings of failure. Sociologist Bonnie Berry (2008) notes that women's pursuit of hegemonic femininity in order to gain power and validation can have the exact opposite effect. In pursuing hegemonic femininity, women can actually be limiting their access to power rather than increasing it, because beauty standards are created and manipulated by elites as a mechanism to control and inhibit women's social mobility (Berry, 2008). This process is manifest in the workforce, among other places, where women are often undermined professionally for failing to meet unachievable standards of beauty (Wolf 1991).

4. In her work on Dominican beauty salons, Ginetta Candelario (2007) positions the salon as a site for women to transform female bodies into culturally scripted displays of femininity. Candelario argues that this transformation of the body and, specifically, the hair is about producing an authentically Dominican version of femininity. It's about creating an ideal Dominican look for women that will distinguish them from other racial/ethnic groups. This transformation is a process women do together, and through it they are active in establishing culturally scripted criteria for beauty and femininity.

5. This is not to say that working-class women don't also do femininity. From within their limited means, working-class women still strive to achieve feminine ideals. Brazil, in particular, recognizing that beauty is essential for poor young women trying to obtain work in the service industry, has established free plastic-surgery clinics so that poor women can "improve" the physical characteristics of the body that impede their work opportunities (Edmonds 2007).

6. Marysol Asencio (2009) finds that parents can link gender displays with sexual orientation, which makes achieving hegemonic femininity important to families as their daughters enter adolescence and adulthood. In part this is due to their investment in promoting heterosexuality (Asencio 2009). Furthermore, Emily Kane (2006) notes that mothers perceive themselves to be accountable for their children's nonconformity and thus worry that when their children resist normative gender ideals, it will reflect badly on them as parents.

7. The participants' desires to disassociate themselves from women who lack outward signs of dominant femininities is similar, though with a reverse gender focus, to the behaviors described by Decena (2011), behaviors that he terms "masculinity as a straitjacket."

CHAPTER 2 — "AND THEN THE FATHER SET ME FREE"

1. The entanglements of religion with women's intimate feelings for one another were relatively common in this sample. Participants recounted meeting their first partners at church or having their first sexual experimentations with other women in the church.

Unfortunately, because of the limitations of the sample, I was unable to explore this issue further. Further research on Latinas' same-sex intimacies should consider the church as a site for love and intense friendships among women.

2. In this way, Maurice Poon and Peter Ho's (2008) findings among gay Asian men are pertinent. They discovered that gay Asian men found ways to restore a sense of positive self by reframing their identities in opposition to the negative stereotypes that prevailed in gay communities regarding their effeminacy and sexual passivity. Instead, Poon and Ho found that gay Asian men emphasized their positive characteristics, such as loyalty, in order to dispel negative stereotypes. By developing a sense of positive self, sexually nonconforming individuals are able to reposition themselves against the social stigmas that confine them.

3. Goffman (1963) candidly notes that the stigma management strategies that individuals use with intimate others are inherently different and perhaps more complicated than those used with strangers.

4. The concept of the Shadow-Beast has rarely been taken up in social science scholarship, even among those who have built liberally upon many of Anzaldúa's other concepts. However, I see the concept of the Shadow-Beast as central to Anzaldúa's larger argument. Those who live on the borderlands and/or those who live in a state of nepantla are plagued by the contradictions of their opposing worlds. The Shadow-Beast provides the mestiza with the strength to resist her oppression. Along with la facultad, the Shadow Beast can help the mestiza survive.

CHAPTER 3 — DOING FAMILY FROM WITHIN
INTERRACIAL/INTERETHNIC RELATIONSHIPS

1. See appendix D for a breakdown of the interracial and interethnic relationships represented in this sample. For a list of the participants, their partners, and the nationalities of both, see appendix B.

2. Cilantro and recao are herbs often used in preparing Puerto Rican meals. They look very similar and can easily be confused for one another if one is not careful.

3. I use the term "Latinidad" here much as it is used by Agustín Laó-Montes in his introduction to *Mambo Montage: The Latinization of New York City*. In it, Laó-Montes writes, "Latinidad is an analytical concept that signifies a category of identification, familiarity, and affinity. In this sense, latinidad is a noun that identifies a subject position (the state of being Latino/a) in a given discursive space. . . . Latinidad, however, does not denote a single discursive formation but rather a multiplicity of intersecting discourses enabling different types of subjects and identities and deploying specific kinds of knowledge and power relations. In these terms, it is not only possible to distinguish between governmental, corporate, and academic discourses of latinidad but also to analyze how latinidad is produced through the work of Latino community institutions and by means of aesthetic practices and social movements" (2001, 4).

4. Elizabeth's family of origin has shown their disapproval of her relationship with Inocencia in multiple ways. Because of the complexities of this relationship, I have chosen to only share one example of cultural ignorance. Many of the other examples pertaining to this couple involve Elizabeth's family's inability to involve Inocencia in their Jewish traditions. Such examples bring up issues of negotiating different religions in a relationship, which go beyond the scope of this chapter.

CHAPTER 4 — PARENTING AMONG FAMILIES OF CHOICE

1. Shortly after meeting Carla, I asked if she was willing to be formally interviewed for this project. She declined to participate in an interview because she thought the process would make her uncomfortable. I respected her wishes.

2. The earliest example of gay and lesbian stepparent literature I could find came from David A. Baptiste Jr.'s (1987) chapter in the edited volume *Gay and Lesbian Parents*. In it, Baptiste explores how gay and lesbian stepparents lack legitimacy both formally and informally to confirm their status as a family. This, he notes, leads them to live a life of secrecy, operating on a daily basis as a family but denying this reality when interacting with the outside public.

3. This work explores how couples choose who will birth their children, divide the household and childcare responsibilities, and construct an understanding of dual motherhood. At times, this work has also explored the role of the family of origin in shaping how same-sex couples construct families of choice.

4. While the sample for this study was overall relatively well educated and middle class, with the exception of Luisa, the mothers discussed here were below average for the sample. Even those who had been professional workers in their countries of origin were not able to attain the same social status after immigrating to the United States.

5. Two of these participants, Carmen and Cassandra, are in a relationship with each other and raising one child together.

6. Moore (2011) found that lesbian stepparents who want to play an active role in raising their partners' biological children can feel alienated from doing so because they lack a legal connection to these children and their role as parent is tied to their relationships with the biological mothers.

7. Moore (2011) makes a distinction between lesbians who become mothers and mothers who become lesbians, arguing that in the latter case the status of mother is separate and distinct from the status of lesbian.

8. Oswald, Fonseca, and Hardesty (2010) report that fears of losing their children and of encountering prejudices from social service workers are major barriers that lesbian mothers face when dealing with intimate partner violence. Perhaps these concerns led Desiree to delay seeking out support for as long as she did.

9. Because so many states have enacted state-level Defense of Marriage Acts, same-sex married couples still need a second-parent adoption for the children born within their relationship because other states are not obliged to recognize the marriage. If a state does not recognize a same-sex marriage, a comother's legal tie to the children could be revoked. See GLAD (Gay and Lesbian Advocates and Defenders) at http://www.glad.org/rights/connecticut/c/family -law-in-connecticut (accessed March 1, 2013) for more information on how this works.

10. In an effort to explore how lesbians manage families of origin and choice, Sullivan asks how becoming a lesbian coparent affects relationships with families of origin (2004). She notes that lesbian comothers must engage in the never-ending process of kinship making, constantly pushing resistant families of origin to recognize their children and their relationships. Furthermore, she finds that families of origin with a biological connection to the children have an easier time accepting their kin's chosen families; whereas those who do not have a biological connection to the children are more reticent to accept them as family. She describes how lesbian comothers struggle to gain visibility from extended family and the tensions that arise within their relationships due to the rejection of families of origin. In another study on "lesbigay" families, Carrington (1999) finds that

lesbian and gay parents have stronger connections to biological families than do lesbian and gay nonparents. He notes that lesbian and gay parents were less likely to see friends as kin and more likely to rely on the biological family for support. He attributes this to lesbigay parents losing their connections with lesbian and gay friends who are not parents and therefore redefining family to include biological grandparents, aunts, and uncles.

11. I put the word "accept" in quotation marks because I recognize there is a limit to this acceptance since it does not really make their relationship visible.

12. Angelica had previously only come to the United States with a tourist visa to visit Miguelina.

CHAPTER 5 — INTEGRATING FAMILIES OF CHOICE AND ORIGIN

1. Pamela's relative financial stability increased her level of acceptance with her family of origin because it enabled her to provide resources for them. In this way, the case of Aurelia and Pamela echoes Cantú's (2009) findings regarding Mexican men who have sex with men, for whom financial independence facilitated familial acceptance. The relative financial independence that Pamela and Aurelia enjoyed coupled with the financial instability of Pamela's family of origin provided them a rare chance for acceptance. Others' subjugated positions within the workplace complicated their ability to use financial resources as an asset in their efforts to obtain acceptance from families of origin.

2. In *The Presentation of Self*, Erving Goffman (1959) notes that in everyday interactions individuals are managing the impression of themselves that others receive: behaving differently on the front stage versus backstage, based on the audience, specific situation, and one's goals for that encounter. However, Goffman did not consider social actors to be feeling beings. His work positions impression management as a surface performance that shapes individuals' outward appearance but not their inner core.

3. Deep acting, Hochschild (1990) argues, is about evoking, shaping, and suppressing one's feelings based on the environment. It involves guiding one's inner feelings according to what one knows to be socially appropriate. Hochschild positions individuals as pursuers of gender strategies who are guided by feelings and rules and who create emotional pathways that will allow them to fulfill the gender strategies that they have set forth as ideal. For Hochschild, emotion work is what people do when their gender strategies do not result in the realization of their ideals. In these instances, one is left to manage the feelings of disappointment and resentment that emerge from not having one's ideals met. Emotion work is how people manage those feelings.

4. Distinct patterns of familial integration can be more satisfactorily explained by differences in socioeconomic status rather than ethnic differences (Sarkisian et al. 2007). Class can affect the form an extended family takes for an individual and if that extended family comes to serve as a resource for survival or a form of back-up support during extenuating circumstances (Gerstel 2011).

5. The key difference between Wendy's arrangement and the MOMs that Wolkomir describes is that Wendy hasn't disclosed her outside relationship to her husband. They did not come to a mutual agreement to stay married while simultaneously pursuing other fulfilling relationships outside the marriage. By not disclosing, Wendy changes the dynamics that we understand MOMs to operate under. For her, it is not a mutual decision; and by virtue of this fact, Wendy reduces her husband to the person with whom she lives, but not with whom she shares any emotional, physical, or otherwise committed relationship.

6. Nepantla is a contradictory space for the study participants. In it, they are able to use the invisibility they experience among their families of origin to their advantage. By introducing their partners to their families of origin as amigas, the participants are able to integrate their two families in a way that is affable, albeit not always without tension.

7. Price (2011) notes that sometimes, for lesbians caring for elderly parents, the reciprocity comes in the form of an opportunity to renegotiate familial relationships and in allowing them to work through previous feelings of rejection from their families of origin.

8. For example, lesbian daughters often get classified as single since their relationships fall outside of the heteronormative paradigm, and thus they risk being constructed as more available to provide care than other siblings who hold recognizable heterosexual attachments (Coon 2003; Raphael and Meyer 2000). As marriage limits the ties that heterosexual children maintain with their parents, the burden of caring for parents can fall disproportionately on "single" children (Sarkisian and Gerstel 2008).

9. The findings I present here are part of an ongoing body of scholarship that addresses familial reactions to disclosure and disclosure as an ongoing process rather than a static event. Looking across race, class, and gender, this work has illustrated the complexities of disclosures or lack of disclosures and the ways in which these processes affect familial relationships (Acosta 2010, 2011; Decena 2008; Yep et al. 2001). Elsewhere, I've argued that the initial process of disclosure fuels the beginning of a whole new process, the journey toward visibility (Acosta 2011).

10. Julie's use of a monogamous heterosexual relationship in order to tend to her own and her mother's emotional needs speaks to the caring these women do for their families of origin, irrespective of their relationship choices. Being in a relationship with a man does not automatically ease familial labor for these women. Parallels can be found with Luz, whose experiences are outlined in the introduction. In both cases these women carefully and meticulously factor in parental reactions to their partnerships with men. They calculate how much information about their relationships to provide their families of origin and when to do it, and consider what the emotional costs will be.

11. Some work has found that a lack of support and acceptance from families of origin can create undue stress for sexually nonconforming couples. Other work has shown that sexually nonconforming couples report support from extended family as being less important to their overall happiness (for a synthesis of this debate, see Goldberg 2010).

12. While Pyke's (1999) work is addressing the physical care needs of the elderly and how those needs impact their relationships with their children, the arguments are applicable to the emotional care needs of family members as well.

CHAPTER 6 — CONCLUSION

1. The process of building families of choice has been compared to the establishment of fictive kin in African American and Latina/o communities (Weston 1991). Kath Weston notes similarities between gay families and fictive kin building in minority groups in that it involves an expansive definition of family and provides individuals with a support system made up of nonbiological sisters and brothers.

2. Oswald (2002) compares gay families of choice to fictive kin among African American and Latina families, noting that while both have flexible understandings of family that include nonbiological relatives, gay families of choice are distinct in that they are often separate from families of origin.

3. On the contrary, previous scholars have begun a dialog that deconstructs the stereotype of machismo and its influence on how Latin American men do fatherhood (González-López 2004; Gutmann 2003). Olavarría (2003) notes that the prevalence of unemployment among Chilean working-class men has transformed patriarchal views of fatherhood and led to men developing stronger emotional connections with their children and becoming more involved in the child-rearing process. In her work on Mexican fatherhood, González-López (2004) found that men's views regarding their daughters' virginity were shaped by their fears for their daughters' safety. These fathers' fears focused on their daughters' economic stability and the risk of single motherhood or not finishing school, more so than on the actual act of their daughters having premarital sex.

REFERENCES

Abel, Emily. 1991. *Who Cares for the Elderly? Public Policy and the Experiences of Adult Daughters.* Philadelphia: Temple University Press.

Acosta, Katie. 2010. "'How Could You Do This to Me?' How Lesbian, Bisexual, and Queer Latinas Negotiate Sexual Disclosure with Their Families." *Black Women, Gender, & Families* 4 (1): 1–23.

———. 2011. "The Language of (In)Visibility: Using In-between Spaces as a Vehicle for Empowerment in the Family." *Journal of Homosexuality* 58 (6–7): 883–900.

Adelman, Miriam, and Lennita Ruggi. 2008. "The Beautiful and the Abject: Gender, Identity, and Constructions of the Body in Contemporary Brazilian Culture." *Current Sociology* 56: 555–586.

Aigner-Varoz, Erika. 2000. "Metaphors of a Mestiza Consciousness: Anzaldúa's 'Borderlands/La Frontera.'" *Melus* 25 (2): 47–62.

Almaguer, Tomás. 1993. "Chicano Men: A Cartography of Homosexual Identity and Behavior." In *The Lesbian and Gay Studies Reader,* edited by Henry Abelove, Michéleaina Barale, and David Halperin, 255–273. New York and London: Routledge.

Anderson, Leon, and David A. Snow. 2001. "Inequality and the Self: Exploring Connections from an Interactionist Perspective." *Symbolic Interaction* 24 (4): 395–406.

Anzaldúa, Gloria. 1999. *Borderlands/La Frontera: The New Mestiza.* 2nd ed. San Francisco: Aunt Lute Books.

———. 2002. "Now let us shift . . . the path of conocimiento . . . inner work, public acts." In *This Bridge We Call Home: Radical Visions for Transformation,* edited by Gloria Anzaldúa and AnaLouise Keating, 540–578. New York: Routledge.

———. 2009. "Border Arte: Nepantla, el Lugar de la Frontera." In *The Gloria Anzaldúa Reader,* edited by AnaLouise Keating, 176–186. Durham, NC: Duke University Press.

Arguelles, Lourdes, and B. Ruby Rich. 1984. "Homosexuality, Homophobia, and Revolution: Notes toward an Understanding of the Cuban Lesbian and Gay Male Experience, Part I." *Signs* 9 (4): 683–699.

Asencio, Marysol. 2009. "Migrant Puerto Rican Lesbians Negotiating Gender, Sexuality, and Ethnonationality." *NWSA Journal* 21 (3): 1–23.

Baca-Zinn, Maxine. 1982. "Familism among Chicanos: A Theoretical Review." *Humboldt Journal of Social Relations* 10 (1): 224–238.

————. 1998. "Race and the Family Values Debate." In *Challenges for Work and Family in the Twenty-First Century,* edited by Dana Vannoy and Paula J. Dubeck, 40–62. Piscataway, NJ: Aldine Transaction.

Baptiste, David A., Jr. 1987. "The Gay and Lesbian Stepparent Family." In *Gay and Lesbian Parents,* edited by Frederick W. Bozett, 112–137. New York: Praeger.

Bates, Aryana. 2005. "Liberation in Truth: African American Lesbians Reflect on Religion, Spirituality, and Their Church." In *Gay Religion,* edited by Edward R. Gray and Scott Thumma, 221–237. Walnut Creek, CA: AltaMira Press.

Bennett, Michael, and Juan Battle. 2001. "'We Can See Them, But We Can't Hear Them': LGBT Members of African American Families." In *Queer Families Queer Politics: Challenging Culture and the State,* edited by Mary Bernstein and Renate Reimann. New York: Columbia University Press.

Berry, Bonnie. 2008. *The Power of Looks: Social Stratification of Physical Appearance.* Hampshire, England: Ashgate Publishing Limited.

Bordo, Susan. 2003. *Unbearable Weight: Feminism, Western Culture, and the Body.* Berkeley: University of California Press.

Calvo, Luz, and Catrióna Esquibel. 2010. "Latina Lesbianas, BiMujeres, and Trans Identities: Charting Courses in the Social Sciences." In *Latina/o Sexualities: Probing Powers, Passions, Practices, and Policies,* edited by Marysol Ascencio. New Brunswick: Rutgers University Press.

Candelario, Ginetta. 2007. *Black behind the Ears: Dominican Racial Identity from Museums to Beauty Shops.* Durham, NC: Duke University Press.

Cantú, Lionel. 2009. *The Sexuality of Migration: Border Crossings and Mexican Immigrant Men,* edited by Nancy Naples and Salvador Vidal-Ortiz. New York: New York University Press.

Carrington, Christopher. 1999. *No Place like Home: Relationships and Family Life among Lesbians and Gay Men.* Chicago: University of Chicago Press.

Chapkis, Wendy. 1986. *Beauty Secrets: Women and the Politics of Appearance.* Boston: South End Press.

Charlebois, Justin. 2011. *Gender and the Construction of Dominant, Hegemonic, and Oppositional Femininities.* Lanham, MD: Lexington Books.

Chito-Childs, Erica. 2005. *Navigating Interracial Borders: Black-White Couples and Their Social Worlds.* New Brunswick, NJ: Rutgers University Press.

Clark-Ibáñez, Marisol, and Diane Felmlee. 2004. "Interethnic Relationships: The Role of Social Network Diversity." *Journal of Marriage and Family* 66 (May): 293–305.

Collins, Patricia H. 2004. "Learning from the Outsider Within: The Sociological Significance of Black Feminist Thought." In *The Feminist Standpoint Theory Reader: Intellectual and Political Controversies,* edited by Sandra Harding, 35–54. New York: Routledge.

Comstock, Gary D. 1996. *Unrepentant, Self-affirming, Practicing: Lesbian/Bisexual/Gay People within Organized Religion.* New York: Continuum.

Coon, David. 2003. *Lesbian, Gay, Bisexual, Transgender (LGBT) Issues in Family Caregiving.* San Francisco: Family Caregiver Alliance.

Dalton, Susan, and Denise Bielby. 2000. "'That's Our Kind of Constellation': Lesbian Mothers Negotiate Institutionalized Understandings of Gender within the Family." *Gender and Society* 14 (1): 36–61.

de Casanova, Erynn Masi. 2004. "'No Ugly Women': Concepts of Race and Beauty among Adolescent Women in Ecuador." *Gender and Society* 18 (3): 287–308.

Decena, Carlos. 2008. "Tacit Subjects." *GLQ: A Journal of Lesbian and Gay Studies* 14 (2–3): 339–359.

———. 2011. *Tacit Subjects: Belonging and Same-Sex Desire among Dominican Immigrant Men.* Durham, NC: Duke University Press.

Denner, Jill, and Nora Dunbar. 2004. "Negotiating Femininity: Power and Strategies of Mexican American Girls." *Sex Roles* 50 (5–6): 301–314.

DeVault, Marjorie. 1991. *Feeding the Family: The Social Organization of Caring as Gendered Work.* Chicago: University of Chicago Press.

———. 1999. *Liberating Method: Feminism and Social Research.* Philadelphia: Temple University Press.

Diamond, Lisa. 2008. *Sexual Fluidity: Understanding Women's Love and Desire.* Cambridge, MA: Harvard University Press.

Díaz, Raphael. 1998. *Latino Gay Men and HIV: Culture, Sexuality, and Risky Behavior.* New York: Routledge.

Diaz-McConnell, Eileen, and Edward A. Delgado-Romero. 2004. "Latino Panethnicity: Reality or Methodological Construction?" *Sociological Focus* 37 (4): 297–312.

Drumm, René. 2005. "No Longer an Oxymoron: Integrating Gay and Lesbian Seventh-Day Adventist Identities." In *Gay Religion,* edited by Edward R. Gray and Scott Thumma, 47–65. Walnut Creek, CA: AltaMira Press.

Duncombe, Jean, and Dennis Marsden. 1995. "'Workaholics' and 'Whingeing Women': Theorising Intimacy and Emotion Work—the Last Frontier of Gender Inequality?" *Sociological Review* 43 (1): 150–169.

Edmonds, Alexander. 2007. "'The Poor Have the Right to Be Beautiful': Cosmetic Surgery in Neoliberal Brazil." *Journal of the Royal Anthropological Institute* 13: 363–381.

Erickson, Rebecca. 1993. "Reconceptualizing Family Work: The Effect of Emotion Work on Perceptions of Marital Quality." *Journal of Marriage and Family* 55 (November): 888–900.

———. 2005. "Why Emotion Work Matters: Sex, Gender, and the Division of Household Labor." *Journal of Marriage and Family* 67 (May): 337–351.

Eriksen, Shelley, and Naomi Gerstel. 2002. "A Labor of Love Itself: Care Work among Adult Brothers and Sisters." *Journal of Family Issues* 23 (7): 836–856.

Espín, Oliva. 1997. *Latina Realities: Essays on Healing Migration and Sexuality.* Boulder, CO: Westview Press.

———. 1999. *Women Crossing Boundaries: A Psychology of Immigration and Transformations of Sexuality.* New York: Routledge.

Esquibel, Catrióna. 2006. *With Her Machete in Her Hand: Reading Chicana Lesbians.* Austin: University of Texas Press.

Fitness, Julie, and Jill Duffield. 2004. "Emotion and Communication in Families." In *Handbook of Family Communication,* edited by Anita L. Vangelisti, 349–375. London: Lawrence Erlbaum Associates, Publishers.

Frankenberg, Ruth. 1993. *White Women, Race Matters: The Social Construction of Whiteness.* Minneapolis: University of Minnesota Press.

Freedman, Rita. 1986. *Beauty Bound.* Lexington, MA: Lexington Books.

Garey, Anita. 2011. "Maternally Yours: The Emotion Work of 'Maternal Visibility.'" In *At the Heart of Work and Family: Engaging the Ideas of Arlie Hochschild,* edited by Anita Ilta Garey and Karen V. Hansen, 171–179. New Brunswick, NJ: Rutgers University Press.

Gerstel, Naomi. 2011. "Rethinking Families and Community: The Color, Class, and Centrality of Extended Kin Networks." *Sociological Forum* 26 (1): 1–20.

Goffman, Erving. 1959. *The Presentation of Self in Everyday Life.* New York: Doubleday.

———. 1963. *Stigma: Notes on the Management of Spoiled Identity.* Englewood Cliffs, NJ: Prentice-Hall.

Goldberg, Abbie. 2006. "The Transition to Parenthood for Lesbian Couples." *Journal of GLBT Family Studies* 2 (1): 13–42.

———. 2010. *Lesbian and Gay Parents and Their Children: Research on the Family Life Cycle.* Washington, DC: American Psychological Association.

González-López, Gloria. 2004. "Fathering Latina Sexualities: Mexican Men and the Virginity of Their Daughters." *Journal of Marriage and Family* 66 (5): 1118–1130.

———. 2005. *Erotic Journeys: Mexican Immigrants and Their Sex Lives.* Berkeley: University of California Press.

———. 2007. "*Confesiones de Mujer*: The Catholic Church and Sacred Morality in the Sex Lives of Mexican Immigrant Women." In *Sexual Inequalities and Social Justice,* edited by Niels Teunis and Gilbert Herdt, 148–173. Berkeley: University of California Press.

Greene, Beverly. 2000. "African American Lesbian and Bisexual Women." *Journal of Social Issues* 56 (2): 239–249.

Gutmann, Matthew. 1996. *The Meanings of Macho: Being a Man in Mexico City.* Berkeley: University of California Press.

———, ed. 2003. *Changing Men and Masculinities in Latin America.* Durham, NC: Duke University Press.

Hammidi, Tania N., and Susan B. Kaiser. 1999. "Doing Beauty: Negotiating Lesbian Looks in Everyday Life." In *Lesbians, Levis, and Lipsticks: The Meaning of Beauty in Our Lives,* edited by Jeanine C. Cogan and Joanie M. Erickson, 55–64. New York: Haworth Press.

Harding, Sandra. 2004. "A Socially Relevant Philosophy of Science? Resources from Standpoint Theory's Controversiality." *Hypatia* 19 (1): 25–47.

Hartsock, Nancy. 2004. "The Feminist Standpoint: Developing the Ground for a Specifically Feminist Historical Materialism." In *The Feminist Standpoint Theory Reader: Intellectual and Political Controversies,* edited by Sandra Harding, 35–54. New York: Routledge.

Hochschild, Arlie. 1979. "Emotion Work, Feeling Rules, and Social Structure." *The American Journal of Sociology* 85 (3): 551–575.

———. 1983. *The Managed Heart: Commercialization of Human Feeling.* Berkeley: University of California Press.

———. 1989. *The Second Shift.* New York: Penguin Group.

———. 1990. "Ideology and Emotion Management: A Perspective and Path for Future Research." In *Research Agendas in the Sociology of Emotions,* edited by Theodore D. Kemper, 117–144. Albany: State University of New York Press.

Hohmann-Marriot, Bryndl E., and Paul Amato. 2008. "Relationship Quality in Interethnic Marriages and Cohabitations." *Social Forces* 87 (2): 825–855.

Holland, Samantha. 2004. *Alternative Femininities: Body, Age, and Identity.* Oxford: Berg.

Itzigsohn, José. 2004. "The Formation of Latino and Latina Panethnic Identities." In *Not Just Black and White: Historical and Contemporary Perspectives on Immigration, Race, and Ethnicity in the United States,* edited by Nancy Foner and George M. Fredrickson, 197–215. New York: Russell Sage Foundation.

Jolicoeur, Pamela, and Teresa Madden. 2002. "The Good Daughters: Acculturation and Caregiving among Mexican-American Women." *Journal of Aging Studies* 16: 107–120.

Kane, Emily W. 2006. "'No Way My Boys Are Going to Be Like That!': Parents' Responses to Children's Gender Nonconformity." *Gender and Society* 20 (2): 149–176.

Keating, AnaLouise, ed. 2000. *Gloria E. Anzaldúa: Interviews/Entrevistas.* New York: Routledge.

———. 2005. *Entre Mundos/Among Worlds: New Perspectives on Gloria E. Anzaldúa.* New York: Palgrave Macmillan.

———. 2009. *The Gloria Anzaldúa Reader.* Durham, NC: Duke University Press.

Kraus, Rachel. 2010. "'We Are Not Strippers': How Belly Dancers Manage a (Soft) Stigmatized Serious Leisure Activity." *Symbolic Interaction* 33 (3): 435–455.

Laó-Montes, Agustín. 2001. Introduction to *Mambo Montage: The Latinization of New York City,* edited by Agustín Laó-Montes and Arlene Dávila, 1–53. New York: Columbia University Press.

Lee, Naomi. 2009. "Women's Discourse on Beauty and Class in the Bolivarian Republic of Venezuela." *Culture Psychology* 15 (2): 147–167.

Lewin, Ellen. 1993. *Lesbian Mothers: Accounts of Gender in American Culture.* Ithaca, NY: Cornell University Press.

Lopéz, Rebecca A. 1999. "Las Comadres as a Social Support System." *Affilia* 14 (1): 24–41.

Mahaffy, Kimberly. 1996. "Cognitive Dissonance and Its Resolution: A Study of Lesbian Christians." *Journal for the Scientific Study of Religion* 35 (4): 392–402.

Manalansan, Martin F., IV. 2003. *Global Divas: Filipino Gay Men in the Diaspora.* Durham, NC: Duke University Press.

Manthorpe, Jill. 2003. "Nearest and Dearest? The Neglect of Lesbians in Caring Relationships." *British Journal of Social Work* 33 (6): 753–768.

Mendez-Luck, Carolyn A., David P. Kennedy, and Steven P. Wallace. 2009. "Guardians of Health: The Dimensions of Elder Caregiving among Women in a Mexico City Neighborhood." *Social Science & Medicine* 68 (2): 228–234.

Moore, Mignon R. 2006. "Lipstick or Timberlands? Meanings of Gender Presentation in Black Lesbian Communities." *Signs: Journal of Women in Culture and Society* 32 (1): 113–139.

———. 2008. "Gendered Power Relations among Women: A Study of Household Decision Making in Black, Lesbian Stepfamilies." *American Sociological Review* 73: 335–356.

———. 2011. *Invisible Families: Gay Identities, Relationships, and Motherhood among Black Women.* Berkeley: University of California Press.

Moraga, Cherríe, and Gloria Anzaldúa, eds. 1983. *This Bridge Called My Back: Writings by Radical Women of Color.* New York: Kitchen Table, Women of Color Press.

Naples, Nancy A. 2001. "A Member of the Funeral: An Introspective Ethnography." In *Queer Families Queer Politics: Challenging Culture and the State,* edited by Mary Bernstein and Renate Reimann, 21–43. New York: Columbia University Press.

———. 2003. *Feminism and Method: Ethnography, Discourse Analysis, and Activist Research.* New York: Routledge.

O'Brien, Jodi. 2004. "Wrestling the Angel of Contradiction: Queer Christian Identities." *Culture and Religion* 5 (2): 179–202.

Olavarría, José. 2003. "Men at Home? Child Rearing and Housekeeping among Chilean Working-Class Fathers." In *Changing Men and Masculinities in Latin America,* edited by Matthew Gutmann, 333–350. Durham, NC: Duke University Press.

Oswald, Ramona. 2002. "Resilience within the Family Networks of Lesbians and Gay Men: Intentionality and Redefinition." *Journal of Marriage and Family* 64 (2): 374–383.

Oswald, Ramona F., Carol A. Fonseca, and Jennifer L. Hardesty. 2010. "Lesbian Mothers' Counseling Experiences in the Context of Intimate Partner Violence." *Psychology of Women Quarterly* 34: 286–296.

Pahl, Ray, and Liz Spencer. 2004. "Personal Communities: Not Simply Families of 'Fate' or 'Choice.'" *Current Sociology* 52 (2): 199–221.

Park, Kristin. 2002. "Stigma Management among the Voluntarily Childless." *Sociological Perspectives* 45 (1): 21–45.

Patterson, Charlotte J. 2000. "Family Relationships of Lesbians and Gay Men." *Journal of Marriage and Family* 62: 1052–1069.

———. 2009. "Children of Lesbian and Gay Parents: Psychology, Law, and Policy." *American Psychologist* 64 (8): 727–736.

Pérez, Emma. 2005. "Gloria Anzaldúa: La Gran Nueva Mestiza Theorist, Writer, Activist Scholar." *NWSA Journal* 17 (2): 1–10.

Pfeffer, Carla A. 2010. "'Women's Work'? Women Partners of Transgender Men Doing Housework and Emotion Work." *Journal of Marriage and Family* 72 (February): 165–183.

Poon, Maurice Kwong-Lai, and Peter Trung-Thu Ho. 2008. "Negotiating Social Stigma among Gay Asian Men." *Sexualities* 11 (1–2): 245–268.

Price, Elizabeth. 2011. "Caring for Mum and Dad: Lesbian Women Negotiating Family and Navigating Care." *British Journal of Social Work* 41 (7): 1288–1303.

Pyke, Karen. 1999. "The Micropolitics of Care in Relationships between Aging Parents and Adult Children: Individualism, Collectivism, and Power." *Journal of Marriage and Family* 61 (3): 661–672.

Qian, Zhenchao, and Daniel Lichter. 2007. "Social Boundaries and Marital Assimilation: Interpreting Trends in Racial and Ethnic Intermarriage." *American Sociological Review* 72 (1): 68–94.

Raphael, Sharon, and Mina K. Meyer. 2000. "Family Support Patterns for Midlife Lesbians: Recollections of a Lesbian Couple, 1971–1997." *Journal of Gay & Lesbian Social Services* 11 (2–3): 139–151.

Reimann, Renate. 1997. "Does Biology Matter? Lesbian Couples' Transition to Parenthood and Their Division of Labor." *Qualitative Sociology* 20 (2): 153–185.

Rodríguez, Clara E. 2009. "Counting Latinos in the U.S. Census." In *How the United States Racializes Latinos: White Hegemony and Its Consequences,* edited by Jose A. Cobas, Jorge Duany, and Joe Feagin, 37–53. Boulder, CO: Paradigm Publishers.

Rodriguez, Eric M. 2010. "At the Intersection of Church and Gay: A Review of the Psychological Research on Gay and Lesbian Christians." *Journal of Homosexuality* 57 (1): 15–38.

Rodriguez, Eric M., and Suzanne C. Ouellette. 2000. "Gay and Lesbian Christians: Homosexual and Religious Identity Integration in the Members and Participants of a Gay-Positive Church." *Journal for the Scientific Study of Religion* 39 (3): 333–347.

Rostosky, Sharon Scales, Beth A. Korfhage, Julie M. Duhigg, Amanda J. Stern, Laura Bennett, and Ellen D. B. Riggle. 2004. "Same-Sex Couple Perceptions of Family Support: A Consensual Qualitative Study." *Family Process* 43 (1): 43–57.

Rumbaut, Rubén G. 2009. "Pigments of Our Imagination: On the Racialization and Racial Identities of 'Hispanics' and 'Latinos.'" In *How the U.S. Racializes Latinos: White Hegemony and Its Consequences,* edited by José A. Cobas, Jorge Duany, and Joe Feagin, 15–36. Boulder, CO: Paradigm Publishers.

Ryan, Maura, and Dana Berkowitz. 2009. "Constructing Gay and Lesbian Parent Families 'Beyond the Closet.'" *Qualitative Sociology* 32: 153–172.

Sarkisian, Natalia, Mariana Gerena, and Naomi Gerstel. 2007. "Extended Family Integration among Euro and Mexican Americans: Ethnicity, Gender, and Class." *Journal of Marriage and Family* 69 (1): 40–54.

Sarkisian, Natalia, and Naomi Gerstel. 2008. "Till Marriage Do Us Part: Adult Children's Relationships with Their Parents." *Journal of Marriage and Family* 20: 360–376.

Schippers, Mimi. 2007. "Recovering the Feminine Other: Masculinity, Femininity, and Gender Hegemony." *Theory and Society* 36 (1): 85–102.

Schmeeckle, Maria, and Susan Sprecher. 2004. "Extended Family and Social Networks." In *Handbook of Family Communication,* edited by Anita L. Vangelisti, 349–375. London: Lawrence Erlbaum Associates, Publishers.

Shallenberger, David. 1996. "Reclaiming the Spirit: The Journeys of Gay Men and Lesbian Women toward Integration." *Qualitative Sociology* 19 (2): 195–215.

Smart, Carol. 2007. "Same Sex Couples and Marriage: Negotiating Relational Landscapes with Families and Friends." *Sociological Review* 55 (4): 671–686.

Smith, Dorothy E. 1987. *The Everyday World as Problematic: A Feminist Sociology.* Boston: Northeastern University Press.

———. 1988. "Femininity as Discourse." In *Becoming Feminine: The Politics of Popular Culture,* edited by L. Roman and L. K. Christian-Smith, 37–59. Philadelphia: Falmer.

Stack, Carol B. 1974. *All Our Kin: Strategies for Survival in a Black Community.* New York: Harper & Row, Publishers.

Sullivan, Maureen. 2004. *The Family of Woman: Lesbian Mothers, Their Children, and the Undoing of Gender.* Berkeley: University of California Press.

Taub, Diane, Penelope McLorg, and Patricia L. Fanflik. 2004. "Stigma Management Strategies among Women with Physical Disabilities: Contrasting Approaches of Downplaying or Claiming a Disability Status." *Deviant Behavior* 25 (2): 169–190.

Thumma, Scott. 1991. "Negotiating a Religious Identity: The Case of the Gay Evangelical." *Sociological Analysis* 52 (4): 333–347.

Trinh Vo, Linda. 2000. "Performing Ethnography in Asian Communities: Beyond the Insider-versus-Outsider Perspective." In *Cultural Compass: Ethnographic Explorations of Asian America,* edited by Martin F. Manalansan, 17–36. Philadelphia: Temple University Press.

Trujillo, Carla, ed. 1991. *Chicana Lesbians: The Girls Our Mothers Warned Us About.* Berkeley, CA: Third Woman Press.

van Dam, Mary Ann A. 2004. "Mothers in Two Types of Lesbian Families: Stigma Experiences, Supports, and Burdens." *Journal of Family Nursing* 10 (4): 450–484.

Vega, William A. 1995. "The Study of Latino Families: A Point of Departure." In *Understanding Latino Families: Scholarship, Policy, and Practice,* edited by Ruth Zambrana, 3–17. Thousand Oaks, CA: Sage.

Villalón, Roberta. 2010. "Passage to Citizenship and the Nuances of Agency: Latina Battered Immigrants." *Women's Studies International Forum* 33: 552–560.

Waters, Mary. 1990. *Ethnic Options: Choosing Identities in America.* Berkeley: University of California Press.

Weedon, Ann. 2009. "Appendix II: Representation of GLBT Scholarship." In "Report to the Committee on the Status of Lesbian, Gay, Bisexual, and Transgender Persons in Sociology," by a committee of sociologists for the ASA, 27–39. Report submitted to the 2009–2010 Council of the American Sociological Association.

Weeks, Jeffrey, Brian Heaphy, and Catherine Donovan. 2001. *Same Sex Intimacies: Families of Choice and Other Life Experiments.* London: Routledge.

West, Candace, and Don H. Zimmerman. 2002. "Doing Gender." In *Doing Gender, Doing Difference: Inequality, Power, and Institutional Change,* edited by Candace West and Sarah Fenstermaker, 3–24. New York: Routledge.

Weston, Kath. 1991. *Families We Choose: Lesbians, Gays, Kinship.* New York: Columbia University Press.

Wilcox, Melissa M. 2002. "When Sheila's a Lesbian: Religious Individualism among Lesbian, Gay, Bisexual, and Transgender Christians." *Sociology of Religion* 63 (4): 497–513.

————. 2003. *Coming out in Christianity: Religion, Identity, and Community.* Blooming-
ton: Indiana University Press.

————. 2005. "A Religion of One's Own: Gender and LGBT Religiosities." In *Gay Religion,*
edited by Scott Thumma and Edward R. Gray, 203–220. Walnut Creek, CA: AltaMira
Press.

Wolf, Naomi. 1991. *The Beauty Myth: How Images of Beauty Are Used against Women.* New
York: Harper Collins Publishers.

Wolkomir, Michelle. 2009. "Making Heteronormative Reconciliations: The Story of
Romantic Love, Sexuality, and Gender in Mixed-Orientation Marriages." *Gender &
Society* 23 (4): 494–519.

Yep, Gust, Karen E. Lovaas, and Phillip C. Ho. 2001. "Communication in 'Asian American'
Families with Queer Members: A Relational Dialectics Perspective." In *Queer Families
Queer Politics: Challenging Culture and the State,* edited by Mary Bernstein and Renate
Reimann, 152–172. New York: Columbia University Press.

Yip, Andrew K. T. 1997a. "Attacking the Attacker: Gay Christians Talk Back." *British Journal
of Sociology* 48 (1): 113–127.

————. 1997b. "Dare to Differ: Gay and Lesbian Catholics' Assessment of Official Catholic Positions on Sexuality." *Sociology of Religion* 58 (2): 165–180.

Zavella, Patricia. 2003a. "'Playing with Fire': The Gendered Construction of Chicana/
Mexicana Sexuality." In *Perspectives on Las Américas: A Reader in Culture, History, and
Representation,* edited by Matthew Gutmann, Félix Matos, Lynn Stephen, and Patricia
Zavella, 229–244. Malden, MA: Blackwell Publishing.

————. 2003b. "Talkin' Sex: Chicanas and Mexicanas Theorize about Silences and Sexual
Pleasures." In *Chicana Feminisms: A Critical Reader,* edited by G. Arredondo, A. Hurtado,
N. Klahn, O. Nájera-Ramírez, and Patricia Zavella, 228–253. Durham, NC: Duke Uni-
versity Press.

INDEX

Abel, Emily, 107
acceptance: from families of origin, 76–81, 98–103, 121; and visibility, 53–57, 101
Adventists, LGBTQ, 54–55
Aigner-Varoz, Erika, 59
alternative femininities, 26–30
American Sociological Association, 3
amigas, 83–84, 144
antigay churches, 40–42
Anzaldúa, Gloria, 7, 55, 59, 108, 129, 134, 135, 147n3, 148n8; *Borderlands/La Frontera*, 12
approval, from families of origin, 121
arrebato (Anzaldúa), 135
Asencio, Marysol, 149n6

Baptiste, David A., Jr., 151n2
barriers to intimacy, 64, 73
Bates, Aryana, 55
beauty and social status, 18–19, 149n3
behavior alterations, 124–127
Berry, Bonnie, 149n3
Bielby, Denise, 91
borderland spaces, 55, 81, 148n8
boundaries, racial and ethnic, 71–75

cages, for Shadow-Beast, 59
Calvo, Luz, 3
Candelario, Ginetta, 19–20, 149n4
Cantú, Lionel, 152n1
capital feminino (González-López), 149n2
caregiving: arrangements, 110, 153n8; in exchange for power, 127; for families of choice and origin, 121; for Latinas, 111
care work and family relationships, 105–107

Carrington, Christopher, 12, 148n10, 151n10
Catholic Church, 41–42, 50, 55, 56, 58
Chapkis, Wendy, *Beauty Secrets*, 18, 149n3
Charlebois, Justin, 17
children, in sexually nonconforming families of choice, 83–104; influence on same-sex relationships, 84–85
chosen families. *See* families of choice
Christian: identity, and gay identity, 46; morals, 39, 49. *See also* Catholic Church; churches
Christians, LGBTQ, 40, 44
churches: antigay, 40–42; gay-friendly, 44, 46, 55; social role, 42
citizenship issues, 68–70, 95–96, 102–104
class status: and family, 152n4; and same-sex relationships, 85
comother family forms, 84, 151n3
comothers: identity, 88; legal recognition, 95, 151n9
compromise with families of origin, 117–120, 126
Comstock, Gary, 40
conocimiento (Anzaldúa), path to, 59–60, 135
contradictions: in integrating families, 128; between religion and sexuality, 12, 39–47, 51–53; within religion, 58
coparenting, resources, 87–88
covering strategy (Goffman), 47
created families of choice and origin, 133
cultural differences vs. racial differences, 63

Dalton, Susan, 91
daughters, obligations of, 111

ABOUT THE AUTHOR

Katie L. Acosta is an assistant professor in the Department of Sociology at Georgia State University.

CPSIA information can be obtained at www.ICGtesting.com
Printed in the USA
BVOW07s0924200913

331534BV00002B/2/P